Choral Pedagogy

Second Edition

Brenda Smith, DMA
Robert T. Sataloff, MD, DMA

PLURAL
PUBLISHING
INC.

SAN DIEGO
OXFORD
BRISBANE

PLURAL PUBLISHING
INC.

5521 Ruffin Road
San Diego, CA 92123

e-mail: info@pluralpublishing.com
Web site: http://www.pluralpublishing.com

49 Bath Street
Abingdon, Oxfordshire OX14 1EA
United Kingdom

Copyright © by Plural Publishing, Inc. 2006

Typeset in 10/12 Palatino by Flanagan's Publishing Services, Inc.
Printed in the United States of America by McNaughton and Gunn

For permission to use material from this text, contact us by
Telephone: (866) 758-7251
Fax: (888) 758-7255
e-mail: permissions@pluralpublishing.com

ISBN-13: 978-1-59756-043-6
ISBN-10: 1-59756-043-X
Library of Congress Control Number: 2005910833

CONTENTS

PREFACE

Choral conducting is a complex activity combining theory with practice. It also merges historical perspectives with pedagogical and literary insights and language. The didactic and creative process leading to the corporate act of choral singing requires a thorough understanding of the vocal instrument. Choral pedagogy, a union of vocal pedagogy, choral conducting, and voice science, seeks to provide the materials and methods necessary for the preservation of healthy vocalization and the promotion of the choral art.

Choral conductors are generally keyboard players or instrumentalists with a love of singing. This book assumes a knowledge of conducting technique and does not review basic beat patterns or other fundamentals readily available elsewhere.[1] However, surprisingly few choral conductors have had formal voice training. Furthermore, the study of solo singing technique differs greatly in content and purpose from the pursuit of choral singing skill. It has been assumed that knowledge of choral literature, proficiency in basic musicianship, and competency in organizational matters were sufficient to extract competent choral performance from a group of singers. The practices of orchestral conducting have been applied liberally to choirs. An orchestral conductor can generally presume a level of individual mastery among the instrumentalists in an ensemble, but an acquaintance with singing technique is unknown to the average choral singer.

Choral singers are amateur performers with a deep commitment to the choir, to its purpose and practice. They commonly share a desire to belong, a need to be hidden in a larger context, and a sincere love of singing. It is rare, however, to find choral singers adept at the rudiments of music or the basic skills of healthy vocalization. Choirs are founded on need and opportunity, enthusiasm and eagerness. The individual singers, relying on a native ability to imitate sound and to recall tuneful melodies, may possess years of choral experience without exposure to a true musical education. Most choirs represent an educational institution to their own membership and the singers expect the conductor to teach them. Too often, the conductor teaches only the notes and basic performance exigencies of the selected repertoire, although the choral rehearsal can be the optimal forum for the study of musicianship. Rhythm, sight-singing, ear training, form and analysis, and historical style studies are all regular topics of consideration in rehearsals. Choral conductors must also incorporate healthy vocalism in each rehearsal.

Choral pedagogy seeks to bridge the gap between choral conducting and choral singing. Choral conductors and singers alike need to recognize the principles of vocal pedagogy and voice science and how they apply to the study and performance of choral music.

This textbook provides an outline for the practical vocal education of a choral conductor. It should prove useful to voice teachers, church musicians, solo singers, and choral singers. Health care providers and speech-language pathologists will find the contents helpful in their evaluation of choral singer patients. In the second edition, we have not only updated the 12 chapters published in the first edition, but we have also added new chapters on "The Aging Voice," "Performing Arts Medicine and the Professional Voice: Risks of Nonvoice Performance," "Voice Disorders Among Choral Music Educators," and "Choral Singing and Children." We have made every effort to keep the book accessible and practical. It should prove useful.

This book contains numerous exercises and specific techniques to help develop healthy choral singing. These are not put forth as the only way to achieve the desired ends, but are examples of the kinds of exercises that have worked well for the authors, Dr. Brenda Smith and Dr. Robert T. Sataloff. They are intended as a guide. The authors hope that anyone who accepts the privilege and responsibility of caring for and training choirs will take the time to master not only the music skills but also the vocal skills that are so important to expressive, successful, healthy, and progressively better choral performance.

Reference

1. Rudolf M. *The Grammar of Conducting.* New York, NY: G Schirmer; 1950.

ABOUT THE AUTHORS

Brenda Smith, DMA

Dr. Brenda Smith teaches studio voice, diction, and vocal pedagogy at the University of Florida in Gainesville. She has been widely recognized for her contributions to the concept of lifelong singing through proper voice care. Dr. Smith is a lyric soprano with special interests in the recital and concert repertoire. In addition, Dr. Smith was translator, collaborator, and assistant to Dr. Wilhelm Ehmann and Dr. Frauke Haasemann, the pedagogues whose work in Germany and the United States developed the concept of voice building for choirs. Dr. Smith works regularly as consultant, clinician, and conductor with amateur and professional choirs throughout the world. She has been associated with the choirs of St. Ignatius Loyola, the Central City Chorus, and the Dessoff Choirs in New York City, the Mendelssohn Club of Philadelphia, the Cathedral Choral Society of the National Cathedral in Washington, D.C., as well as the choirs of the Epiphany Cathedral in Venice, Florida. Because of her interest in public and private music education, Dr. Smith has been the Two-College Choir Interest Chair for the Southern Division of the American Choral Directors Association.

Dr. Smith has collaborated with Dr. Robert Thayer Sataloff, implementing projects to promote vocal health through the choral experience and has presented her work regularly at the International Symposium on the Care of the Professional Voice, sponsored by the Voice Foundation. In June 2000, Dr. Smith was honored by the Voice Foundation and the National Association of Teachers of Singing as the recipient of the Van Lawrence Award in recognition of her demonstrated excellence in teaching of singing and her active interest in voice science and pedagogy. As the Van Lawrence winner, she traveled to the Royal Institute of Technology in Stockholm, Sweden during May 2001 to pursue topics in the acoustics of the voice with Dr. Johan Sundberg.

As Coordinator of Musical Activities at the German School of Middlebury College in Vermont, Dr Smith founded and directed the

"German for Singers" program, a curriculum combining culture and language study with vocal performance. Annually, Dr Smith presents workshops at colleges and universities throughout the United States, Germany, and Switzerland.

She is the translator of the book *Voice Building for Choirs* by Wilhelm Ehmann and Frauke Haasemann (Chapel Hill, NC: Hinshaw Music, Inc.; 1980). Dr. Smith is the author of the forthcoming book, *Cantare et Sonare: A Handbook of Choral Performance Practice* (Hinshaw Music, Inc.) as well as numerous articles on issues of vocal/choral music pedagogy and performance.

Dr. Smith earned a bachelor of music degree at the University of Evansville with further study at the Hochschule für Kirchenmusik der Evangelischen Kirche-Herford and the Hochschule für Musik und darstellende Kunst/Hamburg in Germany. She holds the master of music degree in voice performance from Westminster Choir College, Princeton NJ and a DMA degree in vocal pedagogy and performance from the University of Maryland, College Park. She taught at Westminster Choir College, Dickinson College, Rowan University of New Jersey, and Manatee Community College in Bradenton Florida.

**Robert T. Sataloff,
MD, DMA, FACS**

Dr. Sataloff is Professor of Otolaryngology at Jefferson Medical College, Thomas Jefferson University in Philadelphia; Chairman of the Department of Otolaryngology-Head and Neck Surgery at Graduate Hospital; Adjunct Professor of Otorhinolaryngology–Head and Neck Surgery, The University of Pennsylvania; on the faculty of the Academy of Vocal Arts; and Conductor of the Thomas Jefferson University Choir and Orchestra; and Director of the Voice Foundation's Annual Symposium on Care of the Professional Voice. Dr. Sataloff is also a professional singer and singing teacher. He holds an undergraduate degree from Haverford College in Music Theory and Composition, graduated from Jefferson Medical College, Thomas Jefferson University, received a Doctor of Musical Arts in Voice Performance from Combs College of Music; and he completed his Residency in Otolaryngology–Head and Neck Surgery and a Fellowship in Otology, Neurotology, and Skull Base Surgery at the University of Michigan. Dr. Sataloff is Chairman of the Board of Directors of the Voice Foundation and of the American Institute for Voice and Ear Research. He has also served as Chairman of the Board of Governors of Graduate Hospital, President of the International Association of Phonosurgery, President of the American Laryngological Association, and President of the Pennsylvania Academy of Otolaryngology–Head and Neck Surgery. He is Editor-in-Chief of the *Journal of Voice*, Editor-in-Chief of *Ear, Nose and Throat Journal*, and on the Editorial Boards of the *Journal of Singing, Medical Problems of Performing Artists*, and numerous otolaryngology journals in the United States. Dr. Sataloff has written over 600 publications, including 35 books. Dr. Sataloff's medical practice is limited to care of the professional voice and to otology/neurotology/skull base surgery.

CONTRIBUTORS

Margaret Baroody, MM
Singing Voice Specialist
Philadelphia Ear, Nose and
    Throat Associates
and American Institute for
    Voice and Ear Research
Philadelphia, Pennsylvania,
    USA

Mary Hawkshaw, RN, BSN
Otolaryngologic Nurse
    Clinician
Executive Director
American Institute for Voice
    and Ear Research
Board of Directors
The Voice Foundation
Philadelphia, Pennsylvania

Richard Miller DHL
Professor of Singing
Director, Otto B. Schoepfle,
    Vocal Arts Laboratory
Oberlin College Conservatory
    of Music
Oberlin, Ohio

Richard N. Norris, MD
Private Practice
Physical Medicine and
    Rehabilitation
Florence, Massachusetts

**Robert T. Sataloff, MD, DMA,
    FACS**
Professor, Department of
    Otolaryngology–Head and
    Neck Surgery
Jefferson Medical College
Thomas Jefferson University
    and Chairman, Department
    of Otolaryngology–Head
    and Neck Surgery
    Graduate Hospital
Adjunct Professor of
    Otorhinolaryngology
University of Pennsylvania
Chairman, Board of Directors
The Voice Foundation
Faculty, Academy of Vocal
    Arts
Chairman, American Institute
    for Voice and Ear Research
Philadelphia, Pennsylvania

Brenda Smith, DMA
Assistant Professor of Music
    (Voice)
School of Music
University of Florida
Gainesville, Florida

*In memory of Dr. Wilhelm Ehmann and
Dr. Frauke Haasemann*

*With love and gratitude to Ronald G. Burrichter
and Dahlia, Ben, and John Sataloff*

PART I

Introduction

CHAPTER

1

Amateur and Professional Choral Singers

Most singing around the world is done by amateur singers in choirs, whether they are affiliated with schools, religious institutions, communities, barbershop quartet clubs, or other organizations. Nearly all choirs have an artistic leader or conductor. Consequently, choral conductors are in a unique cultural and epidemiologic position to educate, protect, or potentially injure singers. They also are often the first people to detect vocal problems that require referral for medical attention.

Choral conductors represent more to choir members than just professional musical leaders. Whether choral conductors wish to be or not, they are often therapists, role models, teachers, advisers, and inspirators. Hence, choral conductors must make an extra effort to not only master the art and science of choral singing, but also to understand the individuality of singers under their leadership. Such insight is essential if conductors are to extract the best musical and vocal performances from their singers, especially in amateur choirs, but in professional groups as well.

The Nature of the Amateur Singer
"I have had singing"

Singing surrounds our lives. From the whispered tunes of memory to the pleading calls of birds, from the mindless chants of youth to the soulful meditations of later life, our world rings with song. In *Akenfield*, a real place with a fictitious name, an 85-year-old horseman defines the periods of his life using concentric circles of song:

> There was nothing in my childhood, only work. I never had pleasure. One day a year I went to Felixstowe along with the chapel women and children, and that was my pleasure. But I have forgotten one thing—the singing. There was such a lot of singing in the villages then, and this was my pleasure, too. Boys sang in the fields, and at night we all met at the Forge and sang. The chapels were full of singing. When the first war came, it was singing, singing all the time. So I lie; I have had pleasure. I have had singing.[1(p51)]

Unlike the professional, whose worth is measured in playbills and recording credits, amateur singers seek only pleasure. They have singing.

The amateur singer, devoted with anonymous ardor, may be the wisest singer of all. The amateur singer tends to love singing unconditionally, having few exalted expectations or inflated ambitions. It is not by chance that untrained musicians are defined by words like *amateur* or *volunteer*, words firmly based in love and commitment. The only selfish desires of an amateur singer are honorable ones—namely, acceptance, companionship, learning, and adventure. Most amateur singers do not seek the limelight, preferring instead to huddle with others of like interest. Community choruses, church choirs, barbershop quartets, and other singing societies crop up wherever a few shy but sincere singers gather. Such singing groups, regardless of size, are potent agents within any culture, a place where love resides and is earnestly expressed.

Many choral-conducting superstars have gone on record in favor of the amateur singer over the professional, stating that better cooperation and deeper commitment outweigh musical talent and training. Amateurs bring no stopwatch to a rehearsal, make no attempt to withhold vocal gifts in favor of better-paying events. Confident in the strength of voices united, they abandon themselves to the act of singing. Void of inhibition or judgment, they blend breath with thought, and drama with music in portions equal to their individual abilities. The freshness of this free expression serves as leaven for the conductor's interpretation of the work in progress. Music made among amateur singers often prompts subconscious recollection of familiar adages such as, "out of the mouth of babes" or "a little child will lead them." The amateur's unencumbered innocence informs the singing and the silence, setting the music itself across uncharted, deep waters.

Amateur singers do not confine their musical life to rehearsal and performance spaces. They sing everywhere—in subways, stairwells, and shower stalls—setting their world into motion with music. Singing soothes the sadness of the day, enlivens the boredom, releases the tensions, or simply provides good company. Singing, be it conscious or subconscious, punctuates moments of being, mundane or meaningful. Like the flow of the tides and the faces of the moon, the whistled tune and hummed jingle respond to the poetic magnetism of Earth's orbit. Many amateurs hover near a sound system, joining with invisible choirs for the singing of recorded masterworks. Signs announcing "Karaoke" invite amateur singers to attempt Olympic greatness, spreading the wings of song in limited sky. With no fear of a rebuke, such voices celebrate fully the collision of air with intelligence known as singing.

The act of singing is a form of therapy for many amateurs, a chance to explore and give order to life. Choral singing is group therapy, inviting self-awareness and communal involvement. The instant of resonant sound is a moment of enlightenment—physical, spiritual, and musical. Aglow with the pride of an athletic achievement, choral singers reach a personal best amid team involvement.

Derived from secret depths, singing is a phenomenon to singers and scientists alike. Medical professionals and musicians marvel at the mysteries of the physical instrument, its efficiency and its resilience, its emotional and melodic range. In fact, the closer the encounter with singing and singers, the more profound the amazement. Singing is an art capable of evoking celestial ecstasies and earthbound anxiety, inducing deep inhalation and utter breathlessness. Its subject matter need not be perfected to be powerful. Its potency is rarely considered, although it is often thoroughly realized. Song unleashes a magic potion, like swirls of an exquisite perfume. Singing is utterly seductive, capturing the imagination, altering life's rhythm, congealing love and loyalty in lyric form. Politicians, athletes, educators, theologians, and advertisers know that texts sung meet the mark missed by dry readings. They encourage charismatic delivery of the simplest information through chants, choruses, and jingles. History recounts tales of soldiers, servants, and slaves maintaining momentum in the midst of monotony or catastrophe by tapping an innermost source of melody.

Standing at a respectful distance, amateur singers savor every suc-
culent morsel of music and thought. Amateurs have accepted themselves as passionate lovers, willingly seduced by song. They would be
satisfied to repeat familiar music season after season, wringing it dry
and immersing themselves anew. Luckily, there is a symbiosis between
the professional and amateur singing set. Each relies on the other for
inspiration and endorsement. Professional singers are amateurs who
have risen through the ranks, ascending on the shoulders of aging
vocal artists. Although there is little room at the top of this pyramid of
song, bountiful space is available at its base. The bricks are laid with
the love of singing, the amateur spirit. There we hear singing, lots of
singing; there we all find pleasure in singing. There we, as choral conductors, find our greatest challenges, most awesome responsibilities,
and often our greatest rewards.

Conducting Professional Singers

Professional singers participate in choral activities at three levels:
"ringers," contractual choral singers, and professional choral organizations. The term "ringers" refers to singers who are invited to join
an amateur choir shortly before a public performance. Ringers fortify
and balance the choral sound, sometimes serving as soloists as well.
Contractual choral singers are freelance artists who accept assignments
with other professional singers to create a choral group that meets the
demands of a concert series, a premiere, or an orchestral work requiring choral singing. Professional choirs, organizations providing regular
employment for a set number of auditioned singers, are somewhat rare
in the United States. They are based on the European prototypes of
radio broadcasting choirs, military choral groups, and opera choruses.
Professional choral singers are not discussed at length in this book
because they represent a small percentage of the choral culture.

Generally, ringers enter the amateur choral scene just as the hard
work of perfecting the music has ended and the joys of performing it
approach. Although amateur singers may appreciate the additional
vocal forces, they react immediately to any lack of preparation or
commitment that ringers present. It is essential that ringers rehearse
with the conductor before they are introduced into the various sections
of the choir.

Contracted choral singers follow union rules and gather around
a project with an eye to the clock. They are providing a service in
exchange for payment. Because of contractual time constraints, the

choral conductor must speak efficiently and clearly. Contractual singers expect to be treated with an "instrumental" tone, without any particular interest in voice building. The blending of voices within a section and the balance of choral sections within the choir may not be priorities to these singers, whose voices are trained for solo perform-ance. Such singers are usually punctual and prepared but may not exhibit deep involvement in the musical result without significant inspiration from the conductor.

Professional choirs are particularly adept at achieving a choral sound and reading a complicated score. They possess significant abili-ties as professional choristers and their expectations of a choral con-ductor are also very high. When addressing a professional choir, the conductor must have a detailed rehearsal plan and an exquisite com-mand of the score, its context, and its idiosyncracies. The conductor should adjust vocabulary and syntax to accommodate the musical and vocal expertise of professional singers. The singers will be very alert to the conductor's gestures and nuances and ready to respond fully to what is seen and said. They require a most delicate mix of respect, challenge, inspiration, and the old-fashioned enthusiasm they may not have experienced routinely since their amateur days. Once they have been inspired and molded into a cohesive unit, they become most gratifying and easy to conduct, as long as the conductor is well-prepared and knows exactly what he or she wants to achieve. While they require smaller gestures and less effort on the podium, they demand absolute precision because they will respond to the conduc-tor's smallest physical nuance.

Although professional choirs consist of trained singers, warm-up and cool-down exercises should not be neglected. They prepare even pro-fessional groups physically and mentally, and they help the ensemble.

Choral music is a different art form to professional singers than to amateurs. It may not hold the same social and emotional properties that amateur singers cherish. The musical score is more accessible, perhaps, but the associated elements of unity and blend may be harder to achieve.

Although their numbers are small, the importance of the best pro-fessional choirs deserves emphasis. They set a standard toward which amateur groups strive. That standard must possess more than wonder-ful voices and luxurious choral textures. Professional choirs offer the possibility of near-perfection in choral sound and musical interpretation. Hence, even though they may sound excellent from day one, conductors must work that much harder to challenge professional choirs to achieve the last bits of artistic and technical perfection within their grasp.

Reference

1. Blythe R. *Akenfield: Portrait of an English Village*. London, England: Penguin Press; 1969:51.

CHAPTER

2

The Rehearsal Process

Every rehearsal should be a lively forum for learning, discussion, and experimentation. By combining their efforts, choral singers and conductors may heighten their musicianship and interpretative skill. Each step of the process must move from simple to complex, from a mere acquaintance with the music to a sincere understanding of it. The path toward performance should be fulfilling, innovative, fortifying, and instructive—never rigorous or routine. Drawing on the resources of the music and its historical, poetic, and stylistic context, a conductor leads the members of the ensemble through a labyrinth of meaningful encounters that inform and improve the ultimate performance of the music. A comprehensive approach to the technical, musicologic, and literary aspects of a choral work will give life to the rehearsal process.

A philosophy for teaching musical repertoires grows from an awareness of the idiosyncratic, idiomatic capabilities of a given musical instrument and its literature. Thus, the vocal instrument cannot be separated from the person for whom the voice is a precious means of communication. The singer's quality of life determines much about the spontaneity and responsiveness of the voice. Physical, mental, and spiritual properties combine in a dynamic way, creating a kaleidoscope of action and reaction in a singer. The conductor must amass an arsenal of pedagogical tools, poetic inspiration, historical knowledge, and personal skills to keep pace with the ever-changing complexion of the choir. It is essential that choral conductors learn to use their own voices well, thereby forming a personal frame of reference for vocal matters.

Posture, quality and tone of voice, use of language, and the shape and timing of choral conducting gestures should each exemplify and encourage good vocal habits.

Conductors must remember that singers have "singers' ways," which include fears and apprehensions as well as patterns and habits specific to the idiom of choral singing. Choral singers are aware of each other. They are unsure of their personal role in the activities of the whole and insecure about the symbols on the musical page. Singers are concerned about vocal health. Choral singers are eager for constructive criticism and praise. They tend to tire easily, as choral singing is not their primary occupation on any given day.

The point of departure for developing choral sound is found at the juncture where the conductor and choir meet on similar intellectual and musical turf. If the singers listen and adapt to the common denominator of the group, the choir can be lifted to a higher level of musical achievement. Lines of communication are defined by the conductor's ability to empathize in language, mentality, and culture with the choir.

No amount of conducting skill or educational background will suffice if a conductor is unable to express information in a manner appropriate and acceptable to the choir. The conductor's vocabulary, well chosen and sincerely spoken, must reflect an appreciation and respect for the choir and its corporate musicality. Conductors should study the idiomatic language spoken among the singers to arrive at modes of speech typical of the choir's milieu. After a season of work together, a choir and its conductor generally establish a vocabulary and syntax specific to the organization and its purposes. It is wise to work within the linguistic framework of the choir, rather than impose a hierarchy of foreign terminology likely to alienate and confuse singers.

The content of the material taught should be ordered as carefully and clearly as possible, creating a logical train of thought and action. Using the Socratic principle that knowledge cannot come from without, exercises and explanations should be drawn from events of daily life. In this way, a link is forged between the podium and the singing personnel, between the musical life within and the world outside the rehearsal hall. References to real-life situations or current events create an even playing field for singers and conductors. By presenting such exercises or points of reference, the conductor follows a direct train of thought from familiar daily life to unfamiliar singing circumstances, from shared experience to uncharted adventure. Choral music making does not depend ultimately on the sum total of vocal gifts. The expressive capacity of a choir equals the quotient of human understanding and pedagogical willingness between conductor and choir. A rehearsal should speak to the spirit of the singers.

It is useful to spend time at the beginning of any rehearsal defining the relationship between the music to be learned and the spirit of its creation, between the phrases to be sung and the personal lyricism they evoke. The architecture of the musical form, the style of singing, and the range of poetic interpretation should all be discussed openly. The logic behind each melodic stroke or harmonic crafting will inform the reading of individual notes and rhythms, relieving the choir of treading tediously through a wilderness of the printed score. Compositional "fingerprints" of composers (tendencies toward repetition or imitation, structures achieving balance or asymmetry, preference for specific climactic or cadential figures) should be identified for the choir. Discipline in a rehearsal is rarely a factor if each singer is engaged in an inner search for commonality with the music and its origin.

Although a choral conductor expects the choir's labors to yield substantial rewards in performance, the rehearsal process, with its rich opportunities for learning and sharing, is equally important. The choral tradition in North America is based on the workings of the Berliner Singakademie, an organization founded in Germany by Friedrich Fasch in 1791 to give expression to the principles of the French Revolution, namely, "freedom, equality, and brotherhood." The Singakademie grew from the intellectual life of the Humboldt Universität in Berlin and offered musical instruction to students and amateur singers of all ages. Its constitution states that performances "should occur only when absolutely necessary," and the Singakademie stressed the value of the rehearsal situation. Musical amateurs from all walks of life were encouraged to share their insights into the music, its text, and its transformation through song. At first, the choral activities of the Singakademie centered on the study of works by the masters of the a cappella tradition, especially Palestrina, Isaac, and Lotti. Perhaps its highest moment came in 1829, when the young Felix Mendelssohn-Bartholdy conducted the Berliner Singakademie in a public performance of JS Bach's *St. Matthew Passion*, fortifying the revival of the masterworks of Germany's extensive choral heritage. Throughout the annals of the Singakademie, there are testimonies to the content and atmosphere of rehearsal circumstances and to the beauty of integrated musical preparation. Members of the Singakademie read and discussed issues of poetry, politics, and philosophy. Friendship, fine art, and critical thinking augmented the rudiments and rigors of music making, creating evenings of true enrichment.

For many choral singers, choral music means companionship around a common interest. For some, the door of the choir room means home and hearth. For others, the choir is a refuge from the world, the place from which one cannot be summoned. It is essential that conductors consider the significance of friendship and harmony within the organization. The spiritual elements of the music pervade the spirit of the group, offering comfort and relief, inspiration and edification. For its members, the choir is often the single most important social outlet. The associated social activities of a choral group generate the loyalty that fosters stamina and commitment for the tasks of choral singing.

The choral art emerges gently from a rehearsal process. Rehearsals provide historical context, follow the compositional process of the composer, and give thought and word to the literary art form set to melodic and harmonic shapes. Such rehearsals require careful planning, exquisite timing, and deep interdisciplinary understanding. The process toward a choral performance can and should be rich and colorful, as fulfilling as the concert itself.

PART II

Vocal Health and Pedagogy

CHAPTER

3

Anatomy and Physiology of the Voice

The human voice is remarkable, complex, and delicate. It is capable of conveying not only sophisticated intellectual concepts, but also subtle emotional nuances. Although the uniqueness and beauty of the human voice have been appreciated for centuries, medical science has begun to understand the workings and care of the voice only since the late 1970s and the early 1980s. To train the voice efficiently and safely, the choral conductor should have knowledge of the anatomy and physiology of phonation. Although it is not necessary to master detailed scientific information about anatomy and physiology to sing in a healthy fashion, at least a basic understanding of the structures and functions is helpful to singers and required of their teachers, including their conductors.

Anatomy
What Body Parts Make Up The Voice?

What is the larynx?

The *larynx* (voice box) is essential to normal voice production, but the anatomy of the voice is not limited to the larynx. The vocal mechanism includes the abdominal and back musculature, the rib cage, the lungs, and the *pharynx*, oral cavity, and nose. Each component performs an important function in voice production, although it is possible to produce voice even without a larynx (eg, in patients who have undergone laryngectomy [removal of the larynx] for cancer). In addition, virtually all parts of the body play some role in voice production and may be responsible for voice dysfunction. Even something as remote as a sprained ankle may alter posture, thereby impairing abdominal muscle function and resulting in vocal inefficiency, weakness, or hoarseness.

The larynx is composed of four basic anatomic units: *skeleton, intrinsic muscles, extrinsic muscles,* and *mucosa.* The most important parts of the laryngeal skeleton are the *thyroid cartilage, cricoid cartilage,* and two *arytenoid cartilages* (Figure 3-1). Intrinsic muscles of the larynx are connected to these cartilages. One of the intrinsic muscles, the *vocalis muscle* (part of the *thyroarytenoid muscle*), extends on each side from the arytenoid cartilage to the inside of the thyroid cartilage just below and behind the "*Adam's apple*," forming the body of the *vocal folds* (popularly called the *vocal cords*) (Figure 3-2). The vocal folds act as the *oscillator* or *voice source* (noise maker) of the vocal tract. The space between the vocal folds is called the *glottis* and is used as an anatomic reference point. The intrinsic muscles alter the position, shape, and tension of the vocal folds, bringing them together (*adduction*), moving them apart (*abduction*), or stretching them by increasing longitudinal tension. They are able to do so because the laryngeal cartilages are connected by soft attachments that allow changes in their relative angles and distances, thereby permitting alteration in the shape and tension of the tissues suspended between them. The arytenoid cartilages are also capable of rock-ing, rotating, and gliding, which permits complex vocal fold motion (Figure 3-3) and alternation in the shape of the vocal fold edge. All but one of the muscles on each side of the larynx are innervated by one of the two *recurrent laryngeal nerves.* Because this structure runs a long course from the neck down into the chest and then back up to the larynx (hence, the name "recurrent"), it is easily injured by trauma, neck surgery, and chest surgery, which may result in vocal fold paralysis. The remaining muscle (cricothyroid muscle) is innervated by the *superior laryngeal nerve* on each side, which is especially susceptible to viral and traumatic injury. It produces increases in longitudinal tension important in volume projection and pitch control. The "false vocal folds" are located above the vocal folds; unlike the true vocal folds, they do not make contact during normal speaking or singing.

Because the attachments of the laryngeal cartilages are flexible, the positions of the cartilages change with respect to each other when the laryngeal skeleton is elevated or lowered. Such changes in vertical height are controlled by the extrinsic laryngeal muscles, or strap muscles of the neck.

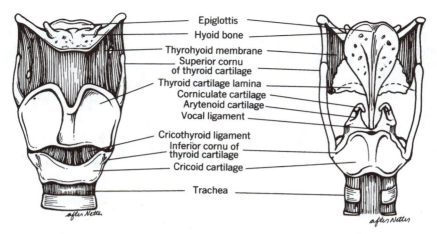

Epiglottis
Hyoid bone
Thyrohyoid membrane
Superior cornu
of thyroid cartilage
Thyroid cartilage lamina
Corniculate cartilage
Arytenoid cartilage
Vocal ligament
Cricothyroid ligament
Inferior cornu of
thyroid cartilage
Cricoid cartilage
Trachea

Anterior   Posterior

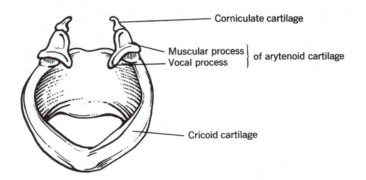

Corniculate cartilage

Muscular process
Vocal process } of arytenoid cartilage

Cricoid cartilage

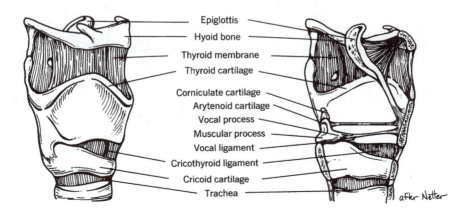

Epiglottis
Hyoid bone
Thyroid membrane
Thyroid cartilage
Corniculate cartilage
Arytenoid cartilage
Vocal process
Muscular process
Vocal ligament
Cricothyroid ligament
Cricoid cartilage
Trachea

FIGURE 3-1. Cartilages of the larynx.

17

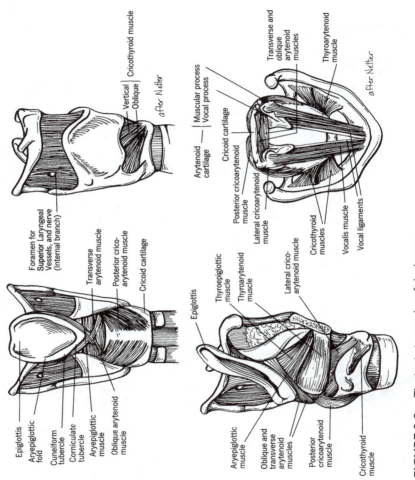

FIGURE 3-2. The intrinsic muscles of the larynx.

Epiglottis

Aryepiglottic fold

Cuneiform tubercle

Corniculate tubercle

Aryepiglottic muscle

Oblique arytenoid muscle

Foramen for Superior Laryngeal Vessels, and nerve (Internal branch)

Transverse arytenoid muscle

Posterior crico-arytenoid muscle

Cricoid cartilage

Vertical ⎫
Oblique ⎬ Cricothyroid muscle

after Netter

Epiglottis

Aryepiglottic muscle

Oblique and transverse arytenoid muscles

Posterior cricoarytenoid muscle

Cricothyroid muscle

Thyroepiglottic muscle

Thyroarytenoid muscle

Lateral crico-arytenoid muscle

Arytenoid cartilage ⎯ ⎫ Muscular process
⎬ Vocal process

Cricoid cartilage

Posterior cricoarytenoid muscle

Lateral cricoarytenoid muscle

Cricothyroid muscles

Vocalis muscle

Vocal ligaments

Transverse and oblique arytenoid muscles

Thyroarytenoid muscle

after Netter

18

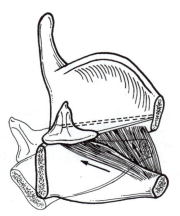

Action of
cricothyroid
muscle

Action of
posterior cricoarytenoid muscles

Action of
lateral cricoarytenoid muscles

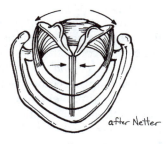

after Netter

Action of
arytenoideus muscle

Action of
vocalis (thyroarytenoid) muscles

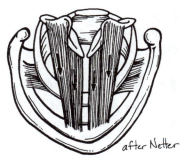

after Netter

FIGURE 3-3. The intrinsic muscles of the larynx and their actions.

When the angles and distances between cartilages change because of this accordion effect, the resting length of the intrinsic muscles is also changed. Such large adjustments in intrinsic muscle condition interfere with fine control of smooth vocal quality. This is why classically trained singers are generally taught to use their extrinsic muscles to maintain the laryngeal skeleton at a relatively constant height regardless of pitch. That is, they learn to avoid the natural tendency of the larynx to rise with ascending pitch and fall with descending pitch, thereby enhancing unity of quality throughout the vocal range. Techniques may be different in certain Asian, Indian, Arabic, and other musical traditions with different aesthetic values.

The soft tissues lining the larynx are much more complex than was originally thought.[1] The mucosa forms the thin, lubricated surface of the vocal folds that makes contact when the two vocal folds are closed. It looks like the mucosa that lines the inside of the mouth. However, the vocal fold is not simply muscle covered with mucosa (Figure 3-4). The thin, lubricated squamous *epithelium* lines the surface. Immediately beneath it, connected by a complex *basement membrane*, is the superficial layer of the *lamina propria*, also known as *Reinke's space*, which consists of loose, fibrous components and matrix. It tends to accumulate fluid, and it contains very few fibroblasts (cells that cause scar formation). The epithelium is connected to the superficial layer of the lamina propria by a sophisticated basement membrane. The intermediate layer of the lamina propria contains primarily elastic fibers and a moderate number of fibroblasts. The deep layer of the lamina propria is rich in fibroblasts and consists primarily of collagenous fibers. It overlies the thyroarytenoid or vocalis muscle. The various layers have different mechanical properties important in allowing the smooth shearing action necessary for proper vocal fold vibration.

Mechanically, the vocal fold structures act more like three layers consisting of the *cover* (epithelium and superficial layer of the lamina propria), *transition* (intermediate and deep layers of the lamina propria), and *body* (the vocalis muscle).

What happens above the larynx?

The *supraglottic* vocal tract includes the pharynx, tongue, palate, oral cavity, nose, and other structures. Together, they act as a *resonator* and are largely responsible for vocal quality (or timbre) and the perceived character of all speech sounds. The vocal folds themselves produce only a "buzzing" sound. During the course of vocal training for singing, acting, or healthy speaking, changes occur not only in the larynx, but also in the muscle motion, control, and shape of the supraglottic vocal tract.

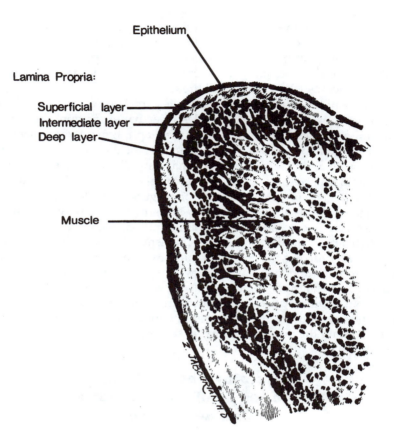

FIGURE 3-4. The structure of the vocal fold.

What happens below the larynx?

The *infraglottic* vocal tract serves as the *power source* for the voice. Singers and actors refer to the entire power source complex as their *"support"* or *"diaphragm."* Actually, the anatomy of support for phonation is especially complicated and not completely understood, and performers who use the terms diaphragm and support do not always mean the same thing. Yet, it is quite important because deficiencies in support are frequently responsible for voice dysfunction.

The purpose of the support mechanism is to generate a force that directs a controlled airstream between the vocal folds. Active respiratory muscles work together with passive forces. The principal muscles of inspiration are the diaphragm (a dome-shaped muscle that extends along the bottom of the rib cage) and the external intercostal (rib) muscles. During quiet breathing, expiration is largely passive. The lungs and rib cage generate passive expiratory forces under many common circumstances, such as after a full breath.

Many of the muscles used for active expiration are also employed in "support" for phonation. Muscles of active expiration either raise the intra-abdominal pressure, forcing the diaphragm upward, lower the ribs or sternum to decrease the dimensions of the thorax, or both, thereby compressing air in the chest. The primary muscles of expiration are the abdominal muscles, but internal intercostals and other chest and back muscles are also involved. Trauma or surgery that alters the structure or function of these muscles or ribs undermines the power source of the voice, as do diseases that impair expiration, such as asthma.

Deficiencies in the support mechanism often result in compensatory efforts utilizing the laryngeal muscles, which are not designed for power source functions. Such behavior can result in decreased voice function, rapid fatigue, pain, and even structural pathology including vocal fold nodules. Current expert treatment for such problems focuses on correction of the underlying malfunction. This often cures the problem, avoiding the need for laryngeal surgery.

Physiology of the Voice
How does it all work together
to make a voice?

What do the brain and the nerves have to do with voice production?

The physiology of voice production is extremely complex.[2,3,4] Volitional production of voice begins in the cerebral cortex of the brain. The command for vocalization involves complex interaction among brain centers for speech and other areas. For singing, speech directives must be integrated with information from the centers for musical and artistic expression. The "idea" of the planned vocalization is conveyed to the precentral gyrus in the motor cortex, which transmits another set of instructions to the motor nuclei in the brainstem and spinal cord. These areas send out the complicated messages necessary for coordinated activity of the larynx, the chest and abdominal musculature, and the vocal tract articulators. Additional refinement of motor activity is provided by the extrapyramidal and autonomic nervous systems. These impulses combine to produce a sound that is transmitted not only to the ears of the listener, but also to those of the speaker or singer. Auditory feedback is transmitted from the ear through the brainstem to the cerebral cortex, and adjustments are made that permit the vocalist to match the sound produced with the sound intended, integrating the acoustic properties of the performance environment. Tactile feedback from the throat and the muscles involved in phonation also helps in the fine tuning of vocal output, although the mechanism and role of tactile (sense of feeling or touch) feedback are not fully understood. Many trained singers and speakers cultivate the ability to use tactile feedback effectively because of expected interference with auditory feedback data from ancillary sound, such as an orchestra, choir, or band.

How is sound produced?

Phonation—the production of sound—requires interaction among the power source, oscillator, and resonator. The voice may be compared to a brass instrument, such as a trumpet. Power is generated by the chest, abdomen, and back musculature, and a high-pressure airstream is produced. The trumpeter's lips open and close against the mouthpiece, producing a "buzz" similar to the sound produced by vocal fold contact. This sound then passes through the trumpet, which has acoustic resonance characteristics that shape the sound we associate with trumpet music. The nonmouthpiece portions of a brass instrument are analogous to the supraglottic vocal tract.

During phonation, the infraglottic musculature must make rapid, complex adjustments because the resistance changes almost continuously as the glottis closes, opens, and changes shape. At the beginning of each phonatory cycle, the vocal folds are approximated, and the glottis is obliterated. This permits infraglottic air pressure to build up, typically to a level of about 7 cm of water, for conversational speech. At this point, the vocal folds are convergent (Figure 3-5, A). Because the vocal folds are closed, there is no airflow. The subglottic pressure then pushes the vocal folds progressively farther apart from the bottom up (Figure 3-5, B) until a space develops (Figure 3-5, C and D) and air begins to flow. *Bernoulli force* created by the air passes between the vocal folds and combines with the mechanical properties of the folds to begin closing the lower portion of the glottis almost immediately (Figure 3-5, E–H), even while the upper edges are still separating. The principles and mathematics of Bernoulli force are complex. It is a flow effect more easily understood by familiar examples, such as the sensation of pull exerted on a vehicle when passed by a truck at high speed or the inward motion of a shower curtain when the water flows past it.

The upper portion of the vocal folds has strong elastic properties that tend to make the vocal folds snap back to the midline. This force

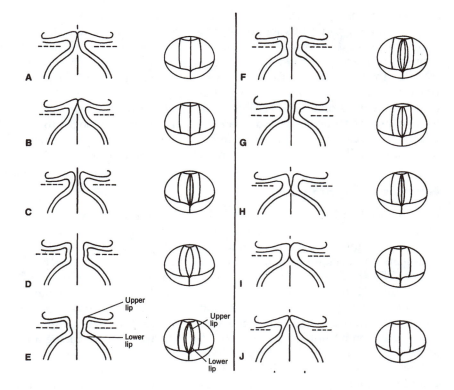

FIGURE 3-5. Movements of the vocal fold edges illustrating vertical phase difference.

becomes more dominant as the upper edges are stretched and the opposing force of the air diminishes because of approximation of the lower edges of the vocal folds. The upper portions of the vocal folds are then returned to the midline (Figure 3-5, I) completing the glottic cycle. Subglottal pressure then builds again (Figure 3-5, J), and the events repeat. The frequency of vibration (number of cycles of openings and closings per second) measured in hertz [Hz] is dependent on the air pressure and on mechanical properties of the vocal folds, which are regulated in part by the laryngeal muscles.[4]

Pitch is the perceptual correlate of frequency. Under most circumstances, as the vocal folds are thinned and stretched and air pressure is increased, the frequency of air pulse emission increases, and pitch goes up. The *myoelastic-aerodynamic mechanism of phonation* reveals that the vocal folds emit pulses of air, rather than vibrating like strings, and also that there is a vertical phase difference. That is, the lower portion of the vocal folds begins to open and close before the upper portion. The rippling displacement of the vocal fold cover produces a mucosal wave that can be examined clinically under stroboscopic light. If this complex motion is impaired, hoarseness or other changes in voice quality may cause the patient to seek medical evaluation.

The sound produced by the vibrating vocal folds, called the voice source signal, is a complex tone containing a *fundamental frequency* and many *overtones*, or higher *harmonic partials*. The amplitude of the partials decreases uniformly at approximately 12 dB per octave. Interestingly, the acoustic spectrum of the voice source is about the same in ordinary speakers as it is in trained singers and speakers.[3] Voice quality differences in voice professionals occur as the voice source signal passes through their supraglottic vocal tract resonator system.

How is the sound shaped?

The pharynx, the oral cavity, and the nasal cavity act as a series of interconnected resonators, which are more complex than that in the trumpet example or other single resonators. As with other resonators, some frequencies are attenuated, while others are enhanced (Figure 3-6). Enhanced frequencies are then radiated with higher relative amplitudes or intensities. Sundberg has shown that the vocal tract has four or five important resonance frequencies called *formants*. The presence of formants alters the uniformly sloping voice source spectrum and creates peaks at formant frequencies. These alterations of the voice source spectral envelope are responsible for distinguishable sounds of speech and song.[2] The *singer's formant* is of special interest. It is a strong acoustical peak at about 2400 Hz to 3200 Hz, depending on voice classification. It is responsible for the "ring" that allows a solo singer to be heard over the sounds of choirs, orchestras, and environmental noise. Even though it is roughly 3½ octaves above middle C, it is an essential component of a singer's sound. If it is filtered out, even a great voice like Pavarotti's will lose its ring and disappear into the surrounding envelope of sound.

While a strong singer's formant is essential for easy, exciting solo singing, it is not always a blessing in choral singers. This energy peak must be adjusted and managed to prevent strong voices from standing out in a choral setting.

How do we control pitch and loudness?

The mechanisms that control two vocal characteristics—fundamental frequency and intensity—are particularly important. Fundamental frequency, which corresponds to pitch, can be altered by changing either the air pressure or the mechanical properties of the vocal folds, although

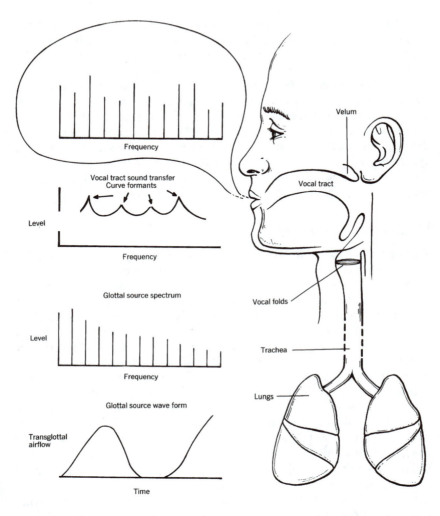

FIGURE 3-6. Function of the vocal tract as a resonator that converts the voice source signal into formants that determine and individual's timbre, vowel intelligibility, and audibility over noise.

changing the latter is more efficient under most conditions. When the cricothyroid muscle contracts, it makes the thyroid cartilage pivot and increases the distance between the thyroid and arytenoid cartilages, thus stretching the vocal folds. This increases the surface area exposed to subglottal pressure and makes the air pressure more effective in opening the glottis. In addition, stretching the elastic fibers of the vocal fold makes them more efficient at snapping back together. As the cycles shorten and repeat more frequently, the fundamental frequency and pitch rise. Other muscles, including the thyroarytenoid, also contribute.[4] Raising the pressure of the airstream also tends to increase fundamental frequency, a phenomenon for which singers must learn to compensate. Otherwise, their pitch would go up whenever they tried to sing more loudly.

Vocal intensity corresponds to loudness and depends on the degree to which the glottal wave motion excites the air molecules in the vocal tract. Raising the air pressure creates greater amplitude of vocal fold displacement from the midline and therefore increases vocal intensity. However, it is not actually the vibration of the vocal fold, but rather the sudden cessation of airflow that is responsible for initiating sound in the vocal tract and controlling intensity. This is similar to the mechanism of the acoustic vibration that results from buzzing lips. In the larynx, the sharper the cutoff of airflow, the more intense the sound.[4]

Can these control systems be assessed?

In the evaluation of voice disorders, clinicians assess an individual's ability to optimize adjustments of air pressure and *glottal resistance*. When high subglottic pressure is combined with high adductory (closing) vocal fold force, glottal airflow and the amplitude of the voice source fundamental frequency are low. This is called *pressed phonation* and can be measured clinically through a technique known as *flow glottography*.[2,4] Flow glottogram wave amplitude indicates the type of phonation used, and the slope (closing rate) gives information about the sound pressure level or loudness. If adductory forces are so weak that the vocal folds do not make contact, the glottis becomes inefficient at resisting air leakage, and the voice source fundamental frequency is also low. This is known as *breathy phonation*. *Flow phonation* is characterized by lower subglottic pressure and lower adductory force. These conditions increase the dominance of the fundamental frequency of the voice source.[2,3,4] Sundberg has shown that the amplitude of the fundamental frequency can be increased by 15 dB or more when the subject changes from pressed phonation to flow phonation.[2] This is a huge increase. If someone in a factory with a large paper machine producing 90 dB turns on a second one, the sound increases by only 3 dB. To get a 15-dB increase, one would need the deafening sound of 32 such machines. If a singer habitually uses pressed phonation, considerable effort will be required to achieve loud voicing. The muscle patterns and force that the singer uses to compensate for this laryngeal inefficiency may cause vocal fatigue and damage.

Conclusion

The vocal mechanism includes the larynx, the abdominal and back musculature, the rib cage, the lungs, and the pharynx, oral cavity, and nose. Each component performs an important function in voice production. The physiology of voice is extremely complex, involving interaction among brain centers for speech and other areas. Signals are transmitted to the motor nuclei in the brainstem and spinal cord, coordinating the activity of the larynx, the chest and abdominal musculature, and the vocal tract articulators. Other areas of the nervous system provide additional refinement. Phonation requires interaction among the power source, oscillator, and resonator. The sound produced by the vocal folds, called the voice source signal, is a complex tone containing a fundamental frequency and many overtones. The pharynx, oral cavity, and nasal cavity act as a series of interconnected resonators. They shape sound quality and enhance audibility by creating a singer's formant. Specific anatomic adjustments control fundamental frequency and intensity and the efficiency of a singer's control strategies can be assessed objectively.

Study Questions

1. What are the cartilages of the larynx?

2. What is the function of the intrinsic muscles of the larynx? Of the extrinsic muscles?

3. Define supraglottic vocal tract and infraglottic vocal tract.

4. What are formants?

5. What is flow phonation?

References

1. Hirano M. Phonosurgery: basic and clinical investigations. *Otologia (Fukuoka)*. 1975;21:239–442.
2. Sundberg J. *The Science of the Singing Voice*. DeKalb, Ill: Northern Illinois University Press; 1987.
3. Scherer RS. Physiology of phonation: a review of basic mechanics. In: Ford CN, Bless DM, eds. *Phonosurgery*. New York, NY: Raven Press; 1991:77–93.
4. Sataloff RT. Clinical anatomy and physiology of the voice. In: Sataloff RT. *Professional Voice: The Science and Art of Clinical Care*. 3rd ed. San Diego, Calif: Plural Publishing, Inc; 2005:143–178.

CHAPTER

Medical Care of Voice Disorders

Robert T. Sataloff and Mary Hawkshaw

What is new in medical care of voice disorders?

Until the 1980s, most physicians caring for patients with voice disorders asked only a few basic questions such as: "How long have you been hoarse?" and "Do you smoke?" The physician's ear was the sole "instrument" used routinely to assess voice quality and function. Visualization of the vocal folds was limited to looking through a mirror placed inside the mouth using regular light or to direct laryngoscopy (looking directly at the vocal folds through a metal pipe) with anesthesia in the operating room. Treatment was generally limited to medicines for infection or inflammation, surgery for bumps or masses; no treatment was recommended if the vocal folds looked "normal." Occasionally, "voice therapy" was recommended, but the specific nature of therapy was not well controlled, and results were often disappointing. Since the early 1980s, the standard of care has changed dramatically.

What kinds of questions are expected from one's doctor?

Good medical diagnosis in all fields often depends on asking the right questions and then listening carefully to the answers. This process is known as "taking a history." Recently, medical care for voice problems has utilized a markedly expanded, comprehensive history, recognizing that there is more to the voice than simply the vocal folds. Virtually any body system may be responsible for voice complaints. In fact, problems outside the larynx often cause voice dysfunction in people whose vocal folds appear fairly normal and who would have received no effective medical care a few years ago.

What is involved in physical examination of a person with voice problems?

In 1854, a singing teacher named Manuel García devised the technique of indirect laryngoscopy. He used the sun as a light source and a dental mirror placed in the mouth to look at the vocal folds of his students. This rapidly became a basic tool for physicians, and it is still in daily use, although they now use an electric light rather than the sun (Figure 4-1). This technique is valuable but has many disadvantages. Effective magnification and photographic documentation are difficult, and standard light does not permit assessment of the rapid and complex motion of the vibratory margin of the vocal folds. After 130 years, technological advances finally addressed these and other shortcomings in the 1980s.

Physical examination of a patient with voice complaints involves a complete ear, nose, and throat assessment and examination of other body systems as appropriate. In the last few years, subjective examination has been supplemented by technological aids that improve the ability to "see" the vocal mechanism and allow quantification of aspects of its function. With phonation at middle C, the vocal folds come together and separate approximately 250 times per second. Strobovideolaryngoscopy uses a laryngeal microphone to trigger a stroboscope that illuminates the vocal folds, allowing the examiner to assess them in slow motion. This technology allows visualization of small masses, vibratory asymmetries, adynamic segments due to scar tissue or early cancer, and other abnormalities that were simply missed in vocal folds that looked "normal" under continuous light. The instruments contained in a well-equipped clinical voice laboratory assess six categories of vocal function: vibratory, aerodynamic, phonatory, acoustic, electromyographic, and psychoacoustic. State-of-the-art analysis of vocal function is extremely helpful in the diagnosis, therapy, and evaluation of progress during the treatment of voice disorders.

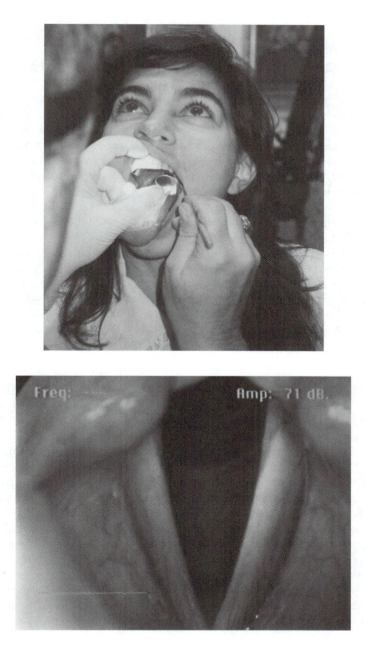

FIGURE 4-1. *Top:* Traditional laryngeal examination. The laryngologist uses a warmed mirror to visualize the vocal fold indirectly. The tongue is grasped, and the patient is asked to say, / i /. *Below:* Normal appearance of the vocal fold oriented as it would be seen through the mirror.

Common Diagnosis and Treatments

Following a thorough history, physical examination, and clinical voice laboratory analysis, it is usually possible to arrive at an accurate explanation for voice dysfunction. Of course, treatment depends on the etiology (cause). Fortunately, as technology has improved voice medicine, the need for laryngeal surgery has diminished. In a great many cases, voice disorders result from respiratory, neurological, gastrointestinal, psychological, endocrine, or some other medical cause that can be treated. Many conditions require prescription of drugs. However, medications must be used with caution because many of them have adverse side effects that alter voice function. Consequently, close collaboration is required among all specialists involved in the patient's care to be certain that treatment of one causal condition does not produce a secondary dysfunction that is also deleterious to the voice. When the underlying problem is corrected properly, the voice usually improves but collaborative treatment by a team of specialists is most desirable to ensure general and vocal health and optimize voice function.

What is hoarseness?

Most people with voice problems complain of "hoarseness" or "laryngitis." A more accurate description of the problem is often helpful in identifying the cause. *Hoarseness* is a coarse, scratchy sound most commonly caused by abnormalities on the vibratory margin of the vocal fold. These may include swelling, roughness from inflammation, growths, scarring, or anything that interferes with symmetric, periodic vocal fold vibration. Such abnormalities produce turbulence that is perceived as hoarseness. *Breathiness* is caused by lesions (abnormalities) that keep the vocal folds from closing completely, including paralysis, muscle weakness, cricoarytenoid joint injury or arthritis, vocal fold masses, or atrophy of the vocal fold tissues. These abnormalities permit air to escape when the vocal folds are supposed to be tightly closed. We hear this air leakage as breathiness.

Fatigue of the voice is inability to continue to phonate for extended periods without change in vocal quality. The voice may fatigue by becoming hoarse, losing range, changing timbre, breaking into different registers, or by other uncontrolled behavior. These problems are especially apparent in actors and singers. A well-trained singer should be able to sing for several hours without developing vocal fatigue. Fatigue is often caused by misuse of abdominal and neck musculature, or overuse (singing or speaking too loudly, too long). Vocal fatigue may be a sign of general tiredness or of serious illnesses such as myasthenia gravis.

Volume disturbance may present as inability to speak or sing loudly or inability to phonate softly. Each voice has its own dynamic range. Professional voice users acquire greater loudness through increased vocal efficiency. They learn to speak and sing more softly through years of laborious practice that involves muscle control and development of the ability to use the supraglottic resonators effectively. Most volume problems are secondary to intrinsic limitations of the voice or technical errors in voice production, although hormonal changes, aging, and neurological disease are other causes. Superior laryngeal nerve paralysis will impair the ability to speak loudly. This is a frequently unrecognized consequence of herpes infections (such as "cold sores") and may be precipitated by an upper respiratory tract infection.

Even nonsingers normally require only about 10 to 30 minutes to warm up the voice. *Prolonged warm-up time*, especially in the morning, is most often caused by reflux laryngitis, a condition in which stomach acid refluxes up the esophagus and ends up burning the throat. *Tickling* or *choking* during speech or singing is associated with laryngitis or voice abuse. Often a symptom of pathology of the vocal fold's leading edge, this symptom requires that voice use be avoided until vocal fold examination has been accomplished. *Pain* while vocalizing can indicate vocal fold lesions, laryngeal joint arthritis, infection, or gastric (stomach) acid irritation of the arytenoids, but it is much more commonly caused by voice abuse with excessive muscular activity in the neck rather than acute pathology on the leading edge of a vocal fold. It does not usually require immediate cessation of phonation pending medical examination.

Does age affect the voice?

Age affects the voice significantly, especially during childhood and older age. Children's voices are particularly fragile. Voice abuse during childhood may lead to problems that persist throughout a lifetime. It is extremely important for children to learn good vocal habits and for them to avoid voice abuse. This is especially true for children who choose to participate in vocally taxing activities, such as singing, acting, and cheerleading. Many promising careers and vocal avocations have been ruined by enthusiastic but untrained voice use. For children with vocal interests, age-appropriate training should be started early. Any child with unexplained or prolonged hoarseness should undergo prompt, expert medical evaluation performed by a laryngologist (ear, nose, and throat doctor) specializing in voice care.

In geriatric patients, vocal unsteadiness, loss of range, and voice fatigue may be associated with typical physiologic aging changes, such as vocal fold atrophy (wasting). In routine speech, such vocal changes allow a person to be identified as "old" even over the telephone. Among singers, they are typically associated with flat pitch and a *"wobble"* often heard in older amateur choir singers. Recent evidence has shown that many of these acoustic phenomena are not caused by irreversible aging changes. Rather, they may be consequences of poor laryngeal, respiratory, and abdominal muscle condition, which undermines the power source of the voice. The medical history usually reveals minimal aerobic exercise and shortness of breath climbing stairs. With appropriate conditioning of the body and voice, many of the characteristics associated with vocal aging can be eliminated, and a youthful sound can be restored.

What are the effects of voice use and training?

The amount of voice use and training also affects voices. Inquiry into vocal habits frequently reveals correctable causes for voice difficulties. Extensive untrained speaking under adverse environmental circumstances is a common example. Such conditions occur, for example, among stock traders, salespeople, restaurant personnel, and people who speak over the telephone in noisy offices. The problems are aggravated by habits that impair the mechanics of voice production, such as sitting with poor posture and bending the neck to hold a telephone against one shoulder. Subconscious efforts to overcome these impediments often produce enough voice abuse to cause vocal fatigue, hoarseness, and even *nodules* (callouslike growths, usually on both vocal folds). Recognizing and eliminating the causal factors through voice therapy and training usually results in disappearance of the nodules and improved voice.

What about singers, actors, and other voice professionals?

It is also essential for the physician to know the extent to which any patient uses his or her voice professionally. Professional singers, actors, announcers, politicians, and others put Olympic demands on their voices. Interest in the diagnosis and treatment of special problems of professional voice users is responsible for the evolution of voice care as a subspecialty of otolaryngology. These patients are often best managed by subspecialists familiar with the latest concepts in professional voice care.

Choral conductors commonly serve as the principal educational resource for amateur singers. The choral conductor is often the first person to recognize hoarseness or some other vocal abnormality, and singers with vocal problems frequently ask their choir conductors for advice and referrals. This opportunity to help, guide, and protect the voices of choral singers is a gratifying part of being a conductor, but it also carries great responsibility. Choral conductors must learn as much as they can about how the voice works and become familiar with the latest concepts and standards of medical practice. They should also investigate the quality and skill of specialists in their areas.

How about smoke and other substances in the air?

Exposure to environmental irritants is a well-recognized cause of voice dysfunction. Smoke, dehydration, pollution, and allergens may produce hoarseness, frequent throat clearing, and voice fatigue. These problems generally can be eliminated by environmental modification, medication, or simply breathing through the nose rather than the mouth, as the nose warms, humidifies, and filters incoming air.

The deleterious effects of tobacco smoke on the vocal folds have been known for many years. Smoking not only causes chronic irritation, but moreover, it can result in histologic (microscopic) alterations in the vocal fold epithelium. The epithelial cells change their appearance, becoming increasingly different from normal epithelial cells. Eventually, they begin to pile up on each other, rather than lining up in an orderly fashion. Then they escape normal homeostatic controls, growing rapidly without restraint and invading surrounding tissues. This drastic change is called squamous cell carcinoma, or cancer of the larynx.

Can foods or drugs affect the voice?

The use of various foods and drugs may affect the voice as well. Some medications may even permanently ruin a voice, especially androgenic (male) hormones, such as those given to women with endometriosis or with postmenopausal sexual dysfunction. Similar problems occur with *anabolic steroids* (also male hormones) used illicitly by bodybuilders. More common drugs also have deleterious vocal effects, usually temporarily. Antihistamines cause dryness, increased throat clearing, and irritation and often aggravate hoarseness. Aspirin contributes to vocal fold hemorrhages because of the same *anticoagulant* properties that make it a good drug for patients with vascular disease. The propellant in inhalers used to treat *asthma* often produces laryngitis. Many neurological, psychological, and respiratory medications cause *tremor* that can be heard in the voice. Numerous other medications cause similar problems. Some foods may also be responsible for voice complaints in people with "normal" vocal folds. Milk products are particularly troublesome to some people because they increase and thicken mucosal secretions.

How about other parts of the body?

The history must also assess the function of the respiratory (breathing), gastrointestinal (gut), endocrine (hormones), neurological, and psychological systems. Disturbances in any of these areas may be responsible for voice complaint. Selected common examples are discussed or illustrated later in this book.

Problems anywhere in the body must be discovered during the medical history. Because voice function relies on such complex brain and nervous system interactions, even slight neurological dysfunction may cause voice abnormalities; voice impairment is sometimes the first symptom of serious diseases, such as myasthenia gravis, multiple sclerosis, and Parkinson's disease. Even a history of a sprained ankle may reveal the true cause of voice dysfunction, especially in a singer, actor, or speaker with great vocal demands. Proper posture is important to optimal function of the abdomen and chest. The imbalance created by standing with the weight over only one foot frequently impairs support enough to cause compensatory vocal strain, leading to hoarseness and voice fatigue. Similar imbalances may occur after other bodily injuries. These include not only injuries that involve support structures, but also problems in the head and neck, especially whiplash. Naturally, a history of laryngeal trauma or surgery predating voice dysfunction raises concerns about the anatomical integrity of the vocal fold but a history of interference with the power source through abdominal or thoracic surgery may be just as important in understanding the cause and optimal treatment of vocal problems.

Do stomach problems or hiatal hernias affect the voice?

Gastrointestinal disorders commonly cause voice complaints. The sphincter between the stomach and esophagus is notoriously weak. In *gastroesophageal reflux laryngitis,* stomach acid refluxes into the throat, allowing droplets of the irritating gastric juices to come in contact with the vocal folds and even to be aspirated into the lungs. Reflux may occur with or without a hiatal hernia. Common symptoms are hoarseness (especially in the morning), prolonged vocal warm-up time, bad breath, sensation of a lump in the throat, chronic sore throat, cough, and a dry or "coated" mouth. Typical heartburn is frequently absent. Over time, uncontrolled reflux may cause cancer of the esophagus and larynx. This condition should be treated conscientiously.

Physical examination usually reveals a bright red, often slightly swollen appearance of the arytenoid mucosa, which helps establish the diagnosis. A barium esophagogram with water siphonage may provide additional information but is not needed routinely. In selected cases,

24-hour pH monitoring provides the best analysis and documentation of reflux. The mainstays of treatment are elevation of the head of the patient's bed (not just sleeping on pillows), use of antacids, and avoidance of food for 3 or 4 hours before sleep. Avoidance of alcohol and coffee is beneficial. Medications that block acid secretion are also useful, including cimetidine (Tagamet), ranitidine (Zantac), famotidine (Pepcid), nizatidine (Axid), omeprazole (Prilosec), lansoprazole (Prevacid), esomepromazole (Nexium) and others. In some cases, surgery to repair the lower esophageal sphincter and cure the reflux may be more appropriate than lifelong medical management. This option has become much more attractive since the development of laparoscopic surgery, which has drastically decreased the morbidity associated with this operation.

Do lung problems cause voice disorders?

Respiratory problems are especially problematic to singers and other voice professionals, but they may cause voice problems in anyone. They also cause similar problems for wind instrumentalists. Support is essential to healthy voice production. The effects of severe respiratory infection are obvious and will not be enumerated. Restrictive lung disease, such as that associated with obesity, may impair support by decreasing lung volume and respiratory efficiency. However, obstructive pulmonary (lung) disease is the most common culprit. Even mild obstructive lung disease can impair support enough to cause increased neck and tongue muscle tension and abusive voice use capable of producing vocal nodules. This scenario occurs even with unrecognized asthma and may be difficult to diagnose unless suspected, because many such cases of asthma are exercise-induced. Vocal performance is a form of exercise, whether the performance involves singing, giving speeches, sales, or other forms of intense voice use. Patients with this problem will have normal pulmonary function clinically and may even have normal or nearly normal pulmonary function test findings at rest in the office. However, as the voice is used intensively, pulmonary function decreases, effectively impairing support and resulting in compensatory abusive technique. When suspected, this entity can be confirmed through a methacholine challenge test performed by a pulmonary specialist.

Treatment of underlying pulmonary disease to restore effective support is essential to resolving the vocal problem. Treating asthma is rendered more difficult in professional voice users because of the need in some patients to avoid not only inhalers but also drugs that produce even a mild tremor. The cooperation of a skilled pulmonologist specializing in asthma and sensitive to problems of performing artists is invaluable.

What about hormones?

Endocrine hormone problems also have marked vocal effects, primarily by causing accumulation of fluid in the superficial layer of the lamina propria, altering the vibratory characteristics. Mild *hypothyroidism* typically causes a muffled sound, slight loss of range, and vocal sluggishness. Similar findings may be seen in pregnancy, during use of oral contraceptives (in about 5% of women), for a few days prior to menses, and at the time of ovulation. Premenstrual loss of vocal efficiency, endurance, and range is also accompanied by a propensity for vocal fold hemorrhage, which may alter the voice permanently. The use of some medications with hormonal activity can also permanently injure a voice. This is particularly true of substances that contain androgens (male hormones) as discussed earlier. Information on these and other hormone problems can be found in other literature.

Does anxiety have anything to do with the voice?

When the principal cause of vocal dysfunction is anxiety, the physician can often accomplish much by assuring the patient that no organic difficulty is present and by stating the diagnosis of anxiety reaction. The patient should be counseled that anxiety-related voice disturbances are common and that recognition of anxiety as the principal problem frequently allows the patient to overcome the problem. Tranquilizers and sedatives are rarely necessary and are undesirable because they may interfere with fine-motor control, affecting the voice adversely. Recently, beta-adrenergic blocking agents, such as propranolol hydrochloride (Inderal), have achieved some popularity in the treatment of preperformance anxiety in singers and instrumentalists. Beta-blockers should not be used routinely for voice disorders and preperformance anxiety. They have significant effects on the cardiovascular system and many potential complications, including hypotension, thrombocytopenia purpura, mental depression, agranulocytosis, laryngospasm with respiratory distress, and bronchospasm. In addition, their efficacy is controversial. If anxiety or other psychological factors are an important cause of a voice disorder, their treatment by a psychologist or psychiatrist with special interest and training in voice problems is extremely helpful. This therapy should occur in conjunction with voice therapy.

Can abusing the voice create problems?

Voice abuse through technical dysfunction is an extremely common source of hoarseness, vocal weakness, pain, and other complaints. In some cases, voice abuse can even create structural problems, such as vocal nodules, cysts, and polyps. Now that the components of voice function are better understood, specialists have developed techniques to rehabilitate and train the voice in speech and singing. Such voice therapy improves breathing and abdominal support, decreases excess muscle activity in the larynx and neck, optimizes the mechanics of transglottal airflow, and maximizes the contributions of resonance cavities. It also teaches vocal hygiene, including techniques to eliminate voice strain and abuse, maintain hydration and mucosal function, mitigate the effects of smoke and other environmental irritants, and optimize vocal and general health. The voice therapy team includes an otolaryngologist (ear, nose, and throat doctor) specializing in voice, a speech-language pathologist specially trained in voice, a singing voice specialist with training in vocal injury and dysfunction, and, when needed, an arts-medicine psychologist, psychiatrist, pulmonologist, neurologist, exercise physiologist, or other specialist. Progress is monitored not only by listening to the patient and observing the disappearance of laryngeal pathology when it is present, but also by quantitative measurement parameters in the clinical voice laboratory. In some cases, however, there are structural problems in the larynx that are correctable only with surgery.

How do tonsil problems affect the voice?

For most singers, noninfected *tonsils* do not affect the voice, although it is possible for extremely large tonsils to alter voice and breathing function. In general, when tonsils cause trouble, they do so by becoming infected. Recurrent *tonsillitis* in singers is particularly problematic. On the one hand, no one is anxious to perform tonsil surgery on a singer. On the other, a singer—particularly a professional—cannot afford to be sick for a week five or six times a year. Tonsil problems can occasionally also cause other difficulties that affect one's performance activities, such as *halitosis*.

In general, singers should be managed using the same conservative approach employed for other patients with tonsil disorders. Every effort should be made to cure tonsil-related maladies through medical management, such as antibiotics and tonsil hygiene (as with a toothbrush or water pick). However, if these methods fail, tonsillectomy should be considered. It is essential that the surgeon remove only the tonsil, avoiding injury to the surrounding muscle and adjacent palate. It commonly takes singers 3 to 4 months to achieve voice stabilization following surgery, although they are usually able to begin vocalizing with supervision within 2 to 3 weeks postoperatively. Usually, tonsillectomy has very little effect on the voice, and sometimes it has a positive effect. However, voice problems can occur following tonsillectomy, especially if there is extensive scarring. As with any surgical procedure, the endotracheal tube used for anesthesia can also result in laryngeal injury.

What are vocal nodules?

Small, callouslike bumps on the vocal folds called nodules are caused by voice abuse (Figure 4-2). Occasionally, laryngoscopy reveals asymptomatic vocal nodules that do not appear to interfere with voice production; in such cases, the nodules need not be treated. Some famous and successful singers have had untreated vocal nodules. In most cases, however, nodules are associated with hoarseness, breathiness, loss of range, and vocal fatigue. They may be due to abuse of the voice during either speaking or singing. Voice therapy always should be tried as the initial therapeutic modality and will cure the vast majority of patients, even if the nodules look firm and have been present for many months or years. Even in those who eventually need surgical excision of the nodules, preoperative voice therapy is essential to prevent recurrence.

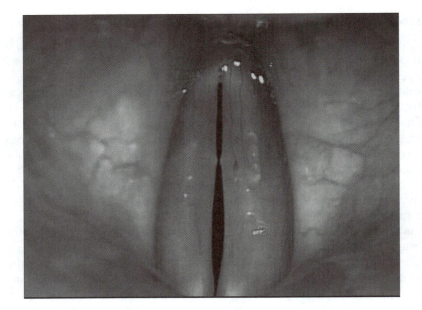

FIGURE 4-2.   Typical appearance of vocal nodules.

Caution must be exercised in diagnosing small nodules in patients who have been speaking or singing actively. In many people, bilateral, symmetrical soft swellings at the junction of the anterior and middle thirds of the vocal folds develop after heavy voice use. No evidence suggests that people with such "physiologic swelling" are predisposed to development of vocal nodules. At present, the condition is generally considered to be within normal limits. The physiologic swelling usually disappears with 24 to 48 hours of rest from heavy voice use.

What are cysts?

Submucosal *cysts* of the vocal folds occur after traumatic lesions that produce blockage of a mucous gland duct, although they may also occur for other reasons and may even be present at birth. They often cause contact swelling on the opposite vocal fold and are usually initially misdiagnosed as nodules. Often, they can be differentiated from nodules by *strobovideolaryngoscopy* when the mass is obviously fluid-filled. They may also be suspected when the nodule (contact swelling) on the other vocal fold resolves with voice therapy but the mass on one vocal fold persists. Cysts may also be found unexpectedly on one side (Figure 4-3) (occasionally both sides) when surgery is performed to

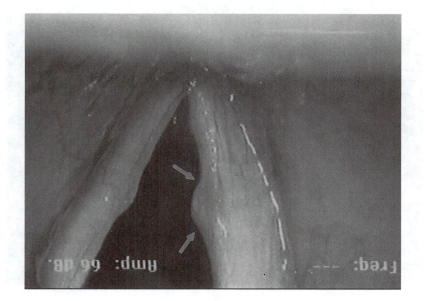

FIGURE 4-3. Right fluid-filled vocal fold cyst and a left reactive nodule in abduction.

remove apparent nodules. Unlike nodules, cysts often do require surgery and are not usually resolved with voice therapy alone. The surgery should be performed superficially and with minimal trauma, as discussed later.

What are polyps?

Many other structural lesions may appear on the vocal folds. Of course, not all respond to nonsurgical therapy. *Polyps* are usually unilateral (on one side), and they often have a prominent feeding blood vessel coursing along the superior surface of the vocal fold and entering the base of the polyp (Figure 4-4). The pathogenesis of polyps cannot be proven in many cases, but the lesion is thought to be traumatic in many patients. At least some polyps start as vocal hemorrhages. In some cases, even sizable polyps resolve with relative voice rest and a few weeks of low-dose corticosteroid therapy, but many require surgical removal. If polyps are not treated, they may produce contact injury on the contralateral (opposite) vocal fold. Voice therapy should be used to ensure good

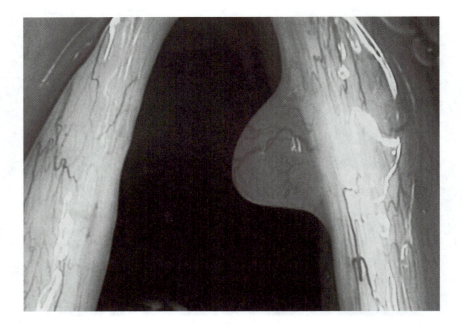

FIGURE 4-4. Typical appearance of a sessile, unilateral polyp of the right vocal fold.

relative voice rest and prevention of abusive behavior before and after surgery. When surgery is performed, care must be taken not to damage the leading edge of the vocal fold, especially if a laser is used.

Do allergy and postnasal drip bother the voice?

Allergies and postnasal drip alter the viscosity (thickness) of secretions, the patency of nasal airways, and have other effects that impair voice use. Many of the medicines commonly used to treat allergies (such as antihistamines) have undesirable effects on the voice. When allergies are severe enough to cause persistent throat clearing, hoarseness, and other voice complaints, a comprehensive allergy evaluation and treatment by an allergy specialist is advisable. Postnasal drip, the sensation of excessive secretions, may or may not be caused by allergy. Contrary to popular opinion, the condition usually involves secretions that are too thick, rather than too abundant. If postnasal drip is not caused by allergy, it is usually managed best through hydration, and mucolytic agents such as those discussed below in the section on drugs for voice dysfunction. Reflux laryngitis can cause symptoms very similar to postnasal drip, and it should always be considered in people who have the sensation of throat secretions, a lump in the throat, and excessive throat clearing.

What is the effect of upper respiratory tract infection without laryngitis?

Although mucosal irritation usually is diffuse, patients sometimes have marked nasal obstruction with little or no sore throat and a "normal" voice. If the laryngeal examination shows no abnormality, a person with a "head cold" should be permitted to speak or sing. They should be advised not to try to duplicate their usual sound, but rather to accept the insurmountable alteration caused by the change in the supraglottic vocal tract. This is especially important in singers. The decision as to whether performing under such circumstances is professionally advisable rests with the singer and his or her musical associates. Throat clearing should be avoided, as this is traumatic. If a cough is present, medications should be used to suppress it, preferably non-narcotic preparations.

How about laryngitis with serious vocal fold injury?

Hemorrhage in the vocal folds (as discussed below) and *mucosal disruption* (a tear) are contraindications to voice use. When these are observed, the therapeutic course includes strict voice rest in addition to correction of any underlying disease. Vocal fold hemorrhage is most common in premenstrual women who are using aspirin products. Severe hemorrhage or mucosal scarring may result in permanent alterations in vocal fold vibratory function. In rare instances, surgical intervention may be necessary. The potential gravity of these conditions must be stressed so that patients understand the importance of complying with voice restrictions.

Should I use my voice if I have laryngitis without serious vocal fold injury?

Mild to moderate *edema* (swelling) and *erythema* (redness) of the vocal folds may result from infection or from noninfectious causes. In the absence of mucosal disruption or hemorrhage, they are not absolute contraindications to voice use. Noninfectious laryngitis commonly is associated with excessive voice use in preperformance rehearsals. It may also be caused by other forms of voice abuse and by mucosal irritation produced by allergy, smoke inhalation, and other causes. Mucous stranding between the anterior and middle thirds of the vocal folds often indicates voice abuse. Laryngitis sicca (dry voice) is associated with dehydration, dry atmosphere, mouth breathing, and antihistamine therapy. It may also be a symptom of diabetes and other medical problems.

Deficiency of lubrication causes irritation and coughing and results in mild inflammation. If no pressing professional need for voice use exists, inflammatory conditions of the larynx are best treated with relative voice rest in addition to other modalities. However, in some instances speaking or singing may be permitted. The more good voice training a person has, the safer it will be to use the voice under adverse circumstances. The patient should be instructed to avoid all forms of irritation and to rest the voice at all times except during warm-up and performance. Corticosteroids and other medications discussed later may be helpful. If mucosal secretions are excessive, low-dose antihistamine therapy may be beneficial, but it must be prescribed with caution and should generally be avoided. Copious, thin secretions are better than scant, thick secretions or excessive dryness. People with laryngitis must be kept well-hydrated to maintain the desired character of mucosal lubrication. Psychologic support may also be extremely valuable, especially in singers and professional speakers.

Infectious laryngitis may be caused by bacteria or viruses. Subglottic involvement frequently indicates a more severe infection, which may be difficult to control in a short period. Indiscriminate use of antibiotics must be prevented. However, when the physician is in doubt as to the cause and when a major voice commitment is imminent, vigorous antibiotic treatment is warranted. Steroids may also be helpful, as discussed below.

Does voice rest help laryngitis?

Voice rest (absolute or relative) is an important therapeutic consideration in any case of laryngitis. When no professional commitments are pressing, a short course (up to a few days) of absolute voice rest may be considered, as it is the safest and most conservative therapeutic intervention. This means absolute silence and communication with a writing pad or other assistive device. The patient must be instructed not even to whisper, as this may be an even more traumatic vocal activity than speaking softly. Whistling through the lips also requires vocal fold motion and should not be permitted. Absolute voice rest is necessary only for serious vocal fold injury, such as hemorrhage or mucosal disruption. Even then, it is virtually never indicated for more than 7 to 10 days. Three days are often sufficient. In many instances of mild to moderate laryngitis, considerations of finances and reputation mitigate against a recommendation of voice rest in professional voice users. In advising performers to minimize vocal use, Dr Norman Punt of London, England, used to counsel, "Don't say a single word for which you are not being paid." His admonition frequently guides the ailing voice user away from preperformance conversations and postperformance greetings. Patients with such vocal problems should also be instructed to speak softly, as infrequently as possible, often at a slightly higher pitch than usual and with a slightly breathy voice; to avoid excessive telephone use; and to speak with abdominal support as they would in singing. This is relative voice rest, and it is helpful in most cases. An urgent session with a speech-language pathologist is extremely valuable in providing guidelines to prevent voice abuse. Nevertheless, the patient must be aware that some risk is associated with performing with laryngitis even when voice use is possible. Inflammation of the vocal folds is associated with increased capillary fragility and increased risk of vocal fold injury or hemorrhage. Many factors must be considered in determining whether a given voice commitment is important enough to justify the potential consequences.

What other treatments may be used for laryngitis?

Steam inhalations deliver moisture and heat to the vocal folds and *tracheobronchial tree* and are often useful. Some people use nasal irrigations, although these have little proven value. Gargling also has no proven efficacy, but it is probably harmful only if it involves loud, abusive vocalization as part of the gargling process. Ultrasonic treatments, local massage, psychotherapy, and biofeedback directed at relieving anxiety and decreasing muscle tension may be helpful adjuncts to a broader therapeutic program. Psychotherapy and biofeedback, in particular, must be supervised expertly if used at all.

What else can be done to help a person with voice problems?

Voice lessons given by an expert teacher are invaluable for singers and even many nonsingers with voice problems. When technical dysfunction is suspected or identified, the singer should be referred to a teacher. Even when an obvious organic abnormality is present, referral to a voice teacher is appropriate, especially for younger singers. Numerous "tricks of the trade" permit a singer to safely overcome some of the disabilities of mild illness. If a singer plans to proceed with a performance during an illness, he or she should not cancel voice lessons as part of the relative voice rest regimen; rather, a short lesson to ensure optimum technique is extremely useful. For nonsingers with voice problems, training with a knowledgeable singing teacher under medical supervision is often extremely helpful. In conjunction with therapy under the direction of a certified, licensed speech-language pathologist, appropriate singing lessons can provide the patient with many of the athletic skills and "tricks" used by performers to build and enhance the voice. Once singing skills are mastered even at a beginner level, the demands of routine speech become trivial by comparison.

Special skills can be refined even further with the help of an acting-voice trainer, who may also be part of a medical voice team. Such training is invaluable for any public speaker, teacher, salesperson, or anyone else who cares to optimize his or her communication skills.

What happens if a blood vessel in a vocal fold ruptures?

Vocal fold hemorrhage is a potential vocal disaster. Hemorrhages resolve spontaneously in most cases, with restoration of normal voice. However, in some instances, the hematoma (collection of blood under the vocal fold mucosa) organizes and fibroses, resulting in the formation of a mass, scar, or both. This alters the vibratory pattern of the vocal fold and can result in permanent hoarseness. In specially selected cases, it may be best to avoid this problem through surgical incision and drainage of the hematoma. In all cases, vocal fold hemorrhage should be managed with absolute voice rest until the hemorrhage has resolved and normal vascular and mucosal integrity have been restored.

This often takes 6 weeks, and sometimes longer. Recurrent vocal fold hemorrhages are usually due to weakness in a specific blood vessel. They may require surgical treatment of the blood vessel.

What are the hazards of laryngeal trauma?

The larynx can be injured easily during altercations and motor vehicle accidents. Steering wheel injuries are particularly common. Blunt anterior neck trauma may result in laryngeal fracture, dislocation of the arytenoid cartilages, hemorrhage, and airway obstruction. Late consequences, such as narrowing of the airway, may also occur.

Laryngeal injuries are frequently seen in association with other injuries, such as scalp lacerations, that may be bleeding and appear much more dramatic. The laryngeal problem is often overlooked initially even though it may be the most serious or life-threatening injury. Hoarseness or other change in voice quality following neck trauma should call this possibility to mind. Prompt evaluation by visualization and radiological imaging should be available. In many cases, surgery is needed.

What about vocal fold paralysis?

Paralysis may involve one or both vocal folds and one or both nerves to each vocal fold. When paralysis is limited to the superior laryngeal nerve, the patient loses his or her ability to control longitudinal tension (stretch) in the vocal fold. Although superior laryngeal nerve paralysis involves only one muscle (cricothyroid), the problem is difficult to overcome. The vocal fold sags at a lower level than normal, and the patient notices difficulty elevating pitch, controlling sustained tones, and projecting the voice. Superior laryngeal nerve paralysis is caused most commonly by viral infection, especially the herpes virus that causes cold sores. The recurrent laryngeal nerve controls all the other intrinsic laryngeal muscles. When it is injured, the vocal fold cannot move toward or away from the midline, although longitudinal tension is preserved, and the vocal fold remains at its appropriate vertical level if the superior laryngeal nerve is not injured. If the opposite (normal) vocal fold is able to cross the midline to meet the paralyzed side, the vocal quality and loudness may be quite good. Compensation often occurs spontaneously during the first 6 to 12 months following paralysis, with the paralyzed vocal fold moving closer to the midline. Unilateral vocal fold paralysis may be idiopathic (of unknown cause), but it is also seen fairly commonly following surgical procedures of the neck, such as thyroidectomy, carotid endarterectomy, anterior cervical fusion, and some chest operations. Vocal fold paralysis should be treated initially with voice therapy. At least 6 months (and preferably 12 months) of observation are needed unless it is absolutely certain that the nerve has been cut and destroyed, because spontaneous recovery of neuromuscular function is common. If voice therapy fails, vocal fold motion remains impaired, and voice quality or ability to cough is unsatisfactory to the patient, surgical treatments are generally quite satisfactory.

What is spasmodic dysphonia?

Spasmodic (or "spastic") *dysphonia* is a diagnosis given to patients with specific kinds of voice interruptions. These patients may have a variety of diseases that produce the same vocal result, which is called a laryngeal *dystonia*. There are also many interruptions in vocal fluency that are incorrectly diagnosed as spasmodic dysphonia. It is important to avoid this error, because different types of dysphonia require different evaluations and treatments and carry different prognostic implications. Spasmodic dysphonia is subclassified into adductor and abductor types.

Adductor spasmodic dysphonia is most common and is characterized by hyperadduction of the vocal folds, producing an irregularly interrupted, effortful, strained, staccato voice. It is generally considered neurologic in etiology, and its severity varies substantially among patients and over time. It is considered a focal dystonia. In many cases, the voice may be normal (or more normal) during laughing, coughing, crying, or other nonvoluntary vocal activities or during singing. Adduction may involve the true vocal folds alone, or the false vocal folds and the supraglottis may squeeze shut. Because of the possibility of serious underlying neurologic dysfunction or association with other neurologic problems as seen in Meige syndrome (*blepharospasm* involving involuntary closing of the eyes, mediofacial spasm, involving muscles of the midface, and spasmodic dysphonia), a complete neurological and neurolaryngological evaluation is required. Adductor spasmodic dysphonia may also be associated with spastic torticollis (wry neck) and extrapyramidal dystonia.

Abductor spasmodic dysphonia is similar to adductor spasmodic dysphonia except that voice is interrupted by breathy, unphonated bursts, rather than constricted and shut off. Like adductor spasmodic dysphonia, various causes may be responsible. The abductor spasms tend to be most severe during unvoiced consonants, better during voiced consonants, and absent or least troublesome during vowels. Both abductor and adductor spastic dysphonia characteristically progress gradually, and both are aggravated by psychological stress.

After comprehensive workup to rule out treatable organic causes, treatment for spasmodic dysphonia should begin with voice therapy. Adductor spastic dysphonia is much more common, and most therapy and surgical techniques have been directed at treatment of this form. Unfortunately, traditional voice therapy is often not successful. Speaking on inhalation has worked well in some cases. Patients who are able to sing without spasms but are unable to speak may benefit from singing lessons. The author's (RTS) voice team has used singing training as a basic approach to voice control and then bridged the singing voice into speech. In a few patients, medications have also been helpful, but these patients are in the minority. When all other treatment modalities fail, various invasive techniques have been used. Recurrent laryngeal nerve section produces vocal fold paralysis and improves spasmodic dysphonia initially in many patients. However, there is a high incidence of recurrence. We do not generally recommend this approach. Other surgical techniques that alter vocal fold length and modify the thyroid cartilage may also be efficacious. A new technique for sectioning the nerve branch to only one muscle also shows promise. However, the most encouraging treatment at present for patients disabled by severe spasmodic dysphonia is botulinum toxin injection. This is usually done with electromyographic guidance, and the technique produces temporary paralysis of selected muscles. This results in relief or resolution of the spasmodic dysphonia. However, the injections need to be repeated periodically in most patients.

Are there other neurological voice disorders?

Many neurological problems commonly cause voice abnormalities. These include myasthenia gravis, Parkinson's disease, essential tremor, and numerous other disorders. In some cases, voice abnormalities are the first symptoms of the condition.

What about cancer of the vocal folds?

Cancers of the larynx are common and are usually associated with smoking, although cancers also occur occasionally in nonsmokers (Figure 4-5). In many cases, the reason is unknown. However, it appears as if other conditions such as chronic reflux laryngitis and laryngeal *papillomas* may be important predisposing factors. Persistent hoarseness is one of the most common symptoms. Laryngeal cancers may also present with throat pain or referred ear pain. If diagnosed early, they respond to therapy particularly well and are often curable.

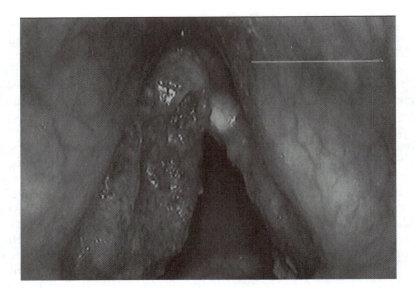

FIGURE 4-5.   Squamous cell carcinoma involving both true vocal folds.

Treatment usually requires radiation, surgery, or a combination of the two modalities. It is usually possible to preserve or restore the voice, especially if the cancer is detected early.

What drugs are used for vocal dysfunction?

Antibiotics

When antibiotics are used to treat vocal dysfunction, high doses to achieve therapeutic blood levels rapidly are recommended and a full course (usually 7 to 10 days) should be administered. Starting treatment with an intramuscular injection may be helpful if there is time pressure.

Antihistamines and mucolytics

Antihistamines may be used to treat allergies. However, because they tend to cause dryness and are frequently combined with sympathomimetic or parasympatholytic agents (decongestants) that further reduce and thicken mucosal secretions, they may reduce lubrication to the point of producing a dry cough. This dryness may be more harmful than the allergic condition itself. Mild antihistamines in small doses should be tried between voice commitments, but they should generally not be used for the first time immediately before performances if the vocalist has had no previous experience with them. Their adverse effects may be counteracted to some extent with *mucolytic* expectorants that help liquefy viscous mucus and increase the output of thin respiratory tract secretions. Guaifenesin is an expectorant that thins and increases secretions. Humibid is one of the convenient and effective preparations available.These drugs are relatively harmless and may be very helpful to patients who experience thick secretions, frequent throat clearing, or postnasal drip. Steroids are a highly effective alternative to antihistamines for treating an acute allergic insult prior to a voice commitment.

Steroids

Corticosteroids are potent anti-inflammatory agents and may be helpful in managing acute inflammatory laryngitis. Although many laryngologists recommend using steroids in low doses (methylprednisolone, 10 mg), the author has found higher doses for short periods to be more effective. Depending on the indication, dosage may be prednisolone 60 mg or dexamethasone 6 mg intramuscularly once, or a similar starting dose orally, tapered over 3 to 6 days. Regimens such as a dexamethasone or methylprednisolone dose pack may also be used. If any question exists that the inflammation may be of infectious origin, antibiotic coverage is generally recommended. Care must be taken not to prescribe steroids excessively. Anabolic steroids, which have received so much attention because of their abuse by athletes, are not used for voice treatment and may damage (masculinize) the voice.

Diuretics

In the premenstrual period, altered estrogen and progesterone levels are associated with changes in pituitary activity. An increase in circulating antidiuretic hormone results in fluid retention in Reinke's space (superficial layer of the lamina propria), as well as in other tissues. The fluid retained in the vocal fold during inflammation and hormonal fluid shifts is bound, not free, water. *Diuretics* do not remobilize this fluid effectively and dehydrate the patient, producing decreased lubrication and thickened secretions but persistently edematous vocal folds. They have no place in the treatment of premenstrual voice disorders. If they are used for other medical reasons, their vocal effects should be monitored closely.

Aspirin and other pain medicines

Aspirin and other analgesics frequently have been prescribed for relief of minor throat and laryngeal irritations. The platelet dysfunction caused by aspirin predisposes one to hemorrhage, however, especially in vocal folds traumatized by excessive voice use in cases of vocal dysfunction. Mucosal hemorrhage can be devastating to a professional voice, and people who depend on extensive voice use should avoid aspirin products altogether unless they are absolutely necessary for treatment of special medical conditions. Acetaminophen is the best substitute, as even most common nonsteroidal anti-inflammatory drugs (NSAIDs) such as ibuprofen may interfere with the clotting mechanism. It is important for singers to avoid aspirin and NSAIDs whenever possible, and to be off aspirin for a least 10 days and off NSAIDs for at least 2 days prior to any vocal fold surgery.

Pain is an important protective physiologic function. Masking it risks incurring grave vocal damage that may be unrecognized until after the analgesic or anesthetic wears off. If a patient requires analgesics or topical anesthetics to alleviate laryngeal discomfort, the laryngitis is severe enough to warrant canceling a vocal performance. If the analgesic is for headache or some other discomfort not intimately associated with voice production, symptomatic treatment should be discouraged until demanding vocal commitments have been completed.

Sprays and inhalants

The use of analgesic topical sprays is extremely dangerous and should be avoided. Diphenhydramine hydrochloride (Benadryl), 0.5% in distilled water, delivered to the larynx as a mist is a formerly popular treatment that may be helpful for its vasoconstrictive properties, but it is also dangerous because of its analgesic effect. It should not be used. Other topical vasoconstrictors that do not contain analgesics may be beneficial in selected cases. Oxymetazoline hydrochloride (Afrin) is particularly helpful in rare, extreme circumstances. Propylene glycol 5% in a physiologically-balanced salt solution may be delivered by large-particle mist and can provide helpful lubrication shortly before performance, particularly in cases of laryngitis sicca after air travel or in dry climates. Such treatment is harmless and may also provide a beneficial placebo effect. Water or saline solution delivered via a vaporizer or steam generator is frequently effective and sufficient. This therapy should be augmented by oral hydration, which is the mainstay of treatment for dehydration. Voice users should monitor the state of hydration by observing urine color ("pee pale").

What should be considered when voice surgery is contemplated?

Principles

Scar tissue occurs in response to trauma, including surgery. If scar tissue replaces the normal anatomic layers, the vocal fold becomes stiff and adynamic (nonvibrating). This results in asymmetric, irregular vibration with air turbulence that we hear as hoarseness, and/or microscopically incomplete vocal fold closure allowing air escape, which makes the voice sound breathy. Such a vocal fold may look normal on traditional examination but will be seen as abnormal under stroboscopic light. Conveniently, most benign pathology (eg, nodules, polyps, cysts) is superficial. Consequently, surgical techniques have been developed to permit removal of lesions from the epithelium or superficial layer of the lamina propria without disruption of the intermediate or deeper layers in most cases. All of these delicate microsurgical techniques are now commonly referred to as *phonosurgery*, although the term was originally introduced by Dr Hans von Leden in referring to operations designed to alter vocal quality or pitch.

Techniques (Endoscopic)

Most voice surgery is performed through the mouth after placement of a metal tube called an operating laryngoscope, utilizing a microscope, and is called endoscopic (or internal) laryngeal surgery. Surgical treatment of laryngeal abnormalities can be performed using microscopic scissors and other instruments or *lasers*. Lesions involving the vibratory margin are still removed most safely using traditional instruments and magnification through an operating microscope. Such lesions include nodules, polyps, and cysts that have not responded to voice therapy. Current techniques allow the surgeon to remove virtually nothing but the diseased tissue. Such atraumatic surgery may not even require postoperative voice rest, and rapid healing with good voice quality usually follows. Although lasers are "high tech," they are not always the best choice for laryngeal surgery—at least not the lasers currently utilized. The potential problem with the carbon dioxide (CO_2) laser in standard use is the associated heat, which may damage surrounding tissues. At the power densities required for surgical ablation and the laser beam spot diameters generally used, there is a heat halo around the beam. When used on the vocal fold edge, the heat may be sufficient to provoke scarring. This produces an adynamic segment on the vocal fold, and hoarseness. The CO_2 laser is, however, extremely useful for selected lesions, such as varicosities, that lead to vocal fold hemorrhages, vaporization of blood vessels that supply laryngeal polyps, papillomas (caused by a virus), and selected cancers. A new pulsed-dye laser (PDL) has become available recently and is useful for some voice problems, especially vascular abnormalities. PDL often can be performed as an office procedure.

When surgery is indicated for vocal fold lesions, it should be limited as strictly as possible to the area of abnormality. Virtually no place exists for "vocal cord stripping" in patients with voice problems. Even when there is good reason to suspect malignancy, more precise surgery can and should be performed in most cases.

Precautions

A detailed discussion of laryngeal surgery is beyond the scope of this book. A few points are worthy of special emphasis, however. Surgery for vocal nodules should be avoided whenever possible and should almost never be performed without an adequate trial of expert voice therapy, including patient compliance with therapeutic suggestions. In most cases, a minimum of 6 to 12 weeks of observation should be allowed while the patient is using therapeutically modified voice techniques under the supervision of a certified speech-language pathologist and possibly a singing teacher. Proper voice use rather than voice rest (silence) is correct therapy. The surgeon should not perform surgery for vocal nodules prematurely under pressure from the patient for a "quick cure" and early return to voice performance. Permanent destruction of voice quality is a very real complication. Even after expert surgery, voice quality may be diminished by submucosal scarring. This situation produces a hoarse voice with vocal folds that appear normal on routine indirect (mirror) examination, although under stroboscopic light the adynamic segment is obvious. No reliable cure exists for this complication.

There are also other potential complications of voice surgery. Although they are uncommon or rare, they may be seen occasionally even if the surgeon and patient do everything right. They include the following: (1) swelling with airway obstruction requiring tracheotomy; (2) chipping or fracture of a tooth by the laryngoscope; (3) bleeding; (4) infection; (5) recurrence of the problem (or a new mass such as a cyst or granuloma) requiring additional therapy (medications, voice therapy, and/or surgery); (6) injury to the larynx, such as arytenoid dislocation; and others.

Techniques (External)

New techniques of external laryngeal surgery to modify the laryngeal skeleton have become extremely useful in treating vocal fold paralysis, a common consequence of viral infection, surgery, and cancer. Until the 1980s, vocal fold paralysis was most often managed by endoscopic injection of Teflon into the tissues beside the paralyzed vocal fold. This pushed the paralyzed side toward the midline, allowing the normal vocal fold to meet it, thus permitting glottic closure and improving voice. Although Teflon is relatively inert, the formation of granuloma in reaction to the foreign body is not uncommon, and stiffness of the vocal fold edge frequently impairs voice quality. Teflon infiltrated into tissues is hard to remove if the results are unsatisfactory. Teflon injection has been largely replaced by injection of fat or other safe materials or thyroplasty. Thyroplasty is a technique in which a skin incision is made and a window is cut in the laryngeal skeleton, and a piece of thyroid cartilage is depressed inward and held in place with a silicone block. This pushes the vocal fold toward the midline fairly reversibly, without injecting a foreign body into the tissues. The author's (RTS) group has also introduced an injection technique similar to Teflon, which uses the patient's own fat, harvested from the abdomen. This eliminates the disadvantages of Teflon, but it may have other problems such as resorption of the fat in some cases. Fat may also be used to improve vocal fold scar in selected cases.

Can surgery change the pitch of a voice?

Surgery of the laryngeal skeleton can also be used to modify vocal pitch. Although such operations are done infrequently, they are valuable in certain circumstances. By closing the space between the cricoid and thyroid cartilages (an extreme version of cricothyroid muscle function), the vocal folds can be lengthened and tensed, and the voice raised. By cutting out vertical sections of the thyroid cartilage, the vocal folds can be shortened and their tension decreased, lowering pitch. Although these techniques are not sufficiently predictable for elective use in singers or other professional voice users, they are valuable in treating selected voice abnormalities and in altering vocal pitch in patients who have undergone transsexual surgery.

What can be done about a voice that is worse after surgery?

Too often, the laryngologist is confronted with a desperate patient whose voice has been "ruined" by vocal fold surgery, recurrent or superior laryngeal nerve paralysis, trauma, or some other tragedy. Occasionally, the cause is as simple as a recently dislocated arytenoid that can be reduced. However, if the problem is an adynamic segment (decreased bulk of one vocal fold after "stripping," bowing caused by superior laryngeal nerve paralysis, or some other serious complication in a mobile vocal fold), great conservatism should be exercised. Voice therapy is nearly always helpful in optimizing compensatory strategies and minimizing fatigue, but it usually will not restore normalcy of the patient's voice. None of the available surgical procedures for these conditions is consistently effective. If surgery is considered at all, the procedure and prognosis should be explained to the patient realistically and pessimistically. It must be understood that the chances of returning the voice to excellent quality are slim, and that it may be made worse. Zyderm collagen (Xomed) injection and fat injection are currently the most common approaches in these difficult cases. A great deal more research is needed to determine the efficacy of the treatments currently available for vocal fold scarring and to establish the treatment of choice.

How can the voice be kept healthy?

Preventive medicine is always the best medicine. The more people understand about their voices, the more they will appreciate the importance and delicacy of the vocal instrument. Education helps us understand how to protect, train, and develop the voice to keep it healthy and handle our individual vocal demands. Even a little bit of expert voice training can make a big difference. Avoidance of abuses, especially smoke, is paramount. If voice problems occur, expert medical care should be sought promptly. Interdisciplinary collaboration among laryngologists, speech-language pathologists, singing teachers, acting teachers, other professionals, and especially voice users themselves has revolutionized voice care since the early 1980s. Technological advances, scientific revelations, and new medical techniques inspired by interest in professional opera singers have brought a new level of expertise and concern to the medical profession and have dramatically improved the level of care available for any patient with voice dysfunction.

How can the voice be made better?

Voice building is possible, productive, and extremely gratifying. Speaking and singing are athletic. They involve muscle strength, endurance, and coordination. Like any other athletic endeavor, voice use is enhanced by training that includes exercises designed to enhance strength and coordination throughout the vocal tract. Speaking is so natural that the importance of training is not always obvious, but endeavors such as running are just as natural. Yet, most people recognize that no matter how well a person runs, he or she will run better and faster under the tutelage of a good track coach. The coach will also provide instruction on strengthening and warm-up and cool-down exercises that prevent injury. Voice training works the same way.

Voice building starts with physical development. Once vocal health has been assured by medical examination, training is usually guided by a voice trainer (with schooling in theater and acting-voice techniques), singing teacher, or a speech-language pathologist. In the author's (RTS) setting, all three specialists are involved under the guidance of a laryngologist, and additional voice team members are utilized, as well, including a psychologist (for stress management), professional interviewer, and others. Initially, training focuses on the development of physical strength, endurance, and coordination. This is accomplished not only through vocal exercises, but also through medically supervised bodily exercise that improves aerobic conditioning and strength in the support system. Singing skills are developed (even in people with virtually no singing talent at all) and used to enhance speech quality, variability, projection, and stamina. For most people, marked voice improvement occurs quickly. For those with particularly challenging vocal needs, voice building also includes training and coordinating body language with vocal messages, organizing presentations, managing adversarial situations (interviews, court appearances, and so forth), television performance techniques, and other skills that make the difference between a good professional voice user and a great one.

The process of voice building is valuable not only for premier professional voice users. Virtually all of us depend on our voices to convey our personalities, ideas, and subliminal messages about our credibility. The right subliminal vocal messages can be as important in selling a product or getting a job as they are in winning a presidential election. The initial stages of voice building are no more complex than the initial stages of learning to play tennis or golf, and their potential value is unlimited. A strong, confident, well-modulated voice quietly commands attention, convinces, and conveys a message of health, strength, youth, and credibility.

Choral singing provides special pleasure and poses vocal risks. More amateur music lovers sing in choruses than in any other setting. Choral music provides joy for its enthusiastic participants and its audiences, but voice abuse during choral rehearsal and performance can damage the larynx. Such damage affects not only an individual's ability to sing, but also the ability to speak and use the voice effectively in social and business settings. Consequently, choral conductors have a great responsibility and liability to treat voices appropriately. Choral conductors also have an exciting opportunity to educate choral singers about vocal health and to strengthen and enhance the vocal abilities of their chorus members. Every choral conductor should be cognizant of these responsibilities and opportunities and learn enough about vocal and choral pedagogy to consistently enhance choral voices and never injure them.

Study Questions

1. Prolonged warm-up time is classically caused by (select one)
   a. Hyperfunctional technique
   b. Hormone disorders
   c. Acid reflux
   d. Vocal fold hemorrhage
   e. Vocal misclassification

2. Which entity most interferes with effective support (select one)?
   a. Hyperthyroidism
   b. Asthma
   c. Acid reflux
   d. Vocal fold hemorrhage
   e. None of the above

3. Vocal nodules can usually be cured without surgery.
   a. True
   b. False

4. Vocal fold cysts can usually be cured without surgery.
   a. True
   b. False

5. If a doctor tells a singer that he or she needs surgical laryngoscopy and "vocal cord stripping," the singer should
   a. Follow the doctor's advice
   b. Be silent for 6 weeks
   c. Expect to return to singing 3 weeks after surgery
   d. Seek another surgical opinion from a laryngologist specializing in professional voice care
   e. None of the above

Suggested Readings

Sataloff RT. *The Professional Voice: The Science and Art of Clinical Care.* 3rd ed. San Diego, Calif: Plural Publishing, Inc; 2005.

Journal of Voice. St. Louis, Mo: Elsevier, Inc; 1997.

Rosen DC, Sataloff RT. *Psychology of Voice Disorders.* San Diego, Calif: Singular Publishing Group Inc; 1997.

Sataloff RT. *Vocal Health and Pedagogy.* San Diego, Calif: Singular Publishing Group Inc; 1997.

Sataloff RT, Castel DO, Katz PO, Sataloff DM. *Reflux Laryngitis and Related Disorders.* 3rd ed. San Diego, Calif: Plural Publishing, Inc; 2005.

CHAPTER

5

The Aging Voice

Margaret Baroody and Brenda Smith

From the instant of conception until the moment of death, our bodies are continuously aging. In our youthful years, the life process advances toward a physical peak. Once that peak is achieved, a brief plateau is possible after which a reversing of momentum ensues. The speed of these incremental changes both toward maximum capacity and away from it varies significantly from person to person. It is impossible to predict the rate and results of the aging process for any two people of the same chronologic age. However, certain kinds of physical deterioration due to aging will have an impact on the vocal instrument, such as loss of muscle bulk and elasticity, lessened neurologic functions, decreased respiratory function and blood flow, and ossification of cartilage. Because the onset of such limitations is idiosyncratic, the corporate singing life of choral singers is particularly beneficial to the aging voice. Regular, prudent vocal exercise will preserve vocal skill while impeding the inevitable losses of range, control, and agility.

At any age, a total body regimen is essential for maintaining a healthy voice. Whether building or maintaining a voice, the singer must remember that the singing instrument involves the entire body, the mind, and the spirit. Aging singers should be encouraged to recycle the pattern of their daily routines, not retire from them entirely. Daily cardiovascular workouts promote muscle tone, flexibility, and circulation. Moderate exercise (swimming, walking, weight training, stretching) should be done with care, but should be done regularly.

Vocal warm-ups for the aging voice begin with relaxation of the mind and body. Sighing, stretching of the neck, arms, and torso as well as tongue and jaw are good first steps. Rolling the shoulders up and back, then around to the front will relieve neck and shoulder tension. Easy oscillation of the head from side to side is also useful. The older the singer, the more gentle the motions should be.

Posture may not be as simple to maintain as one ages. Some older singers may be limited in their ability to execute preparatory exercises such as knee bends or toe touching. For those with limited mobility, the most balanced singing posture may be a seated one. Whether standing or sitting, every singer should have the rib cage elevated and expanded to breathe freely. The shoulders should be broad and the head relaxed, with the chin parallel to the floor. If a seated posture is required, the singer should be encouraged to keep the feet directly in front of the chair with weight on the metatarsals. Crossing the ankles or retracting the feet will cause tension in the abdominal region.

The respiratory system is the primary power source for the voice. Once relaxation exercises and posturing bring the desired results, a few minutes of deep, abdominal breathing should follow. If it is possible for the singer to extend the arms, the sense of release in the rib cage and abdominal areas will be enhanced. All breath exercises begin with exhalation with attention given to the posture. The chest must not fall when air is expelled. Inhalation should be done calmly and effortlessly. Singers should not gasp or stiffen during inhalation. The conductor should create imagery situations that induce a welcoming of breath into the body. Watch for tension in the neck and jaw during inhalation. A joyful attitude toward breathing ensures flexibility in the entire process.

Although every singer has experienced an inadequacy of available air near the end of a phrase, older singers are likely to recall more such negative vocal moments than younger singers. Therefore, the fear of "running out of breath" is more intense among aging voices. Some may have respiratory limitations like asthma or emphysema that could impede inhalation. Deep breathing exercises will increase lung capacity to a given extent in each singer. When assisting aging voices, the conductor should temper breath gestures, encouraging reasonable but not vigorous inhalation. It is also necessary to be alert to hyperventilation in singers whose reduced muscle flexibility impedes full exhalation.

Achieving resonance in singers should start with activities from daily living that bring breath to pitch without involving vowel sounds. By considering the spirit and sophistication of the ensemble, the conductor will arrive at the right routines, be they the buzzing of bees and the mooing of cows or glides on voiced consonants such as r [r], v [v], z [z], or lip trills [br]. Senior citizens can be very fanciful and, therefore, eager to imitate; others may be more intellectual, preferring concrete exercises. In either situation, it is useful to engage the connection of breath with pitch on consonants first, followed by simple gliding patterns of consonants with vowel sounds. The patterns should begin just above the speaking range and glide downward. The tongue should be relaxed and passive, the posture tall and buoyant. The aging singer is struggling against the effects of muscle atrophy and decreased coordination of the vocal instrument. Thus, exercises for resonance should be systematic and gentle, stretching the vocal folds and improving the coordination of timing between breath support and vocal fold coordination.

Light, easy staccato exercises will lead to increased agility and stamina. Because the vocal folds tend to lose muscle bulk with age, exercises involving sustained pitches such as *messa di voce* (a consistent crescendo and decrescendo on one pitch) are effective. In both staccato and sustained exercises, range and volume should be moderate. Incremental increase of syllables and pitches will maintain flexibility of the voice. Extremely rapid passages should, however, be avoided. In multigenerational choirs, the older singers should not be expected to sing every note in florid, bravura music. Asking the older singers to sing only the first of each group of sixteenths can assist the younger singers in maintaining a steady tempo as they execute the intervening note values.

The acquisition of the vocal skills described above will be different for each singer. Muscles have the ability to remember instilled behaviors. The conductor must expect some older singers to spring quickly to a higher level, as instinctive muscle responses are awakened. At the same time, not all singers develop positive muscle memory in singing during earlier life. In addition, mental and spiritual factors play a role. Concentration and coordination are related issues for all ages. In the older singer, mental agility and body awareness are particularly difficult to predict. As life progresses, losses accumulate. Older singers have fewer friends and family their own age than younger singers do. An element of sadness at these personal and spiritual deficits affects, for many, quickness of mind and body. A conductor who works with older singers should be mindful of this reality. A lack of physical wellbeing or mental quickness in an older singer may have an emotional or spiritual base.

In truth, older singers pose a dynamic teaching puzzle for the conductor. Psychologists, physicians, and educators have studied the growth and learning curves of young people for decades. Curricula have been adopted to accommodate the common ground of each age range from preschool through college students. Gerontology is a developing specialty in medical and academic research, yielding at present more hypotheses than conclusions. As our population ages, seniors are living longer under improved circumstances. More of them are seeking to maintain a role in society through communal activities like singing. Choral conducting manuals rarely speak to the issue of the older singing voice, because older singers usually did not continue to participate. Therefore, the choral conductor of an aging choir cannot refer to numerous articles or call upon trusted mentors for tested solutions to vocal or teaching problems.

Older singers can possess a rich array of skills not always found in younger singers. In general, older singers are much more familiar with the conventions of any given musical composition, having sung it in a variety of situations over the years. Aware of their lessening physical powers, they may be more disciplined and more willing to listen than youthful choristers. The learning skills of an older singer are usually more refined and, thus, more obvious to the astute choral conductor. Finally, the absence of the ego so necessary for success in a younger singer creates a relaxed, productive learning atmosphere. Singing to maintain a voice is much less stressful than singing to develop one. The selection of repertoire and the pacing of rehearsals are keys crucial to the work of the choral conductor and the older choral singer. When these two factors are combined with resilient spirits on either side, an adult choir of older singers can be the choral instrument of choice for a resourceful, pedagogic conductor.

To optimize choral sound and the choristers' health, age and size-appropriate singing should be the goal of any conductor. An older singer will benefit from a conductor's advice regarding vocal tone quality, vibrato rate, and agility expectations. It is important to remember that any singer relies upon the ears of another when evaluating the results. Honest information delivered with kindness will be appreciated. In addition, the conductor should suggest strategies.

To improve tone quality, be it strident or breathy, the conductor should create short exercises in descending patterns that will be sung on each of the basic Italian vowels ([a], [ɛ], [i], [ɔ], [u]). It is likely that the open sounds of ah [a] and [ɔ] will be the most problematic. Once an optimal vowel shape has been determined, each vowel sound can be related to it. The conductor then designs exercise patterns that intersperse the more resonant vowels with the less resonant ones in logical order. For example, the conductor invites the singers to sing a sustained tone on a pitch of medium range beginning with the syllable me

[mi] and moving to ma [mɑ] and back to me [mi] or moo [mu] to maw [mɔ] to moo [mu]. If the conductor evaluates the results, indicating the positive aspects found in the well-centered vowels, the older singers will begin to understand the sensations of resonance that are best for them and for the choir. Subsequent exercises will exploit increasingly larger intervals and ranges.

Imagery is perhaps the quickest way to assist older singers in minimizing motion in the tone. Asking older singers to imagine the singing tone of a choir boy generally limits the vibrato instantly. Images of gentle breezes, poignant scents or soothing sounds will lessen the tendency toward vibrato rich tone. Eavesdropping and echoing are useful imaginary tools. If the singer strokes an arm as if petting a kitten or puppy while singing, a calmer tone will emerge.

In addition, the maintenance of tone in the muscles that support the breath will increase the possibility for a more youthful sound. The exercises described in earlier chapters using gentle gliding patterns, sirens, and lip trills are also useful. Vocalises using staccato articulation increase mind and body coordination. The patterns should be short, in a medium range, and accompanied by frequent feedback regarding their execution. Alternating staccato with legato singing trains the ear and body to maintain focus and support. If the conductor tailors exercise patterns with an eye to the melodic material of the repertoire, the choral technique of the choir will advance even faster. Singing segments of the repertoire using first staccato and then legato technique is a good warm-up exercise.

The more the older singer "audiates" (hears mentally) a slender tone, the more the voice and musculature will produce one. In a choir of older singers, it is best to select repertoire based on texts of a cooler, more intellectual nature. Dramatic or emotive texts will be set with expansive vocal ranges and harmonic structures that encourage less controlled singing. It is essential to recognize that older singers will not be able to execute agile passages as rapidly as younger ones. If repertoire contains such passages, older singers should be encouraged to sing the first of each group of sixteenth notes, allowing younger singers to carry the remaining ones. Some older singers may find their voices will become more flexible as they develop a familiarity with the melisma. However, older singers should not be pressured to sing exposed, agile passages. Choral repertoire makes it possible for older singers to participate in the singing of complicated, contrapuntal music without having to be responsible for every single note.

In matters of range and dynamic, it is necessary to make adjustments for older singers as well. It is unlikely that older singers will be able to sing comfortably in extreme registers or dynamics. A conductor can revoice chords, allowing older singers to sing lower pitches while the higher ones are carried by young voices. When repertoire demands sudden pianissimo singing, the choir can be divided between a solo group and a tutti one. By reducing forces, the effect of softer singing can be achieved. The ability of the singers should always be a major factor in repertoire selection. If the membership of the choir is primarily older, tuneful text settings in medium range will prove to be more satisfying.

If the older singers are properly seated in the choir, according to the acoustic properties of their voices, blending their voices into a choral tone should not be difficult. Depending upon the physical condition of an older singer, the best location in the choral unit may not be possible. Some older singers may not be able to stand on risers or be able to climb stairs to reach higher levels in a choir loft. In these cases, a compromise must be sought. Slow, careful attention to vocal technique will be helpful for the entire choir, but especially fortifying to the older singer.

Lifelong singing is evidence of a good vocal technique. Singing should not be halted because a voice no longer sings at its optimal range or agility. The cycle of aging is real and healthy. If expectations are adjusted, every singer can make music throughout life. As our population ages and medical research advances, the choral culture expands too. When a young voice changes to an adolescent one, we rejoice in the newness while mourning the departure of the unchanged voice's characteristic purity. As we age, our voices mature with us. In each season of life, our voices shed certain timbres and acquire others. Elderly singers present with vocal qualities appropriate to their idiosyncratic physical, spiritual, and mental state. Older voices need and deserve to be heard just as much as younger ones do. In the choral setting, older singers provide a richness of life experience invaluable to the music making of the whole. The singer retired from the workforce may be the most dependable member of the choir, able to assist with fund-raising, administrative matters, and social functions. The enthusiasm of such a singer will inspire the continued growth and aspirations of every other member of the choir. Singing is a universal pastime as well as profession, available to all human beings in their most private as well as public moments. The choral art itself honors the capacity of voices lifted in song from infancy to the end of life. Through study, practice, and composition, our choral culture must pursue vigorously the development of tools and strategies for the aging singer.

Study Questions

1. How does singing benefit an older person?

2. What physical activities encourage vocal fitness?

3. Name the physical limitations of the aging population that are related to vocal technique.

4. Create a warm-up and a cool-down routine targeted for an ensemble of older singers.

5. How do older singers enhance a choir?

CHAPTER

Performing-Arts Medicine and the Professional Voice User: Risk of Nonvoice Performance

The developing specialty of arts medicine is extremely valuable for voice professionals. The physician caring for professional vocalists will find it useful to be aware of developments in related fields.[1] Through the National Association of Teachers of Singing, the *Journal of Singing*, the *Journal of Voice*, the Voice Foundation Symposia, and many other sources, enlightened singing teachers have become familiar with recent advances in the care of professional voice users. Many of these arose from interdisciplinary teamwork, and new insights have resulted in better methods of history taking, physical examination, and objective voice measures, as well as wider availability of educational information about the voice. All of these have produced better informed, healthier singers. Although voice medicine is the most advanced area of arts medicine, there are several other specialities that may be helpful during a singing career. As singers must often do other jobs as well, such as acting, dancing, or playing piano, it is useful for singers and singing teachers to be aware of developments in related fields.

What is different about arts medicine?

For physicians, arts medicine and sports medicine pose special interests, challenges, and problems. Traditional medical training has not provided the background necessary to address them well. Consequently, development of both fields has required understanding and interaction among physicians, performers (artistic athletes), and members of other disciplines. Such cooperation and interaction have taken a long time to develop because of language problems. For example, when a singer complains of a "thready midrange," most doctors do not know what he or she is talking about. To the traditional physician, if such a singer looks healthy and has "normal" vocal folds on mirror examination, he or she is deemed "normal." General medicine enjoys a broad range of physical condition that is considered "normal." The biggest difference we encounter in the fields of arts and sports medicine is the patient's sophisticated self-analysis and narrow definition of normal. In general, doctors are not trained to recognize and work with the final percentages of physical perfection. The arts medicine specialist is trained to recognize subtle differences in the supranormal to near-perfect range in which the professional performer's body must operate. To really understand performers, physicians must either be performers themselves or work closely with performers, teachers, coaches, trainers, and specific paramedical professionals. In voice, this means a laryngologist working with a singing teacher, voice coach, voice trainer, voice scientist, speech-language pathologist, and often other professionals. In other fields, the specialities vary, but the principles remain the same.

Hand Medicine

After voice medicine, hand medicine is the most advanced specialty of arts medicine. Like voice problems, problems of pianists, violinists, harpists, and other instrumentalists who depend on their hands are treated best by a team. An arts medicine hand clinic usually includes a hand specialist (generally a surgeon), physical therapist, radiologist, and, perhaps, music coaches, teachers, and trainers. Facilities are available to observe the musician while playing his or her instrument, as many problems are due to subtle technical quirks. Hand medicine really catapulted arts medicine to public prominence. A great many musicians have health problems. A self-completion questionnaire study of the 48 affiliated orchestras of the International Conference of Symphony and Opera Musicians (ICSOM)[2] resulted in return of questionnaires by 2,212 of the 4,025 professional musicians studied. Of the musicians responding, 82% reported medical problems, and 76% had a medical problem that adversely affected performance. Many of these musicians had problems caused or aggravated by musical performance. Yet, until the past few years, this was not widely known, and musicians were afraid to admit their difficulties for fear of losing work. Moreover, those who did seek medical attention usually were disappointed with the evaluation and results. World-class pianist Gary Graffman changed all of that almost single-handedly. When he developed difficulty controlling his right hand, he persevered until he found a physician who was willing to look at the possibility that his piano playing had caused his problem. Together, they came to understand his overuse syndrome. When Graffman made his difficulties known to the general public and Leon Fleischer followed suit, thousands of musicians discovered they were not alone and began seeking help. Gradually, the medical profession has learned to provide the specialized care that musicians need. Moreover, far-sighted music schools like the Curtis Institute, which Graffman directs, are beginning to incorporate scientifically based practice and development techniques in their curricula.

Vague, incomplete control over one's hands at the keyboard or on the strings is one of the primary symptoms of overuse syndrome. This often comes from excessive, ineffective practicing with unbalanced muscle development, which may result in nearly crippling problems that end an instrumentalist's career. Chronic pain is also a common concomitant symptom. In an earlier paper, Hochberg et al[3] reported that the most common hand complaints among musicians were (in order of frequency): pain, tightening, curling (drooping or cramping), weakness, stiffness, fatigue, a "pins and needles" sensation, swelling, temperature change, and redness. They resulted in tension, loss of control, and decreased facility, endurance, speed, or strength. Many of the musicians with these problems had either stopped playing, altered their practice, or changed their fingering, technique, or repertoire. Some of them also had related problems in their forearms, elbows, upper arms, or shoulders. Arts medicine centers now provide accurate diagnosis and helpful treatment for most of the conditions that cause these problems, if they are diagnosed early. Hand problems are not limited to pianists, violinists, and harpists, of course. Clarinetists, for example, often develop pain in the right thumb from the weight of the instrument and the position used to hold it up.

Orthopedics and general arts medicine

Lower extremity orthopedic problems are discussed below in the section on dance medicine. Like swimmer's shoulder and tennis elbow in sports medicine, many instruments produce localized pain. Among the most common are cymbalist's shoulder, flutist's forearm, and guitarist's nipple. Brass players may develop problems in their lips, jaws, tongue, and teeth. Changes in tooth alignment, which may follow dental wear, work, or injury, also present special and potentially disabling problems for wind players in whom *embouchure* is critical. There are arts-medicine specialists in the field of dentistry who are especially skilled at handling such problems. Wind players may also develop *pharyngoceles* or *laryngoceles* that present as large airbags in the neck, which stand out as they play. They sometimes interfere with performance and require treatment.

Performance-related problems may also occur in other parts of the performer's body. For example, neck and back problems are almost routine in violinists and violists. Skin abrasions and even cysts requiring surgery occur under the left side of the jaw at the contact point of the instrument in many string players. Dermatologic problems also occur in flutists. Lower back pain is also a problem in many instrumentalists, especially in pianists who sit on benches without back support for 8 hours of practice. In many performers, such problems exist throughout a career. In established performers, they are often precipitated by illness or slight changes in technique of which the performer may be unaware. Skilled analysis in an arts-medicine center can now usually help.

Dance medicine

Ballet and modern dance are among the most demanding of all athletic pursuits. Various forms of popular and show dancing, and especially break dancing, also place enormous demands on the body. The stresses caused by unusual positions (such as dancing *sur les pointes*), hyperextension, and leaps and lifts result in injury. In young dancers, hip injuries are especially common. Ankle, foot, and lower leg problems are more common in older dancers. Even a mild muscle strain may interfere with performance for weeks or months and may produce minor technical changes that predispose to other injuries. Major injuries, such as rupture of the Achilles tendon, also occur. Stress fractures in the hips, legs, and feet, which cause persistent pain, are often missed on X-ray but can now be diagnosed early with computerized tomography or bone scan.

The esthetic requirements of dance may result in other problems. Excessive weight loss, bulimia, and even anorexia are disturbingly common, although in their most severe forms, they are usually encountered in students rather than in established dancers. The prevalence of malnutrition among classical dancers of all ages is most disturbing, however. Dancers also have other special problems that may be less obvious. Menarche (the age when the first menstrual period occurs) is approximately 2 years later among young dancers than it is in the general population. This is believed to be due to low body weight and extreme exercise and may be aggravated by malnutrition from weight loss. Amenorrhea (cessation of menstrual periods) is also common. The incidence of reversible infertility is increased among female dancers. Vaginal yeast infections are common because of the tights worn by ballet dancers. Physicians specializing in dance medicine recognize immediately these and other problems. Often, these physicians are orthopedists who also are directors of sports medicine centers. Participation by members of the arts medicine clinic in the educational programs of dance schools and professional companies is already helping many dancers avoid such problems.

Respiratory dysfunction in wind instrumentalists

Just as asthma may undermine support and impair a singer's technique, pulmonary dysfunction can undermine a wind instrumentalist's support and result in lip dysfunction in brass players (especially trumpeters), and cause analogous problems in other musicians. The most common complaints reported by wind instrumentalists are fatigue during playing, lip and throat pain, loss of upper range, and loss of ability to sustain long notes. In some cases, embouchure was seriously impaired by rapid fatigue of lip muscles, asymmetry of muscle contraction, lip tremor, or apparent hypertrophy with nearly constant contraction, and some patients had been diagnosed as having lip dystonias. As in singers with similar performance problems, some of these instrumentalists appear to have developed performance dysfunctions because of pulmonary dysfunction, particularly unrecognized asthma. When the pulmonary condition is treated, performance ability generally improves. Anecdotal, unpublished reports indicate that other centers have had similar experiences. Because reversible pulmonary dysfunction often causes performance impairment and the fact that this association is not widely recognized, this preliminary report is presented to review the subject.

Performance using woodwind or brass musical instruments requires consistent control over the stream of expired air. This is also true for singers, in whom pulmonary and glottal aerodynamics have been studied more extensively. The musical community has recognized the importance of respiratory training and endurance for optimal playing and singing for generations. In fact, there is extensive pedagogical literature on similarities and differences in breathing requirements for singers and instrumentalists and on the advisability of concurrent study of voice and wind instruments. The consensus is that optimal breathing technique and techniques for abdominal support are essentially the same for singers and most instrumentalists despite specific differences in resistance, flow rate, and flow volume associated with reeds and mouthpieces of varying sizes.

Recent studies have also confirmed the importance of laryngeal activity and vocal tract shape in instrument playing.[4,5] Although such interactions have not been clearly documented until recently, musicians have recognized them for many years. These interactions are responsible for standard language in instrumental teachings, such as "play with an open throat." For example, Eckberg[6] discusses the importance of proper breathing and pharyngeal relaxation in his study of breathing for instrumentalists. He states, "As for the music teacher who instructed you to 'use more air' and 'blow harder,' you may have subconsciously decided to protect that slowly developing embouchure from the overpowering air pressure by tightening your throat. But when you add resistance to the airflow by closing off the throat, you need to 'push' harder from the abdominal muscles—and with more push, the throat muscles constrict even tighter to keep the air from overblowing the embouchure. So it becomes a hopeless tension-producing cycle that can cause a thin, pinched-sounding tone and a limited range."[6(p18-19)]

It is clear that the larynx plays a significant role in shaping the quality of sound for many instrumentalists, such as flutists during *trills*, trombonists, trumpeters, saxophonists, and others. Consequently, illness or technical abuses, such as excessive constriction of neck muscles that cause laryngeal dysfunction (as demonstrated in singers), also appear to produce dysfunction among wind instrumentalists. This may be due in part to the fact that such conditions can alter intrapulmonic pressure and airflow.[7]

Breath support is fundamental in traditional training of wind and brass players, as well as of singers. In singers, the oscillator of the musical "instrument" is the larynx, specifically the vibrating vocal folds. The resonator is the supraglottic vocal tract. For the instrumentalist, the lips and mouthpiece or reed constitute the oscillator, and the rest of the instrument itself is the resonator. The resonator is responsible for much of the quality or timbre. The importance of the lungs, thorax, and abdominal muscles as the power source for sound production has been established for all wind instrumentalists and vocalists. Large muscle groups in these areas generate a vector of force that directs the expired air through the oscillator. Using more delicate muscles for fine control, the lips or vocal folds interrupt the stream of air to produce the desired sound. Abrupt, irregular, or uncontrolled changes in the flow of air require large compensatory muscular adjustments at the oscillator that interfere with controlled tone production, quality, and endurance. Moreover, if the column of air is not sufficiently constant and powerful to drive the instrument or voice, the performer usually attempts to compensate with excessive muscle contraction not only at the oscillator, but also elsewhere in the head or neck. This is observed most easily in singers as hyperfunctional activity in the face, jaw, and strap muscles, and as tongue retraction.[8]

Similar changes occur in instrumentalists. Tightening of the lips, increased pressure of the mouthpiece against the mouth, and forceful biting of single-reed instruments are the most prominent changes. However, tongue retraction, tightening of neck muscles, and pharyngeal constriction also occur and appear to affect sound quality and the performer's endurance. These problems are also well-recognized in music literature. Bouhouys notes that "the maintenance of a tone of constant pitch and loudness on a wind instrument requires a constant mouth pressure and a constant airflow rate."[9] Gradwell adds that trouble "starts for a musician if he has not taken in adequate air to last the phrase, as he now forces air out with his abdominal muscles and automatically the neck muscles will contract to help with the forced breathing. This causes strain, stiffens the shoulders, exhausts the player and of course ruins the sound of the note he is playing."[10] Any condition that impairs respiratory function (such as asthma) may produce the same effects as if the performer had not taken in adequate air.

The effect of musical performance on pulmonary function remains uncertain in healthy patients,[11-13] although it appears that musical training probably produces little significant increase in total lung capacity but a higher tidal volume and lower residual lung volume. The adverse effects of respiratory dysfunction on performers have been established clearly.[14,15]

Various conditions may undermine respiratory support and cause performance dysfunction, the most common being improper technique. In many performers, especially the elderly, lack of exercise and poor aerobic conditioning are responsible. The results are unfortunately often mistaken for irreversible changes associated with aging, resulting in the premature conclusion of salvageable performance careers. Respiratory disease is a particularly important cause of technical dysfunction in young singers and instrumentalists, as well as in performers who strain with inappropriate muscles in neck, face, and lips to compensate for deficient support by impaired breathing.

The most common obstructive airway disease is asthma, affecting 8 million people in the United States. The problems that obstructive pulmonary disease creates for singers are now well-recognized.[16] Our clinical observations suggest that the treatment of asthma in performers is somewhat different from that of the general population.

Psychiatry

Performance careers are stressful. The demand for daily perfection, public scrutiny, constant competition, critics, and old-fashioned stage fright may all exact a heavy toll. The additional strain on the performer and his or her family that accompanies an extensive tour may be particularly trying and often results in marital strife or even divorce. Such problems are shared by many successful performers, and usually they can be kept under control. However, when the stress has become unmanageable or interferes excessively with the performer's life or artistic ability, the intervention of a professional may be appropriate. Fortunately, there are now psychologists and psychiatrists who have special skills and insight into these problems. Many of them are performers themselves. They can be most helpful in controlling the effects of these stresses, managing stage fright, overcoming writer's block, and in teaching the performer to regain sufficient control over his or her life to permit continuation of his or her career. Most arts medicine centers have access to psychological professionals with special interests in this area.

Other arts-medicine problems

Many other special problems occur in performers. Hearing loss may be an occupational hazard for musicians, for example. This occurs not only in rock musicians, but also in members of symphony orchestras. Rock musicians may help avoid the problem by standing behind or beside their speakers rather than in front of them. Satisfactory solutions in the orchestra environment have not yet been advanced. Instrumentalists sitting in front of the brass section have particular problems. Certain instruments may actually cause hearing loss in performers who play them. For example, the left ear of a violinist is at risk. Occupational hearing loss in general is a complex subject, and the special problems of hearing loss in musicians require a great deal more study.

Bagpiper's disease, a little-known problem within the medical profession, is also potentially serious. The skins used to make bagpipes are cured in glycerine and honey. Bags make an excellent culture medium for growth of bacteria and fungi. Chronic fungal pneumonias occur among bagpipers. They are usually caused by *Cryptococcus* bacteria, and occasionally by aspergillosis infection. Bagpipers may also develop a spastic, "hourglass" stomach, which makes frequent rumbling noises. Many similar problems exist among other performers but are beyond the scope of this review. Many more will be recognized no doubt as sensitivity to performers increases.

Conductor's health issues

Health issues related to conducting have received little attention in medical or musical literature but are worthy of consideration. Conductors live longer than people in other professions. It has been assumed that this is due to increased aerobic exercise of the upper body, but this explanation has not been confirmed scientifically.[17] Nonetheless, conducting is not entirely advantageous to one's health.

Numerous medical problems have been associated with conducting. The most famous injury occurred to composer/conductor Jean-Baptiste Lully in the 17th century. In that era, a large wooden stick was used instead of using a baton to beat time against the floor. History records that Lully missed the floor, striking his own foot. This injury led to gangrene, which caused his death. In the modern era, batons can also be hazardous. Baton injuries usually occur to audience or orchestra members when the baton flies out of a conductor's hand, but eye injuries to the conductor have also occurred.

More commonly, conductors experience numerous musculoskeletal problems, including pain in the neck, shoulders, and back. Cumulative trauma disorders (associated with repetitive motion) are common, including carpal tunnel syndrome, DeQuervain's tenosynovitis, ganglion cysts, trigger finger, tennis elbow, golfer's elbow, biceps tendinitis of the shoulder, rotator cuff tendinitis, and thoracic outlet syndrome. More serious acute traumatic injuries also occur, particularly from falls off the podium. Some conductors guard against this potential catastrophe by placing a warning bar or railing at the back of the podium.

Hearing loss is also a hazard of conducting, even classical or orchestral conducting. For example, the author (RTS) treats a world-class conductor who developed one-sided hearing loss and tinnitus (ear noise) caused by exposure to the noise of brass instruments at Wagner rehearsals in a small, wooden rehearsal hall in Europe.

Voice problems are also common among conductors, especially choral conductors. Conductors who have not completely mastered the techniques and craft of choral conducting often sing routinely during choir rehearsals. To correct errors within sections, they may sing each of the parts (alto one moment, soprano the next) at volumes louder than the entire choir. This approach to choral conducting can lead to hoarseness, vocal nodules, and vocal fold hemorrhage and can occasionally result in permanent vocal injury.

Virtually all the health hazards associated with conducting can be avoided through mastery of excellent and ergonomically sound conducting technique, attention to rehearsal and performance environments, and proper rehearsal planning.

Importance for singers

Singers are often called on for performance functions other than singing. Both singers and their teachers should be aware of the potential hazards of nonvocal performance and should recognize signs of problems early. Fortunately, they can usually be corrected. However, if left unattended, they may worsen and interfere not only with playing and dancing but also with a singing career. Help is usually available through arts medicine centers.

Education in arts medicine

Arts medicine is a newly established specialty that poses unique educational challenges. The field involves basic research and specialized clinical care for singers, instrumentalists, dancers, visual artists, and others who place unique demands on their bodies and minds and require function much closer to optimal than virtually any other patients in medicine. The demands on some performing artists are extraordinary. For example, in a study of 55 "sports" by a sports medicine center, ballet dancing was determined to be the most difficult and challenging.[18]

A great deal of information remains to be discovered to understand the anatomy, physiology, physics, and other fundamentals that allow efficient, healthy development of artists and rational clinical management by physicians and teachers of the arts. The research and clinical challenges are more difficult due to the fact that available information is scattered among diverse professions, each with its own literature, educational traditions, and institutions. Traditionally, even the language used by the various professions is incomprehensible to practitioners of fields now interacting through arts medicine. Although recently there has been a substantial increase in basic research, in the opening of clinical "arts medicine centers," in the development of scientifically based pedagogy courses within music schools, and in the publication of arts medicine literature,[19-21] there are few places one can go to obtain the necessary training. At present, no academic programs or degrees are offered in arts medicine. To educate oneself, it is necessary to either obtain multiple degrees, which frequently requires time and information not applicable to the student's goals, or to find informal "apprenticeships" to fill in gaps left by traditional educational categorization.

A couple of programs have been proposed to address these problems. Titze suggested a curriculum in vocology.[22] This program was conceived as a modification of the master's program in speech-language pathology. It combines techniques offered in theater arts and music with those traditionally taught in speech-language pathology programs. It is designed to optimize training in vocal habilitation and rehabilitation. For singing teachers who wish to become singing voice specialists and who are willing to obtain a master's degree and clinical certification in speech-language pathology, the vocology program offers many advantages over most speech-language pathology programs. Vocology training has been initiated and is available at the University of Iowa.

Sataloff proposed a doctoral program in arts medicine.[23] The degree was intended to ensure and promote the development of academic excellence in arts medicine. The proposal had four tracks from which a student could choose: voice, hand, dance, or other. Although there was some overlap in the proposed curriculum, course requirements were different for each concentration. Detailed curriculum requirements were proposed, and considerable interest was generated. So far, no school has initiated such a program, however. Consequently, physicians and other health care providers must still find less efficient ways to educate themselves in this important, multifaceted specialty.

Conclusion

Many voice professionals participate in other performance or athletic endeavors. Others sustain accidental bodily injuries that may affect performance. It is important to understand the complexity of arts medicine, interrelations of all body systems, and the necessity for expert evaluation and treatment of any injury or malfunction in a performer.

Study Questions

1. Medical problems severe enough to adversely affect performance
   have been reported in approximately what percentage of professional instrumentalists?
   a. About 10%
   b. About 25%
   c. About 50%
   d. About 75%
   e. About 100%

2. Delayed menarche (first menstrual period) is common among
   a. Singers
   b. Flutists
   c. Ballerinas
   d. Cellists
   e. None of the above

3. Scientific studies indicate that singers should not study
   wind instruments.
   a. True
   b. False

4. Playing instruments in classical orchestras can result in
   noise-induced hearing loss.
   a. True
   b. False

5. Conducting is safe and generally not associated with injuries or
   health problems.
   a. True
   b. False

References

1. Sataloff RT, Brandfonbrener AG, Ledermann RJ. *Performing Arts-Medicine.*
   New York: Raven Press; 1991.
2. Fishbein M, Middlestadt SE, Ottati V, et al. Medical problems among
   ICSOM musicians: overview of a national survey. *Med Prob Perform Art.*
   1988;3:1–8.
3. Hochberg FH, Leffert RD, Heller MD, Merriman L. Hand difficulties
   among musicians. *JAMA.* 1983;249:1869–1872.

4. King AL, Asby J, Nelson C. Laryngeal function in wind instrumentalists: the woodwinds. *J Voice.* 1988;1:365–367.
5. King AL, Asby J, Nelson C. Laryngeal function in wind instrumentalists: the woodwinds. Presented at the Seventeenth Symposium: *Care of the Professional Voice.* June 9, 1976; The Voice Foundation, New York.
6. Eckberg JC. Better breathing: the key to better playing. *Accent.* 1976;1: 18–19.
7. Tanaka S, Gould WJ. Vocal efficiency and aerodynamic aspects in voice disorders. *Ann Otol Rhinol Laryngol.* 1985;94: 29–33.
8. Sataloff RT. Professional singers, part II. *J Voice.* 1987;1:191–201.
9. Bouhouys A. Pressure-flow events during wind instrument playing. *Ann NY Acad Sci.* 1968;155:266–268.
10. Gradwell J. Breathing for woodwind players. *Woodwind World.* 1974;8: 17–37.
11. Gould WJ, Okamura H. Static lung volumes in singers. *Ann Otol.* 1973;82: 89–95.
12. Schorr-Lesnick B, Teirstein AS, Brown LK, Miller A. Pulmonary function in singers and wind-instrument players. *Chest.* 1985;82:202–205.
13. Heller SS, Hick WR, Root WS. Lung volumes in singers. *J Appl Physiol.* 1960;15:40–42.
14. Spiegel JR, Sataloff RT, Cohn JR, Hawkshaw M. Respiratory function in singers: medical assessment. *J Voice.* 1988;2:40–50.
15. Shigemorei Y. Some tests related to the air usage during phonation: clinical investigations. *Otologia (Fukuoka).* 1977;23:138–166.
16. Cohn JR, Sataloff RT, Spiegel JR, Fish JE, Kennedy K. Airway reactivity-induced asthma in singers (ARIAS). *J Voice.* 1991;5:332–337.
17. Sataloff RT, Brandfonbrener AG, Letterman RJ. *Performing Arts Medicine.* 2nd ed. San Diego, Calif: Singular Publishing Group Inc; 1998:23.
18. Nicholas JA. Risk factors, sports medicine and the orthopedic system: an overview. *J Sports Med.* 1975;3:243–259.
19. *Journal of Voice.* New York, NY: Elsevier, Inc.
20. *Medical Problems of Performing Artists.* Philadelphia, Pa: Hanley & Belfus.
21. Sataloff RT, Brandfonbrener A, Lederman RJ. *Textbook of Performing-Arts Medicine.* New York, NY: Raven Press; 1991.
22. Titze IR. Rationale and structure of a curriculum in vocology. *J Voice.* 1992; 6:1–9.
23. Sataloff RT. Proposal for establishing a degree of doctor of philosophy in arts medicine. *J Voice.* 1992;6:17–21.

CHAPTER

7

Seating Problems of Vocalists

Richard Norris

When is a chair not a chair? When it is an instrument of torture! Singers, along with other seated workers and students, are often unintentional victims of poorly designed seating. As Dr AC Mandal points out in his book *The Seated Man*,[1] the human body was not designed to sit with the hips and knees bent at a 90° angle. The chair as we know it seems to have been derived from the ancient throne designed for ruling, not for working, singing, or playing musical instruments. The chair as a symbol of power gives us the modern-day titles of chairperson and the chair.

The International Conference of Symphony and Opera musicians conducted a survey in 1986 regarding the incidence of musculoskeletal problems of instrumentalists.[2] This survey revealed a rather high incidence of lower back and upper back pain. Another study published in the science section of the *New York Times* (Oct 13, 1989) reported a very high incidence of back pain in instrumentalists. There have been no studies of back pain related to seating problems of vocalists to date.

Back pain in the sitting position has several causes: poorly designed chairs, deconditioned backs of the performer, inadequate back awareness, and physical and emotional tension. Having a properly designed chair is no more a substitute for proper physical conditioning and body awareness than taking vitamin pills excuses one from eating properly.

There are many physical therapists, Alexander technique specialists, and Feldenkrais practitioners who are skilled in working with performing artists and can be good resources for exercises and body awareness. Of course, thorough medical evaluation to rule out serious causes of back pain is always advised before beginning an exercise program.

The Mechanics of Sitting

When the hips are flexed to 90°, the femur (thigh bone) can only rotate 60° in the hip socket. The remaining 30° comes from a posterior (backward) rotation of the pelvis[1(p33)] (Figure 7-1). Because the spine is

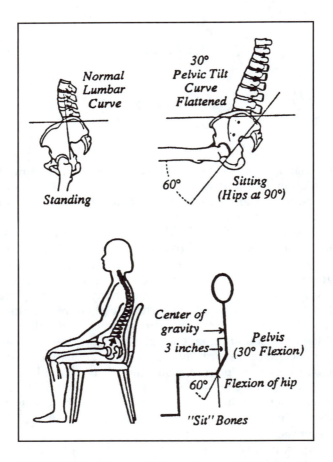

FIGURE 7-1.   The mechanics and anatomy of the spine, hips, and pelvis.

attached to the pelvis, backward rotation of the pelvis causes flattening of the lumbar curve (lordosis), thereby placing the center of gravity of the torso approximately 3 inches (8.5 cm) behind the "sitting bones," creating a torque or turning force on the back. This flattening of the lumbar curve and posterior pelvic tilt results in a slumped "C" curve to the entire spine. To resist these forces, one can sit up straight; but the back extensor muscles, abdominal muscles, and hip flexor muscles have to continually contract to overcome the physical forces that are trying to make the back slump. Continual contraction of a muscle reduces its blood flow, resulting in the buildup of metabolites (waste products of muscle work). When metabolites accumulate, they cause pain, resulting in muscle spasm, and a vicious cycle ensues.[3] Flattening of the lumbar curve has other painful consequences, such as increased pressure on the intervertebral disks[4,5] and stretching the capsules of the small facet joints[6] (the place where each vertebra contacts the one above and below).

For singers, a further consideration is diaphragmatic function. The diaphragm is a large dome-shaped muscle arising from the lower aspect of the ribs and sternum (breastbone) and inserting on the upper lumbar vertebrae. Flattening in the lumbar spine results in flattening of the diaphragm, limiting its range of motion and thereby impeding the airflow (Figure 7-2).

Some suggestions for back support

The use of a forward-sloping seat can alleviate many of the aforesaid problems arising from the flattening of the lumbar curve, such as strain on the back muscles and ligaments and diminished breathing capacity. As mentioned previously, with hips at 90°, the center of gravity is 3 inches (8.5 cm) behind the sitting bones, with the lumbar curve flattened 30°. If the seat is sloped forward, the torso is brought directly over the sitting bones, eliminating the torque which would otherwise force the back into a "C"curve,[3] and then one can maintain an erect posture with little muscular effort (Figure 7-3). This naturally occurs while in the standing position and also while sitting on a horse with the thighs sloping downward. No backrest is needed. A full 30° slope is neither necessary nor desirable, for many people feel pitched forward. A 15° or 20° slope seems to be adequate.

Historical perspective

The forward-sloping principle is seen in historical illustrations of seated workers from Egypt to 19th century Europe, but it seems to have been forgotten by the designers of "modern" chairs until the relatively

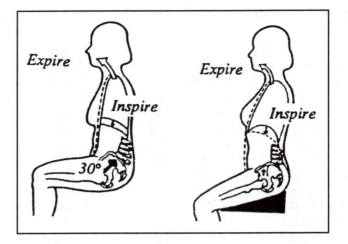

FIGURE 7-2. A forward sloping seat reduces the stresses of sitting, restores a more natural hip-pelvis-spine relationship, and restores full diaphragmatic function.

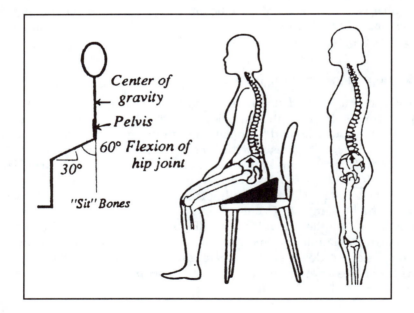

FIGURE 7-3. By bringing the center of gravity of the torso directly over the sit bones, a forward sloping seat eliminates the torque acting on the spine and affords an upright posture with a minimum of muscular effort, similar to that found in the standing posture.

recent arrival of kneeling chairs from Scandinavia, which have gained some popularity among seated workers (Figure 7-4). The chief disadvantages of the kneeling chairs are knee discomfort, as the knees are flexed to about 130°, lack of easy portability (critical to musicians), and expense (even more critical to musicians).

A more practical solution for singers who travel and therefore are subjected to sitting on chairs provided by the theater (often standard folding chairs), or for anyone who spends the working day in a chair, is a lightweight, portable wedge cushion (the Ergo Cush No. 1777, AliMed Inc., Dedham, Mass, or similar product) to temporarily modify the existing chair seat. The back is placed in a position of comfort similar to that of kneeling chairs, but without the accompanying knee discomfort. A unique, dual-layered design provides a top layer of soft foam for comfort, with a dense foam layer underneath for support.

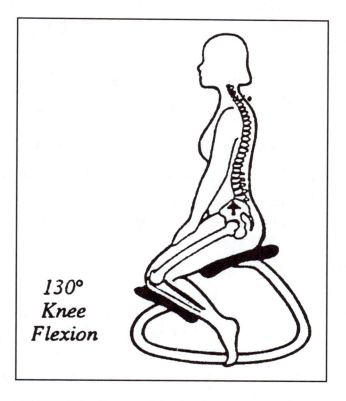

130° Knee Flexion

FIGURE 7-4. Illustration of a kneeling chair. This posture is good for the back, but can be hard on the knees.

Other less expensive alternatives, such as placing a rolled-up towel at the rear of the seat or placing a 2 × 4-inch (5 × 10 cm) board under the back legs of the chair work well. While observing a recent youth symphony orchestra rehearsal, the author (Richard Norris) noted that several of the wind and string players tipped their chairs with backward-sloping seats onto the front legs to attain a forward-sloping effect.

Conclusion

In summary, seat modification is only a battle in the war against back discomfort. Through a good exercise program designed for strengthening flexibility, frequent breaks to change position during practice, attention to body awareness by such means as yoga, the Alexander technique, or Feldenkrais work, and relaxation techniques such as meditation, biofeedback, or stress management programs, the singer can avoid much of the physical discomfort that so often takes some of the joy out of singing and may undermine technique as well.

Study Questions

1. What are the main causes of lower back pain?

2. What can be done to ease physical tensions when seated?

3. What can be done to eliminate emotional stress in a rehearsal situation?

4. What are the best resources for exercises and body awareness to facilitate choral singing?

5. Name at least two practical solutions to ease seating stress for choral singers.

References

1. Mandal AC. *The Seated Man.* Copenhagen, Denmark: Dafania Press; 1985:33.
2. Middlestadt SE, Fishbein M. The prevalence of severe musculoskeletal problems among male and female symphony orchestra string players. *Med Prob Perform Artists.* 1989;4(1):44.
3. Caillet R. *Low Back Pain Syndrome.* Philadelphia, Pa: FA Davis; 1983:214.

4. Nachemson A. The load on lumbar discs in different positions of the body. *Clin Orthoped.* 1966;45:107–122.
5. Nachemson A. Intervertebral dynamic pressure measurement in lumbar discs. *Scand J Rehab Med.* 1970(suppl 1):98–100.
6. Keegan JJ. Alterations of the lumbar curve related to posture and sitting. *J Bone Joint Surg.* 1953;35A(3):589.

CHAPTER

8

Historical Overview of Vocal Pedagogy

Richard Miller

The vocal instrument does not need to be constructed; it is available for immediate use. Lodged in a physical machine, it receives its impetus from mental and spiritual parameters of human personality. Its adaptability in channeling communication is the foundation on which human civilizations are built.

The capacity to communicate through vocal sound inevitably led to the voice of singing. Singing predates all other forms of music performance. In every primitive society, a few individuals were more attuned to the inherent emotive power of voicing than were others. They are the ancestors of the solo singer. As the potentials of the singing voice became increasingly evident, techniques for the realization of enhanced vocal skills were developed and passed on.

People of all ages and cultures have crafted indigenous styles of singing. Witness the Greek tragedian searching beyond the boundaries of normal speech for the best method by which to become audible in the amphitheater (however grateful its architectural acoustic); the citharoedus accompanying himself on the lyre or cithara in public Olympic competition; David singing and playing his harp privately before distressed King Saul; the cantor leading vigorously sung ancient liturgies—the synagogue *hazan*, the mosque *muezzin*; the ascetic monk intoning initial phrases of subdued Gregorian chant; the occult shaman inciting emotive responses in his listeners; the operatic soprano and tenor bringing down the house with ringing high Cs.

In early records of secular song, the late Medieval Goliard[1] students who protested the moral strictures of the universities, the early Renaissance trouvères and troubadours, the Minnesingers, and the Meistersingers exemplify solo balladeering. Almost no evidence exists as to how these singers executed technical aspects of their art. References to breath management, laryngeal action, and resonation (the three components of the tripartite vocal instrument) are so minimal as to be of little use in determining how vocal color was achieved. Internal evidence from existing musical fragments suggests that vocal demands seldom exceeded those of speech.

Treatises written before the 19th century restrict themselves largely to matters of style. To the 16th-century and the 17th-century writer, codification of performance rules was of primary concern. Even in the 18th century, technical aspects of the singing voice were only tangentially treated. Indeed, there is peril in applying information from those centuries to vocal literature of general performance because much of what was written about performance practice could not pertain to the singing voice. Given the structure of the vocal instrument, it is clear that a singer was never expected to match the sounds of the mechanically constructed instruments with which he or she performed.

Current assessments of the character of pre-19th-century vocalism are largely speculative, based on personal tonal preferences that enjoy minimal scholarly documentation. Beyond general aesthetic guidelines, both pedagogic and critical period literatures reveal little as to how vocal qualities were produced. Especially regarding late Baroque vocal literature, current "historically authentic performance" most probably remains wide of the mark.

A 15th-century voice-pedagogy note comes from Franchinus Gaffurius in the *Practica musicae* of 1496[2]:

> Singers should not produce musical tones with a voice gaping wide in a distorted fashion or with an absurdly powerful bellowing, especially when singing at the divine mysteries; moreover they should avoid tones having a wide and ringing vibrato, since these tones do not maintain a true pitch and because their continuous wobble cannot form a balanced concord with other voices.

Clearly, for Gaffurius a wide *vibrato* and a bellowing voice were as common and as undesirable in his day as are broad vocal oscillations and shouting in present-day singing. He did not suggest that the singing voice should avoid natural vibrancy but that an uncontrollable vibrato was not acceptable. Gaffurius offered no instruction as to how these technical errors were to be avoided.

In 1592, in his *Prattica di musica utile e necessaria se al compositore per comporre i canti suoi regolamente, si anco al cantore*, Ludovico Zacconi recommended continuous use of vibrato, which he termed tremolo[3]:

> This tremolo should be slight and pleasing; for if it is exaggerated and forced, it tires and annoys; its nature is such that, if used at all, *it should always be used*, [italics added], since use converts it into habit . . . it facilitates the undertaking of passaggi [ornamentation]; this movement . . . should not be undertaken if it cannot be done with just rapidity, vigorously and vehemently.

Bénigne de Bacilly (c. 1625–1690) in *Remarques curieuses sur l'art de bien chanter* (Paris, 1668) made a distinction between *cadence* and *tremblement*. A.B. Caswell[4] translates Bacilly's *cadence* as "vibrato," a phenomenon not to be equated with the rapid oscillatory *tremblement*. Bacilly indicated that the singer's *cadence* is a "gift of nature" that sometimes becomes too slow or too fast. The *tremblement* may produce an undesirable *voix chevrotante* (*bleating* or wobbling). Slow and rapid oscillations are used only as ornaments. Clearly, there was no intention of outlawing natural vibrato. For Bacilly a pretty voice "is very pleasing to the ear because of its clearness and sweetness and above all because of the nice *cadence* [here, *vibrato*], which usually accompanies it.[5]

Other treatises from the late Renaissance make frequent reference to unwanted nasality and to the common fault of singing out of tune. They insist on beauty and consistency of timbre but remain mostly silent as to how desirable vocal quality can be managed. A chief reason for lack of attention in early treatises to the training of the singing voice is that extensive individual solo artistic expression did not emerge until the close of the 16th century. Prior to the "invention of opera" by the Florentine camerata in the late years of the 16th century and the early decades of the 17th century, vocal literature had largely been directed to ensemble, not soloistic concerns. It was, however, replete with complex technical and musicianly demands that required high-level performance, It is clear that early singers were highly trained and capable of executing pyrotechnical passages for individual voices, but singing was still adjunctive to social or religious functions, taking place in monastery, chapel, cathedral, salon, or parlor. In the 17th century, individual solo singers became public performers in their own right, exhibiting remarkable ascendancy by midcentury.

Passing references to vocal technique prior to 1600 are of limited practical value to current performers of the vocal music from those eras. Further, aesthetic tastes are by no means stable from decade to decade, let alone century to century. To achieve "authenticity" by imitating each assumed aesthetic stratum of the past, the professional singer would need to develop technical maneuvers deleterious to vocal health, although it is tempting to react to the layers of stylistic information available by nostalgically looking back to some period of lost vocal perfection. Today's lyric artist must distinguish among vocal styles appropriate to diverse literatures, but Herbert Witherspoons's remark[6] may provide a needed counterbalance:

> There have always been few good singers and fewer great ones so a tirade about present-day conditions in comparison with the glorious past is of no use. . . . Perhaps if we heard the singers of a century or two ago we should not care for them. . . . Our task is with today, not yesterday.

Nonetheless, to understand the several current strands of today's vocal pedagogy, a knowledge of their roots is essential.

All solo vocal performance must include technical prowess for all solo vocal performance that goes beyond speech or folksong idioms. In order to discover and disseminate technical principles for extended tasks, the discipline of vocal pedagogy arose. Vocal pedagogy of the 17th century was mostly directed to the male voice, not to the castrato and female instruments as is sometimes falsely assumed. During the 18th century, a number of treatises concerned the castrati, whose techniques, as documented by such researchers as Duey,[7] Heriot,[8] and Pleasants,[9] were clearly of the highest order. However, it is easy to overlook the fact that public esteem for the female soprano at times rivaled that afforded the castrati. During the first half of the 18th century the low female voice also gradually gained acceptance as a viable vocal instrument for the stage. Puberty affects male and female larynges differently. (The effects of puberty were largely avoided with the castrato.) But techniques of breath management and articulation apply to both sexes and to every category of singer. It is not the case that 17th- and 18th-century vocal instruction was intended only for the altered male larynx.

One must turn to 18th-century Italy to trace the origins of an international vocal pedagogy capable of matching the tasks found within the vocal literature. Even today, much of the early Italian heritage remains dominant among competing national and regional schools. A brief survey of the pedagogic tenets of the historic Italian school follows.

Francesco Antonio Pistocchi (1659–1726) founded a Bolognese singing school around 1700. In pyrotechnical skill, it rivaled the proficiency of string playing. He was the teacher of Antonio Bernacchi (c. 1690–1756), who in turn taught two of Handel's favorite castrati, Senesino and Carestini.

Another school of outstanding singers flourished under the tutelage of the tenor and composer Nicola Porpora (1686–1768) at Naples and quickly became international. The ability to sustain (*cantabile*) and to move (*cabaletta*) the voice were the pedagogic aims of the Neapolitan vocal school. (These skills became pre-eminent in the *cavatina/cabaletta* aria form of the following century.) Among Porpora's many successful pupils were two famous castrati, Caffarelli and Farinelli, and the highly regarded female sopranos Mingotti and Gabrielli.

Jean-Baptiste Bérard (also known as Jean-Antoine Bérard), discussing respiration for singing in his *L'art du chant* of 1755,[10] is in accord with the international Italianate school by advocating an outwardly raised rib cage, diaphragmatic descent, and controlled breath emission as technical essentials.

An early significant written source on solo vocal pedagogy[11] comes from the hand of the castrato Pier Francesco Tosi. His *Opinioni de' cantori antichi e moderni sieno osservazioni sopra il canto figurato* was first published in Bologna in 1723, when Tosi was more than 70 years old. It thereafter (1742) appeared in an English translation by a German emigrant to England, Johann Ernst Galliard and has long been known in British and North American vocal pedagogy circles as *Observations on the Florid Song*. A German translation with commentary by JH Agricola, *Anleitung zur Singkunst*, was issued in 1757. Although largely concerned with the execution of embellishments such as the appoggiatura and the shake, and with the management of roulades and scales, Tosi makes general references to technical matters, but he mostly avoids specific advice. For example, with regard to breath management:

> to manage his respiration . . . [the singer must] always be provided with more breath than is needful; and may avoid undertaking what, for want of it, he can not go through with.

Castrato Tosi designated the vocal registers as *voce di petto* (chest voice) and *voce di testa* (head voice) without precise advice as to how they were to be facilitated. He offered more specific information as to the effects of the articulators on the resonator tract. In keeping with the age-old Italian preference for front vowels over the back vowels in upper range, he maintained that the vowels [i] and [e] were less fatiguing than the vowel [o].

Although singing technique may not have adhered to uniform instructional ideals endorsed by all, common technical threads run throughout early treatises. Despite the commonality of pedagogic viewpoints on breathing and enunciation, one is struck by the frequent complaint from renowned teachers that the rest of the pedagogic world has lost the true art of singing (reminiscent of some of today's pedagogic and critical lamentation). Tosi was not happy with the existing status of the singing art:

> Gentlemen! Masters! Italy hears no more: [1723] such exquisite voices as in times past, *particularly among the women* [italics added], and to the shame of the guilty I'll tell the reason. The ignorance of the parents does not allow them to perceive the badness of the voices of their children, as their necessity makes them believe, that to sing and grow rich is the same thing, and to learn music, it is enough to have a pretty face. Can you make anything of her?

Tosi's comments on the role of the performing artist as teacher of singing are as sagacious for our era as for his:

> It may seem to many, that every perfect singer must also be a perfect instructor but it is not so; for his qualifications (though ever so great) are insufficient if he cannot communicate his sentiments with ease, and in a method adapted to the ability of the student.

Giambattista Mancini is another oft-cited 18th-century source on the art of singing,[12] yet his *Pensieri, e riflessioni pratiche sopra il canto figurato* of 1774 is, as its title implies, largely devoted to practical reflections on vocal ornamentation. Mancini (b. 1714, Ascoli; d. 1800, Vienna) had studied singing with Bernacchi and must have had a good grasp of the accepted singing techniques of the period. Much of his pedagogic comment is directed to the resonator system, with particular attention to the maintenance of natural postures of the buccal cavity, and to the smiling posture as an adjustor of the vocal tract. Berton Coffin was struck by Mancini's awareness of the variation in physiologic structure among singers:[11]

> He acknowledged that all faces differ in structure, and some are better proportioned for singing than are others; nevertheless certain positions [of the mouth] were best for a smooth, pure quality of tone, and certain positions would bring out a suffocated and crude tone (too open) or a nasal tone (too closed). He thought the Italian vowels [ɑ, e, o, u] could be sung on each note in the position of a smile with the [o] and [u] being slightly rounded. . . . Mancini felt the [ɪ] vowel was difficult and should be sung in the position of a "composed smile."

Another Mancini pedagogic tenet was that to be distinct and executed with the greatest possible velocity, all runs and agility passages should be supported by a robust chest, assisted by graduated breath energy, and with light "fauces" (the passage from the mouth into the pharynx).

W. Crutchfield[13] remarks that Domenico Corri (1746–1825) is "probably the most valuable single theorist as far as the provision of practical examples is concerned." Corri's extensive variations and cadenzas on Sarti's *Lungi dal caro bene,*[13] is cited as an example of vocal embellishment practices of the period. E. Harris[14] quotes Corri's 1810 comment on performance and style[15]:

> The vocal art affords various characters—the sacred, the serious, the comic, anacreontic, cavatina, bravura, etc., etc.—and though each style requires different gifts and cultivation, yet true intonation, the swelling and dying of the voice, with complete articulation of words, is essential to all.

Corri suggested that the voice should increase in volume as it rises and decrease in volume when descending. However, he does not offer significant advice to a reader searching for clues on how best to accomplish the technical complexities of the vocal literature considered.

Tenor Manuel del Popolo Vincent Garcia Rodriguez (1775–1832) is known as Garcia *père* to distinguish him from his son Manuel Patricio Rodriguez Garcia (1805–1906). His vocal technique book, *Exercises pour la voix,*[16] was published in Paris between 1819 and 1822. It was fully within the pedagogical tradition of the 18th-century Italian school. (An English translation was published in London in 1824.) One of Garcia's teachers was Giovanni Ansoni, a member of the Neapolitan singing school. Having already established himself as a premier singer in his native country, Garcia left Spain in 1808 to build an international opera career, performing in Paris, Turin, Rome, and Naples. The role of Count Almaviva (*Il barbiere di Siviglia*, by Rossini) was written for him: it is ample evidence of the capability of Garcia *père* and presents explicit pedagogic advice:

> The position of the body must be erect, the shoulders thrown back, with the arms crossed behind; this will open the chest and bring out the voice with ease, clear and strong, without distorting the appearance of either face or body.

> . . . [the singer ought] never to commence singing in a hurry, always to take breath slowly and without noise, which would otherwise be unpleasant to those who listen, and injurious to the singer.

> . . . The throat, teeth and lips, must be sufficiently opened so that the voice may meet with no impediment, since the want of a strict attention

to either of these three is sufficient to destroy the good quality of the voice and to produce the bad one, of the throat, nose, etc.; besides, proper attention to the mouth will give that perfect and clear pronunciation indispensable to singing, and which unfortunately, few possess.

Early 19th-century Garcia *père* resides solidly in the tradition of the 18th-century Italian school. Among his pupils were his daughters (Viardot and Malibran, perhaps the most celebrated female vocal artists of the era), his son Manuel, and Adolphe Nourrit, the leading French tenor of the first half of the 19th century until the advent of Gilbert Duprez.

A thorough examination of the contribution of his son, Manuel Garcia *fils* (1805–1906), becomes all the more intriguing because much subsequent critical comment implies that the younger Garcia introduced technical directions that withdrew from previous tenets of the Italian school. When accounts of his entire teaching career are taken into consideration, it becomes doubtful that such a break with tradition took place. A case (admittedly controversial) could be made that Garcia the younger used his new knowledge of laryngeal and vocal tract anatomy and physiology to verify and enhance what he had learned from his father.

Manuel Garcia's appearance in New York at age 20 as Figaro in Rossini's *Il barbiere di Siviglia* (with his father as Almaviva, his sister as Rosina, and his mother as Berta) indicates that 10 years of vocal study with his father had produced a precocious baritone voice. (It also makes one question if performance standards were as high as current idealization of past vocal eras may imagine.) Garcia's strenuous performing routine while still so young (sometimes even acting as substitute in tenor roles for his ill father) may well have contributed to his early vocal deterioration. In any event, he was unable to emulate the performance successes of his father and his siblings, and he turned to teaching. His *Traité complet de l'art du chant*[17] appeared in 1840.

In 1841, *Manuel Garcia's Mémoire sur la voix humaine*[18] was presented to the French Academy. His growing curiosity about physical function was further sparked by anatomical observations made at military hospitals. In 1854, these interests led him to the invention of a primitive laryngoscope. (Note that it was a voice teacher, not a physician, who first saw the vocal folds in action during spoken and sung phonations.)

Garcia devised register terminology with the designations chest voice, falsetto voice, and head voice, based on physiologic information and practical knowledge of then-current performance practice. These registration divisions are confusing to modern-day voice researchers.

He discussed laryngeal positioning in detail as well as the *coup de glotte* (the stroke of the glottis). His descriptions later generated a variety of pedagogic assumptions, some of which, if one is to believe reports of his students, went far beyond principles he himself taught. In a summary of his method, undertaken in 1870 and published in 1872,[19] one finds distinct parallels with what his father had proposed, even to the inclusion of similar technical exercises. For example, he advised that the head and neck should remain erect on the torso, that the shoulders ought to be well back without stiffness, that the chest must remain in an expanded position, and that inspiration should occur silently and slowly without sudden diaphragmatic lowering. He recommended the use of a breath-management exercise that had come down by word of mouth from the previous century, Farinelli's exercise, in which the breath cycle is accomplished through a slow tripartite maneuver consisting of an inspiratory gesture, a subsequent suspension of either inhalation or exhalation, and a concluding expiratory gesture, the three segments being of equal duration. He recommended use of the *attacco de suono* (onset) as a basic exercise for the development of breath-management skill. His "open" and "closed" vocal timbres are in line with the *voce aperta/voce chiusa* (open voice/closed voice) and the *copertura* (cover) terminology of the traditional Italian school. Laryngeal posture should be low and stable. His instruction on the relationship of vowel integrity to vowel modification in ascending pitch is a pillar of today's vocal art.

A thorough analysis of Manuel Garcia's technical principles requires extensive consideration not possible here. Proof of the efficacy of his teaching lies in the large number of outstanding singers of many nationalities who were among his pupils. Further insight into Garcia's pedagogy is to be found in an *Essay on Bel Canto* written by his pupil and close associate Herman Klein.[20] Never in the history of solo singing has one individual so influenced vocal pedagogy as did Manuel Garcia. It is fair to suggest that current international mainstream vocalism and many of its divergent nationalist rivulets can be traced directly to interpretations of Garcia's admonitions. His own assessment of the state of singing (when many thought it at its peak) was that singing had become as much a lost art as that of the manufacture of Mandarin china or the varnish used by the old string-instrument masters.

An interim figure, surfacing in the Italian school between the Garcias and the Lampertis, is the Neapolitan Luigi LaBlache (1794–1858), whose career as outstanding *basso* of the era took him to La Scala, Vienna, Paris, and London. Yet his *Méthode de chant*, published undated in Paris, as was the English edition,[21] came late in life. It offers little precise information as to how the art of singing ought to be taught. Evidence of his successful teaching lies in the number of his pupils who managed professional careers.

A *Treatise on the Art of Singing*[22] by Francesco Lamperti (1813–1892) is undated but is presumed to have appeared after 1860. F. Lamperti's chief contribution to the historic Italian school is his description of the *lutte vocale* (It. *lotta vocale*), the basis for the *appoggio* breath management that is a fundamental precept of the 19th-century Italian School:

> To sustain a given note the air should be expelled slowly; to attain this end, the respiratory [inspiratory] muscles, by continuing their action, strive to retain the air in the lungs, and oppose their action to that of the expiratory muscles, which is called the *lutte vocale* or vocal struggle. On the retention of this equilibrium depends the just emission of the voice, and by means of it alone can true expression be given to the sound produced.

Although the term *appoggio* appears to have first come into use in the second half of the 19th century, the *lutte vocale* (which is analogous to the appoggio technique) already existed in the exercise that Farinelli is reputed to have learned a century earlier from Porpora (see above) to acquire his phenomenal breath management.

Francesco Lamperti held to the three-register designation of the 19th-century Italian school (allowing for gender differences), and he was adamant that whether singing softly or loudly, timbre must be consistent. The *messa di voce* (sung on a single note or phrase beginning at piano or pianissimo dynamic level, crescendoing to forte or fortissimo, then returning to the original decibel level) was an important part of his pedagogy. He stressed the need for full, complete tone production at all dynamic levels.

His son, Giovanni Battista (Giambattista) Lamperti (1839–1910), left an even more enduring mark on international vocal pedagogy. He taught singers who would become identified with the "second golden age" of vocalism, and these students carried on his system well into the first half of the 20th century. Lamperti's advice regarding general posture and events of the breath cycle[23] parallels that of his predecessors: "The shoulders [must] be slightly thrown back to allow the chest due freedom in front." For GB Lamperti, breath management was the prime factor in skillful singing. He recognized the unique relationship of vocal registers to each vocal category and to the individual instrument. Breath renewal should be silently incorporated into the release of the tone at each phrase termination, with subsequent precise onset (attack). Singing piano was in all regards the same as singing forte, only softer. Above all, good singing necessitated command of the art of legato, which depended on efficient breath management.[23] Lamperti's opposition to the "relaxed" posture then being advocated by the German school is eminently clear. In contrast to that school's lowered thoracic postures, the singer was to feel broad-shouldered, high-chested, and straightened-up like a soldier. Despite the reputation of many turn-of-the-century singing artists, Lamperti lamented the general deterioration of the art of singing and of voice teaching:

> There has never been much enthusiasm for the singing art, nor have there been so many students and teachers as of late years. And it is precisely this period that reveals the deterioration of this divine art and the almost complete disappearance of genuine singers and worse, of good singing teachers.

Could Giambattista Lamperti have had in mind the inroads that the national schools were making into the historic international Italianate school?

A telling influence in 20th-century North America vocal pedagogy is William Earl Brown's *Maxims of G.B. Lamperti*. The book first appeared in print in America in 1931,[24] but the maxims were collected in 1891–1893 when Brown was Lamperti's student and assistant in Dresden. He maintained that the quoted maxims were directly from studio notes he made during that period.

> At no time during the song or series of exercises must you relax while replenishing the breath or you [will] lose the feeling of suspension. Only when the song is over may you let go . . . [Maintain] sustained intensity of initial vibration and continuous release of breath-energy . . . Tone and breath "balance" solely when harmonic overtones appear in the voice, not by muscular effort and "voice placing."

He said legato was achievable only through the presence of constant vibrancy, a result of the appoggio. Lamperti held that loose breath escaping over the vocal folds and not turned into tone was destructive to good function, causing irregular vibration and disruption of breath energy.

> Until you feel the permanency of your vibration you cannot play on your resonances . . . [E]nergy in regular vibration is constructive. The violence in irregular vibration is destructive.

The influence of the Lamperti maxims has never been surpassed by other pedagogic writing of the 20th century.

In the interest of chronology, the treatises of two other representatives of the Lamperti school, William Shakespeare and Herbert Witherspoon, are considered later. For additional commentary regarding the influence of this school's appoggio technique on modern vocal pedagogy, the reader is directed to C Timberlake's astute remarks on historic pedagogy and performance styles.[25]

The historic Italian school dominated all European professional vocalism; its proponents taught in the major cities of Europe (Garcia in London and Paris, GB Lamperti in Munich and Dresden, for example). In the latter half of the 19th century, with the emergence of European nationalism, the conscious development of indigenous regional cultures, and divergences stemming from application of new scientific findings to the art of singing, the reign of Italian vocalism became less encompassing. Whereas opera, the chief performance vehicle for professional singing, had been Italian-centered during the 17th, 18th, and early 19th centuries, in the latter half of the 19th century, other performance literatures, such as the *Lied*, the *mélodie*, the orchestrated song, and the oratorio, began to flower. These literatures continued to burgeon as the 20th century dawned, garnering new impetus in subsequent decades. Even though the Italian model was still pre-eminent in the international world of professional vocalism, disparate, identifiable tonal aesthetics began to flourish in France, in Germany and Northern Europe, and in England, while Italy persistently held firm to historic tradition through at least the first third of the 20th century. It is worthy of note that Manuel Garcia is frequently cited in support of the many pedagogic strands that became alternative to the original Italianate model. National digressions resulted from differing emphases in tonal ideals, from emerging vocal literatures, and above all, from an increasing interest in achieving synthesis of word and music, transcending the traditional Italian emphasis on vocalism as the chief aesthetic concern.

The unification of the German political states into a national body, the increasing importance of liturgical choral traditions (such as the Germanic/Scandinavian Lutheran and the Anglican), the emergence of the public *Liederabend*, the rise of Romantic German opera, the impact of Wagner, and the shift from royal to public patronage altered the dominant role of the international Italian school, but it did not obliterate its influence on national schools. (All pedagogic threads were woven into the North American vocal-pedagogy garment.)

The modern pedagogue may best understand the wide diversity among systems of vocal technique, most of which had their origins in the late 19th century, by gauging the extent to which they break away from the earlier international model and the extent to which they retain its premises. In a number of instances, divergent modern pedagogics continue the late 19th-century search for justification of techniques by applying modern scientific measurement. Some treatises of the latter half of the 19th century were written by teachers with one foot located south of the historic Italian pedagogic Alp, the other foot planted north of it. "New" 20th-century pedagogic systems are seldom more than extensions of those diverse formulae.

Julius Stockhausen was born in Paris in July, 1826, and died in Frankfurt-am-Main in September, 1906. Beginning in 1845, Stockhausen undertook theoretic studies at the Paris Conservatoire but privately studied voice with Manuel Garcia, whom he followed to London in 1849. Despite Stockhausen's future impact on Germanic/Nordic and North American vocal pedagogy, he did not excel chiefly in opera. He was second baritone at the Mannheim theater from 1852 through 1853. Stockhausen's chief performance successes lay in oratorio and *Lieder* repertoires. His public performance of *Die Schöne Müllerin* took place with great success in 1856 at Vienna. Brahms and Stockhausen first collaborated in recital in Hamburg in 1861, performing a program that included Schumann's *Dichterliebe*. Stockhausen's subsequent selection over Brahms as the director of the Hamburg Philharmonische Konzertgesellschaft and of the Singakademie did not interfere with their continued artistic coalition. Stockhausen premiered the baritone role of Brahm's *Ein deutsches Requiem* in 1868; the rangy, dramatic vocal writing was considered ungrateful to Stockhausen's instrument. The composer's remarkable Magelone cycle was written with Stockhausen in mind. It demands stamina and sensitivity, two facets that the singer seemed able to deliver equally well in the *Lieder* of Schubert, Schumann, and Brahms. After serving as a singing teacher at several institutions, Stockhausen founded his own school of singing in 1880. In 1884, *Gesangsmethode,*[26] translated as *Method of Singing*, appeared.

Stockhausen's publication is a significant step in the history of vocal pedagogy because of its continuing influence on the Germanic/Nordic vocal schools and on a sizable segment of North American pedagogy and because it raises questions as to the accuracy of Stockhausen's interpretation (and that of his disciples) of Manuel Garcia's pedagogic orientation. One of Stockhausen's chief departures from the tenets of the 18th- and 19th-century Italian school lies in his advocacy of a constantly low laryngeal position while singing. Although it remains unclear as to how low Stockhausen's "low larynx' was, he advised a position lower than that of the normal speaking voice. In itself, this admonition is not in conflict with the historic Italian pedagogic tenet that requests the noble posture and silent breath renewal, in which limited laryngeal descent will occur and remain. But most of Stockhausen's followers interpret him as having taught retention of the yawn position, with depressed larynx, as being ideal for sung phonation. His avoidance of a pleasant facial expression, together with his promotion of the lowered jaw, diminished the supraglottic vocal tract flexibility so characteristic of the Italianate school. However, Stockhausen specifically outlawed both nasal and pharyngeal timbres. Inasmuch as it is difficult to envision how distended pharyngeal timbre can be avoided while one consciously induces throat-wall expansion, Stockhausen's comments may invite varying pedagogic interpretations.

Stockhausen requested that the lips be drawn backward on back and mixed vowels, and that for [e] and [ɑ] the lips be pursed in forward position. These are withdrawals from the *si canta come si parla* (one sings as one speaks) maxim of the traditional Italian school. Yet, more in keeping with the Italian pedagogic heritage, Stockhausen recommended the use of closed vowels in ascending pitch patterns, and of open vowels in descending pitch patterns.

Although he did call for full rib expansion in the *respiro pieno* (full breath), another departure from the Italian school was Stockhausen's minimal attention to breath management. His passaggio registration points are located similarly to those of Garcia. He advocated the use of the messa di voce so dear to the Lampertis. The modern pedagogue must conclude that Julius Stockhausen severely adapted traditional Italianate-schooled principles to the performance of the emerging Germanic repertoire in which he excelled and to national tonal preferences. Given his commitment to non-Italianate technical devices, one wonders how well Stockhausen may have managed vocalism and diction in the Italian and French operatic repertories during his 3-year stint in the Paris Opéra Comique (1856–1859). Stockhausen's pedagogic orientation raises the question as to how far vocal technique can be altered for the performance of different literatures.

Not even a brief overview of historic vocal pedagogy can dispense with at least passing reference to Emma Seiler (c. 1875). Her own experiences as a singer, which she describes as having been in both Italian and German traditions, appear to have been frustrating. She finally associated herself with the eminent physicist and acoustician Hermann Helmholtz, who expressed indebtedness to her in his formulation of acoustic theories of voice production. Some of Seiler's assumptions regarding the function of the laryngeal mechanism are insupportable. In explaining her vocal registration hypotheses, she heavily relied on proprioceptive sensations of mouth, throat, stomach, and sternum. Her treatise[27] is largely important as a prototype of forthcoming Germanic pseudoscientific pedagogic literature that attempts in imaginative ways to apply physiology and acoustics to the singing voice.

British vocal pedagogy was not immune to Germanic influences. Emil Behnke's *The Mechanism of the Human Voice*, published in 1880,[28] and his *Voice, Song and Speech*,[29] in collaboration with Lennox Browne, were highly regarded in turn-of-the-century British pedagogy circles. Yet he was not a follower of Stockhausen, nor were his ideas in line with the Germanic techniques later developed by Armin. Behnke was particularly enamored of the male falsetto.

Enrico Delle Sedie (1822–1907) was a highly successful baritone in Italy, Paris, and London, singing the Verdian roles Di Luna (*Il trovatore*), Renato (*Un ballo in maschera*), and Germond (*La traviata*). Figaro (*Il barbiere di Siviglia*) and Malatesta (*Don Pasquale*) were in his repertoire. In 1876, he published *Arte e fisiologia del canto*, and in 1886, *L'estetico del canto e l'arte melodrammatica*. In 1894 *A Complete Method of Singing*,[30] which included material from his earlier publications, appeared in New York. Drawing on physiologic and acoustic information of the time, Delle Sedie exemplified those singers and teachers who increasingly began to turn to science as a means for verifying tenets of the historic Italian school. His method deals with the resonator tract as a filtering source for laryngeally generated sound. He unites the registration and timbre terminologies of the historic Italian school with emerging acoustic information, especially as regards vowel modification. As such, his writing has had considerable impact on North American vocal pedagogy.

A North American publication containing accurate drawings of the larynx and confirmable explanations of diaphragmatic function was EB Warman's *The Voice: How to Train It and Care for It* (1889). This treatise[31] is a successful effort to undergird the tenets of the Italianate school with scientific information.

A teacher of singing who left no written advice but whose outstanding pupils indicated his impact on vocal pedagogy, is the Neapolitan tenor Giovanni Sbriglia (1832–1916). Sbriglia made his debut at San Carlo in 1853 and his 1860 New York debut at the Academy of Music, where he appeared in *La sonnambula* with Adelina Patti. Both Edward de Reszke and his brother Jean (who underwent change from baritone to tenor), Pol Plançon (who also studied with Duprez), and Lillian Nordica were products of the Sbriglia studio.

Summaries of Sbriglia's teaching have been recorded by his pupils. Assuming these reports to be reliable, it appears that Sbriglia lies within the historic Italian school that extends from Garcia *père* through the Lampertis and into the 20th century. Sbriglia opposed the *Bauchasussensstütze* (outward abdominal-wall thrusting) that became characteristic of the late 19th- and 20th-century Germanic school. According to Byers[32]:

> he believed that all great singers breathed alike—"the same natural way." He did not like what he called "the new pushing method of

singing with the back of the neck sunk in the chest, and the muscularly
pushed out diaphragm. . . . "

> The foundation of this teaching is perfect posture. Foremost is a high
> chest (what nature gives every great singer), held high without tension
> by developed abdominal and lower back muscles and a straight spine—
> this will give the uplift for perfect breathing. . . . Your chest literally must
> be held by these abdominal and back muscles, supported from below,
> and your shoulder and neck will be free and loose.

It is easy to assume that Mathilde Marchesi was a proponent of the
Italian school. However, Mathilde Marchesi (b. 1821, Frankfurt-am-
Main; d. 1913, London) was a German mezzo-soprano who in 1852
married the singer Salvatore Marchesi. Her early training took place in
Germany. In 1845, she went to Paris to study with Manuel Garcia for a
period of several years. Although she had some success as a public performer, her energies were largely devoted to teaching. Outstanding
female singers were numbered among her pupils, among them Eames,
Calvé, Garden, and Melba.

Theoretical and Practical Vocal Method[33] and *Ten Singing Lessons*[34]
attest to Marchesi's organized approach to vocal pedagogy. Her description of the singing voice as a three-part instrument consisting of motor,
vibrator, and resonator system has a remarkably modern ring. In
regard to posture for singing, she is directly in the lineage of Garcia
père, Manuel Garcia, and both Lampertis, as evidenced by her suggestion that students should position the arms at the back in order to
achieve proper chest elevation and to induce low breathing. She taught
the *coup de glotte* (probably the balanced *attacco del suono*), which she
described as producing firm, complete approximation of the glottis
and which she believed used minimal air to set the vocal folds in vibration. She adhered to the three-register concept of the Italian school.
Marchesi modified the Italianate model by suggesting that the jaw
drop into low position and remain nearly immobile during singing.
Much of her success as a teacher appears to have been a result of
her systematic approach, which was summarized in the maxim, "First
technique, afterwards aesthetics."

Lilli Lehmann's *Meine Gesangkunst* (1902), published in 1914[35] as
How to Sing (later revisions appeared), has exerted lasting influence on
aspiring North American, European, and Asian singers. It is not easy
to classify Lehmann (1848–1929) by school because her language, both
subjective and specific, borrows from several traditions and appears
ultimately to be a search for justification of her personal vocal technique
through physiologic and acoustic verification, much of it inaccurate.

This combining of the subjective and the objective were expressed as follows:

> Technique is inseparable from art. Only by mastering the technique of his material is the artist in a condition to mold his mental work of art . . . [M]uscles contract in activity, and in normal inactivity are relaxed . . . [W]e must strengthen them by continued vocal gymnastics so that they may be able to sustain long-continued exertion; and must keep them elastic and use them so. It includes also the well-controlled activity of diaphragm, chest, neck, and face muscles. . . . Since these things all operate together, one without the others can accomplish nothing; if the least is lacking, singing is quite impossible, or is entirely bad.

One of the most influential pages in vocal pedagogy contains Lehmann's schema for subjective tone-placement sensations that move upward into the bony skull in response to ascending pitch. Lehmann's reputation as a gifted artist who could sing widely diverse roles, together with the longevity of her career, helped establish the importance of her opinions.

A major figure in 20th-century, German-language vocal pedagogy literature is Franziska Martienssen-Lohmann, who precisely describes breath-management procedures, registration practices, and timbre designations without the Germanic/Nordic School.[36-38] By taking exception at times to typical Germanic practices of heavy *Deckung* (covering), excessive *Kopfstimme* (head voice), and the *Tiefstellung* (low positioning) of the larynx, Martienssen-Lohmann appears to move in the direction of the international Italianate school, as do many contemporary Germans.

The teaching of Georg Armin, beginning in the 1930s, left a lasting imprint on the "heroic" segment of the German School and on its North American derivative. His breath-damming *Staumethode*,[39] by which he believed the *Urkraft* (primal strength) of the vocal instrument could be rediscovered,[40] led to several techniques of induced low-trunk breath-management maneuvers, including anal-sphincteral occlusion and the cultivated grunt (extension of the vocal fold closure phase during phonatory cycles, with sudden release of glottal tension at phrase terminations).

Frederick Husler, with his collaborator Yvonne Rodd-Marling, made a 20th-century attempt to recover a presumed primitive vocal Atlantis. Through a series of exercises (including what he considered to be prespeech maneuvers), he meant to re-establish the vocal freedom he believed to have been lost through civilization's harnessing of the vocal instrument to the functions of speech.[41] A large group of teachers follow the Husler method; they are found mostly in German, British, and Canadian conservatory enclaves.

The great Polish artist Jean de Reszke (1850–1925) stated that he did not wish to establish a method but only to express his personal ideas about the art of singing, yet his influence on the future of singing in France was monumental. Despite some study with Cotogni (a representative of the Lamperti school), de Reszke did not advocate postural attitudes of the Italian school, preferring that the student discover "relaxed" breathing by sitting with collapsed and rounded shoulders and by dropping all muscles of the torso except the diaphragm. According to reports,[42] he advised, "Imagine yourself to be a great church bell, where all the sonority is round the rim." He aimed for local control of the diaphragm and recommended that "the body sit down on the diaphragm." He suggested the use of the sigh, together with hot-air expulsion to be felt on the hand, as means for "relaxing" the glottis, the throat, and the tongue. These admonitions are in line with a number of non-Italianate models that would take root in mid-20th century North American soil. De Reszke also advocated principles that remain characteristic of current (but by no means all) 20th-century French voice instruction: (1) raised head posture (singing to the gallery); (2) placement of the tone in the masque and at the bridge of the nose; and (3) producing "the singer's grimace" (*la grimace de la chanteuse*) for high notes. One of his favorite exercises was based on a phrase containing a series of French nasals: *Pendant que l'enfant mange son pain, le chien tremble dans le buisson.*

For years, however, Paris was the international operatic center of the world. With a few notable exceptions, however, French singers have not enjoyed international careers in the later decades of the 20th century. Many observers, including French singing teachers, tend to view 20th-century French vocalism as being, at least in part, a de Reszke heritage. A return to international pedagogic orientation is increasingly in progress in France.

At the close of the 19th century, the international Italianate pedagogy model was represented by non-Italian pupils of Giovanni Battista Lamperti. Englishman William Shakespeare's end-of-the-century treatises, made available in 1921 versions called *The Art of Singing*[43] and *Plain Words on Singing*, reiterate the *lutte vocale* of the Lamperti School: opposition between the muscles that draw in the breath. Noiseless and imperceptible breathing was the aim; a phrase was never to be terminated by allowing the torso to collapse. Although some aspects of traditional British vocal technique (such as spreading of the upper back) entered into Shakespeare's pedagogy, in general he was in line with the historic international school.

The same is true of Shakespeare's countryman H Plunket Greene, who at the close of his 1912 book, *Interpretation in Song*,[44] appended two chapters, one devoted to breath management, the second to legato. Both could have been written by either of the Lampertis. Plunket Greene wanted an axial posture "with the chest as high as ever it will go." He detailed techniques for inducing the appoggio and delineated factors that contribute to legato singing.

Current British vocal technique seems to be of two minds, one filled with historic Italianate pedagogic ideals, the other aimed at "purity" of timbre based on influences from the treble-voice liturgical tradition—"cathedral tone." However, the one concept tumbles into the other, so that typical British tonal ideals often take on a recognizable insular flavor. (It is hardly possible to mistake British-trained operatic tenors, sopranos, or mezzo-sopranos for Italian-trained singers.)

At the beginning of the 20th century, the EG White Society proposed the theory of sinus tone production.[45] Despite a lack of scientific verification for its basic tenet, the society still claims more than 200 active members, most of them English and North American. It is closely allied with British notions of "tonal purity."

More recently, E Herbert-Caesari attempted in several volumes[46-48] to fuse the mystical with the mechanical. His books remain influential in British vocal pedagogy.

In 1953, Herbert Witherspoon became director of the Metropolitan Opera Company, where he had already sung for eight seasons. He was a key figure in the performance world and in academia and was one of the founders of the oldest voice-teacher organizations in the world, the American Academy of Teachers of Singing and the Chicago Singing Teachers Guild. As mentioned earlier, Witherspoon is a direct descendant of the historic international Italian school. His 1925 *Singing*[49] remains a classic of modern vocal pedagogy. He studied with GB Lamperti and continued that tradition. Witherspoon's unique contribution originated in his convictions that (1) the singing voice primarily is a physical instrument that obeys the laws of efficient physical function and (2) the singing voice is an acoustic instrument that must be produced naturally in accordance with the laws of vocal acoustics. His dictum that we do not perform any physical act through relaxation, but with correct tension and action, places him in direct opposition to Germanic/Nordic techniques of the lowered, relaxed torso. His "lifts of the breath," meaning breath-energy increases at registration pivotal points, correspond to the passaggi registration demarcations of the Lamperti school. His treatment of vocal tract filtering is in complete accord with that school. A typical passage reads:

> as pitch ascends . . . the tongue rises coordinately upwards and forwards, changing the shape of the throat and the mouth, the fauces point forward

and narrow, or approximate; the uvula rises and finally disappears, the soft palate rises forward, never backward; while the epiglottis, rising up against the back of the lower tongue, seems to have a law of its own regarding quality, clear or veiled.

Not all of his observations precisely corresponded to what modern investigation verifies, yet Witherspoon masterfully combined past international vocalism with then-available scientific and acoustic information; tradition and modern pragmatism found a happy marriage. He based his pedagogy on the language of function, yet Witherspoon stressed that singing deals not simply with mechanics ("muscles and organs cannot be locally controlled") and that it is linguistic and musical interpretation that finally control technique.

In the period immediately before and following World War II, a plethora of writings on vocal technique emerged in Germany. In general, they tend to support low-abdominal breath-management techniques and fixated resonator tracts. Some American pedagogues were not far behind in building on those premises. Pedagogic cultivators of all the national schools flourish on the North American continent, yet the international Italian model is still the predominant exemplar for the professional singer.

The influence of Douglas Stanley, beginning with his 1929 *The Science of Voice*,[50] has been enduring on a small but devoted segment of American voice teaching circles. His viewpoints on register separation and unification have been further expanded by the skillful writing of Cornelius Reid.[51-53]

Among publications that have exerted influence on mid-20th-century vocalism, none has been more forceful than William Vennard's *Singing, the Mechanism and the Technic*.[54] This volume is a reliable source for the study of anatomy, physiology, and acoustics of the vocal instrument. With regards to his use of the yawn/sigh device and to his stances on "belly breathing," the *passaggi*, vocal registration, and postures of the vocal tract, Vennard indicates partial allegiance to the historic Germanic/Nordic camp. In other respects, he appears to be in tune with international vocalism.

Another important pedagogic strand in recent North American pedagogy comes from the prolific Berton Coffin,[55-57] whose premises unite his knowledge of the phonetic properties of the singing voice with scholarly interest in historic vocalism. Coffin's advocacy of elevated laryngeal and head postures described as "the sword-swallowing position," and his championing of male falsetto as a legitimate extension of the upper voice, ally him with segments of the modern French school, although in most other respects, he retains allegiance to the international Italianate school.

A splendid singer himself, Ralph Appelman attempted to unite vocal pedagogy and scientific principles in his ground-breaking volume, *The Science of Vocal Pedagogy*,[58] which is filled with detailed information on physiology and acoustics. It has been difficult for Appelman's admirers to translate his highly systematized pedagogy into accessible lay language.

Even the briefest survey of vocal pedagogy must append a list (by no means all-inclusive) of voice professionals, past and present, who have contributed significant articles or books on the relationships of function, artistic singing, and vocal pedagogy: L Bachner, RM Baken, W Bartholomew, M Benninger, MP Bonnier, D Brewer, M Bunch, VA Christy, T Cleveland, D Clippinger, R Colton, A Cranmer, R Edwin, J Estill, VA Fields, T Fillebrown, V Fuchs, WJ Gould, JW Gregg, T Hixon, CH Holbrook, H Hollien, R Husson, J Klein, J Large, V Lawrence, P Lohmann, R Luchsinger, M Mackenzie, MS MacKinley, L Manén, PM Marafiotti, W McIver, B McClosky, J McKinney, C Meano, DC Miller, DG Miller, F Miller, R Miller, GP Moore, RC Mori, M Nadoleczny, G Newton, D Proctor, A Rose, R Rosewal, RT Sataloff, HK Schütte, N Scotto di Carlo, C Seashore, R Sherer, T Shipp, D Slater, A Sonninen, A Stampa, RH Stetson, J Sundberg, J Tarneaud, R Taylor, J Teachey, I Titze, JB van Deinse, W Van den Berg, H von Leden, K Westerman, HW Whitlock, J Wilcox, C Wilder, PS Wormhoudt, and BD Wyke.

Recent contributors to the literature on vocal pedagogy apply fiberoptic stroboscopy, spectrography, fluoroscopy, and other forms of measurement to the events of voicing. Their intention has not been mostly to invent new ways to sing but to objectively compare traditional, international, national, regional, and idiosyncratic pedagogies in matters of their vocal efficiency and their relationship to vocal aesthetics and vocal health.

Conclusion

The history of vocal pedagogy may be traced over a period of centuries. The earliest writings discussed in this chapter date from the 15th century. The Italianate school developed in the 18th century, and a subsequently diverse school of pedagogy emerged. A variety of influences have determined the progress of singing pedagogy and the techniques of singing and teaching utilized most widely today.

Study Questions

1. Which school of pedagogy has most strongly influenced international singing pedagogy?
   a. Greek
   b. Italian
   c. Russian
   d. German
   e. French

2. Which of the following individuals was most influential in the development of modern day pedagogy?
   a. Benigné de Bacilly
   b. Pier Francesco Tosi
   c. Berton Coffin
   d. Manuel Garcia
   e. Francesco Lamperti

3. What is the name given to the fundamental breath-management precept of the 19th-century Italian school of singing, a precept still in wide use today?
   a. arpageretora
   b. arpeggio
   c. appoggia
   d. ascension
   e. allegro

4. Singing a single note that begins softly, crescendos to a louder volume, and then softens to the original level, is an exercise known as:
   a. mezza voce
   b. modulation
   c. marcato
   d. marking
   e. messa di voce

5. Who is the singer whose teaching career and vocal pedagogy book, *The Method of Singing*, influenced significantly the German/ Nordic vocal schools, as well as North American pedagogy?
   a. Julius Stockhausen
   b. Manuel Garcia
   c. Giambattista Lamperti
   d. Johannes Brahms
   e. Giovanni Sbriglia

References

1. Jander O. Singing. In: Sadie S, ed. *The New Grove Dictionary of Music and Musicians.* New York, NY: Grove's Dictionaries of Music; 1980:17.
2. Tosi P-F. *Observations on the Florid Song.* Gailliard JE, trans. London, England; 1742.
3. Harris E. The Baroque era voices. In: Brown HM, Sadie S, eds. *Performance Practice: After 1600.* New York, NY: WW Norton; 1989.
4. De Bacilly B; Caswell A, trans. 1968 (Originally published as *Remarques curieuses sur l'art de bien chanter.* Paris, France; 1668.)
5. Coffin B. Vocal pedagogy classics: practical reflections on figured singing by Giambattista Mancini. In: Miller R, ed. *The NATS Bulletin.* 1981;37(4) 47–49.
6. Witherspoon H. *Singing.* New York, NY: G Schirmer; 1925.
7. Duey P. *Bel Canto in Its Golden Age.* New York, NY: King's Crown Press; 1950.
8. Heriot A. *The Castrati in Opera.* New York, NY: Da Capo Press, 1964.
9. Pleasants H. *The Great Singers.* New York, NY: Simon and Schuster; 1966.
10. Bérnard J-B (J-A). *L'Art du Chant.* Paris, France; 1755.
11. Tosi P-F. *Observations on the Florid Song.* Gailliard JE, trans. London, England; 1742.
12. Mancini G. *Practical Reflections on the Art of Singing.* Buzzi P, trans. Boston, Mass: Oliver Ditson; 1907.
13. Crutchfield W. The 19th century: voices. In: Brown HM, Sadie S, eds. *Performance Practice: Music After 1600.* New York, NY: WW Norton; 1989.
14. Tosi P-F. *Observations on the Florid Song.* Gailliard JE trans. London, England; 1742.
15. Corri D. *The Singer's Preceptor.* London, England; 1810.
16. Garcia MPVR. *Exercices pour la voix.* Paris, France: A Parite; c. 1820.
17. Garcia MPVR. *Trait complet de l'art du chant.* Paris, France: French Academy of Science; 1840.
18. Garcia MPVR. *Mémoire sur la voice humaine.* Paris, France: E Suverger; 1841.
19. Garcia MPVR. *Garcia's Complete School of Singing.* London, England: Cramer Beal & Chappell; 1872.
20. Klein H. *An Essay on Bel Canto.* London, England: Oxford University Press; 1923.
21. Lablache L. *Lablache's Complete of Singing: or, a Rational Analysis of the Principles According to Which the Studies Should Be Directed for Developing the Voice and Rendering It Flexible.* Boston, Mass: Oliver Ditson; n.d.
22. Lamperti F. *A Treatise on the Art of Singing.* Griffith JC, trans. New York, NY: G Schirmer; 1905.
23. Lamperti G-B. *The Techniques of Bel Canto.* Baker T, trans. New York, NY: G Schirmer; 1905.
24. Brown WE. *Vocal Wisdom: Maxims of Giovanni Battista Lamperti.* New York, NY: Crescendo Press; 1957.
25. Timberlake C. Apropos of appoggio, parts I and II. *The NATS Journal.* 1995;52(3,4).

26. Stockhausen J. *Method of Singing.* London, England: Novello; 1884.
27. Seiler E. *The Voice in Singing.* Philadelphia, Pa: JB Lippincott; 1875.
28. Behnke E. *The Mechanism of the Human Voice.* London, England: J Curwen & Sons; 1880.
29. Browne L, Behnke E. *Voice, Song and Speech.* New York, NY: G Putnam's Sons; 1900.
30. Delle Sedie E. *A Complete Method of Singing.* New York, NY: private printing; 1894.
31. Warman EB. *The Voice: How to Train It and Care for It.* Boston, Mass: Lee & Shepard; 1889.
32. Byers MC. Sbriglia's method of singing. *The Etude.* May 1942.
33. Marchesi M. *Theoretical and Practical Vocal Method.* New York, NY: Dover; 1970.
34. Marchesi M. *Ten Singing Lessons.* New York, NY: Harper & Brothers; 1901.
35. Lehmann L. *How to Sing.* New York, NY: Macmillan; 1903.
36. Martienssen-Lohmann F. *Das bewusste Singen.* Leipzig, Germany: CF Kahnt; 1923.
37. Martienssen-Lohmann F. *Der Opernsänger.* Mainz, Germany: B Schott's Söhne; 1943.
38. Martienssen-Lohmann F. *Der wissende Sänger.* Zurich: Atlantis-Verlag; 1963.
39. Armin G. *Die Technik der Breitspannung: In: Beitrag über die horizontal-vertikalen Spannkräfte beim Aufbau der Stimme nach dem "Stauprinzip."* Berlin, Germany: Verlag der Gesellschaft für Stimmkultur; 1932.
40. Armin G. *Von der Urkraft der Stimme.* Lippstadt, Germany: Kistner & Siegel; 1921.
41. Husler F. Rodd-Marling Y. *Singing: The Physical Nature of the Vocal Organ.* London, England: Faber & Faber; 1960.
42. Johnstone-Douglas W. The teaching of Jean de Reszke. *Music and Letters.* July 1925.
43. Shakespeare W. *The Art of Singing.* Bryn Mawr, Pa: Oliver Ditson; 1898.
44. Greene HP. *Interpretation in Song.* London, England: Macmillan; 1912.
45. White EG. *Sinus Tone Production.* Boston, Mass: Crescendo Press; 1970.
46. Herbert-Caesari E. *The Alchemy of Voice.* London, England: Robert Hale; 1965.
47. Herbert-Caesari E. *The Science and Sensations of Tone.* Boston, Mass: Crescendo Press; 1968.
48. Herbert-Caesari E. *The Voice of the Mind.* London, England: Robert Hale; 1969.
49. Witherspoon H. *Singing.* New York, NY: G Schirmer; 1925.
50. Stanley D. *The Science of Voice.* New York, NY: Carl Fischer; 1929.
51. Reid C. *Bel Canto Principles and Practices.* New York, NY: Coleman-Ross; 1950.
52. Reid C. *Psyche and Soma.* New York, NY: J Patelson Music House; 1975.
53. Reid C. *The Free Voice.* New York, NY: Coleman-Ross; 1965.
54. Vennard W. *Singing, the Mechanism and the Technic.* 5th ed. New York, NY: Carl Fischer; 1967.

55. Coffin B. *Historical Vocal Pedagogy.* Metuchen, NJ: Scarecrow Press; 1989.
56. Coffin B. *Overtones of Bel Canto.* Metuchen, NJ: Scarecrow Press; 1982.
57. Coffin B. *The Sounds of Singing: Vocal Technique with Vowel-Pitch Charts.* Metuchen, NJ: Scarecrow Press; 1977.
58. Appelman R. *The Science of Vocal Pedagogy.* Bloomington: Indiana University Press; 1967.

CHAPTER

9

Choral Pedagogy and Vocal Health

Choral conductors engage groups of amateur singers in the act of re-creating the masterworks of the choral art, blending voices to shape longer, larger phrases of music than any single singer performs in an aria or song. The goal in choral singing is the blending of individual vocal and intellectual components to achieve a choral sound. The sound of any choir is indicative of its singers, weaving a unity made of threads from each voice. Some, but not all, of the tools learned for solo singing are helpful in this process. Three basics of singing, namely, relaxation, posture, and breathing, are beneficial in solo and choral singing in equal measure. Resonance for choral singing must be adjusted to avoid the maximum acoustic properties of any one voice (ie, the singer's formant) to be exposed, thus disrupting the choral fabric. Singers must be taught how to make these adjustments. If not, conflicts arise between the choral conductors and studio teachers. Every singer should enjoy a cooperative association between choral and solo singing instructors. Both play significant roles in the lives of singers. Portions of this chapter appeared in the *Journal of Singing* in January/February 2003, with the intention of assisting members of the National Association of Teachers of Singing in evaluating the needs of solo singers who participate in choral ensembles.

When evaluating the health of a singer engaged in choral activities, a health care professional or singing teacher should pose a number of questions.

Is the choral conductor primarily a singer? An instrumentalist?

Does the choral rehearsal begin with a period of warm-up and end with a period of cool-down? If so, what is the nature of the warm-up?

What is the nature of the cool-down?

Is there a policy regarding choral posture for sitting and for standing?

Does the singer sight-sing music easily?

Is music taught in the rehearsal using the piano or the voice?

Are the text and music taught simultaneously?

What is the level of discipline within the choral group?

Does the conductor offer the choir a breath gesture?

Does the conductor teach tools for adjusting resonance from a solo technique to a choral one?

Is there a seating chart for the choir? Is the seating arrangement determined by vocal and acoustic qualities? By height of each chorister?

How long does the rehearsal last?

Is the rehearsal space spacious? Well-ventilated?

How frequently does the choir perform? What level of difficulty is the repertoire?

Is it sung with piano? Orchestra? Organ? A cappella?

Is there a break during the rehearsal? Is food served? Are caffeinated beverages consumed?

Warm-Up and Cool-Down Procedures

If the choral conductor is a singer, the rehearsal is likely to begin with a warm-up period. The purposes of any warm-up period are the same, namely: (1) to adjust the voice from speaking to singing, (2) to align the body and free the breathing mechanism for the act of singing, (3) to create a physical awareness of the vocal mechanism being used correctly, and (4) to stretch gently and exercise the skeletal muscles used in phonation. In the latter case, one follows the principles of physiology that highlight the importance of muscle warm-up prior to any athletic activity.

In a choral rehearsal, these adjustments are best made when a well-trained singer or qualified conductor gives verbal instructions and sings short, simple patterns. The exercises should be organized with consideration of the needs of the singers. In one rehearsal, additional time may be spent on relaxation or posture, while in another, breath may be more difficult to train. Resonance should not be addressed until the first three steps have been successfully achieved. The warm-up leader must be able to model the exercises effectively and should have a sensitive eye and ear to the results. The piano is unnecessary during the warm-up period, except as a harmonic support. In the introduction to the book *Voice Building for Choirs*, the authors wrote:

> A choral conductor who feels incapable of presenting choral voice building exercises to a choir may wish to call upon a professional voice teacher or a trained choir member to fulfill the assignment. In any case, one must resist the temptation to employ the organ or the piano as a mechanism for voice building because of the percussive nature of both instruments. The conductor who is involved with performing as an accompanist for the choir is not capable of hearing critically.[1(p xi)]

The singers need to prepare their bodies for the task of singing and remind themselves of the lyric quality of the singing voice before attempting more difficult assignments.

If the choral conductor is an instrumentalist who has chosen to assume the role of leadership with a choir, it is probable that the preparation for singing will be a series of tuning exercises or a set of patterns played upon the piano. Without proper vocal warm-up, either of these methods can result in vocal distress for the singers. First, if tuning exercises begin the choral rehearsal, singers may attempt to sustain the speaking voice to achieve proper pitch levels. Second, the mechanism of the piano is percussive, the action consisting of hammers hitting metal strings. Singers instinctively imitate the sound of the piano by pressing on the back of the tongue while producing tone. Constriction and tension then follow in the pharyngeal and laryngeal areas. Generated by pressed phonation, this initial choral sound may continue for an entire rehearsal. This is not only tiring, but also potentially abusive to the vocal mechanism. Finally, for the vocal mechanism to operate efficiently, the singer must "audiate" or hear the pitch mentally. The body coordinates to phonate the sound imagined. This mental activity requires immense concentration. When tuning exercises precede or replace a real vocal warm-up or the piano is used to accompany vocal exercises, the singer does not practice this basic aural skill. This is not to say that the piano can never be used during warm-ups. Many good choral conductors and singing teachers use the piano without adverse effect, allowing the piano to give tonal cues or harmonic foundation to the voice-building process. However, one must be aware of the pitfalls should the piano become a crutch instead of an aid. To train a fine choral ensemble, the desired vocal sounds must be demonstrated and their repetitions monitored during the warm-up period.

Only recently have voice pedagogues realized the importance of a cool-down at the conclusion of singing. Just as the voice adjusts during a warm-up from speaking to singing, a cool-down returns the voice to a comfortable speaking condition, after a workout in higher and lower registers. Physiologically, cool-down vocal exercises are analogous to stretching exercises advised after running or weight-lifting. In general choral rehearsals last from 90 minutes to as long as 3 hours. After an extended period of vocal activity, it is helpful to assist the vocal mechanism in identifying the speaking range of the voice and to reinforce or restore appropriate muscle relaxation, tone, and flexibility. As stated in Chapter 16, the cool-down period can be brief but must not be overlooked. Two examples of useful cool-down routines are:

- A steady, well-supported sigh beginning on an easily reached upper tone and descending through the middle range, followed by a gentle shrug of the shoulders, to relax the body and voice.

- Chanting selected poetry or prose at various pitch levels and moving from the head voice through the middle voice to prepare the voice for conversation speaking tones.

A brief sequence of this nature is wise and healthy for returning choral voices back to conversational ranges. A cool-down should be comforting, an act of closure. A choral conductor holds the voices of the ensemble in trust and promises them a satisfying musical, spiritual, and educational experience. It is essential that every effort be made to protect the voices from misuse and abuse. Warm-up and cool-down procedures are essential vocal habits for every singer and, therefore, should be used in the choral setting.

A special word of caution is necessary for church musicians, especially those for whom the pipe organ is the primary performing medium: Frequently, organists or choirmasters ask church choir members to rehearse the hymns for the coming worship service as an act of warm-up or cool-down. This may seem like a good use of time, but it can be detrimental to the singers. Many choral singers cannot read text and music simultaneously with ease. A good warm-up separates vowel shapes from consonants, allowing the voice to flow on the breath before introducing the complexities of consonant formation. When text and music are required under pressure in rehearsal, inexperienced singers may tighten their jaw and neck muscles and sing without proper support for several verses of music. Their voices will fatigue unnecessarily and vocal injury may result.

In some choirs, singers are asked to arrive at the rehearsal prepared to sing. Because most choral ensembles convene in the midst of an academic schedule or in the evening after a full day's work, few singers can be expected to have either the time or the discipline to complete a useful warm-up prior to arrival. When the conductor arrives, the singers may be at risk, as it is likely that musical demands will be placed on them without full knowledge of their vocal, physical, and mental capacities at the given moment. Without a clear understanding of the practice of an organization, it is difficult to arrive efficiently at the moment of readiness for effective learning. In some choirs, an assistant conductor will be sent to warm up the choir before the conductor arrives. Choral conductors have only one musical outlet—the choir. The choir must be treated as an instrument to be studied and cherished. The wise conductor meets the singers at the door of the rehearsal space ready to aid and nurture them as creative people who sing.

If a voice student complains of hoarseness or vocal fatigue after choral singing, the private voice teacher should investigate the pedagogic steps that open and close the choral rehearsal. The seeds of tension are often planted there. Should warm-ups be unproductive or cool-downs absent from the rehearsal plan, the studio teacher must provide the choral singer with a short regimen of exercises that will ensure adequate preparation for the task of choral singing. Ideally, if the voice teacher can communicate delicately these suggestions to the choral conductor as well, the entire choir may benefit.

In summary, choral singing should be refreshing to the voice, not fatiguing. The choral rehearsal should be a forum for developing singing techniques that are healthy with or without piano accompaniment. Most importantly, the vocal instrument should be built upon proper posture, breath support, and resonance techniques under expert guidance in both solo and choral settings.

Posture

Choral conductors must be responsible for the seated and standing posture of the singers in the choir. Posture is important because of its effect on the positioning of the vocal mechanism and breath support musculature. Posture affects vocal fold contact forces and injury potential, as well. Fearing the appearance of tyranny or nagging, many choral conductors refrain from admonishing their choral singers regarding poor posture. Others may assume that singers, like instrumentalists, have learned their singing techniques, including proper posture, through years of private instruction. Such a presumption can be very harmful to the vocal health of choral singers, most of whom are untrained. Peer pressure is a powerful agent. If other singers sit or stand in an unproductive manner without correction, new members of the ensemble will follow suit. Remember: In the eyes of the choral singer, the choral conductor is an authority in the area of vocal music. If the conductor allows poor posture habits among the singers, this failing can produce not only bad singing technique in untrained choral singers, but also a wide gap between studio teaching and choral training.

It is important for choral conductors, vocal coaches, and teachers of singing to discuss the maintenance of good posture at all times. To date, there are few chairs designed to encourage proper support of the spine for singing. For more information, see Chapter 7, Seating Problems of Vocalists, by Richard Norris. Students of singing must be taught to stand, sit, and walk with erect, balanced posture–even if the matter is not addressed by the choral conductor.

Teaching Choral Repertoire

Music

A healthy singing tone evolves from a process of neurologic signals that are expressed through the vocal tract. Therefore, a clear mental image of the pitch and the vowel must be created before a clear, ringing tone can emerge. The act of "audiation," the term used in music education for hearing the vocal sound mentally before phonation, requires training, practice, and timing. In the corporate setting of a choral rehearsal, participating singers present with various levels of musical skill. Some may sing music readily at sight, whereas the majority relies heavily on the power of imitation to learn notes, rhythms, and words. Thus, choral singers who read music readily tend to lead those with less skill. This practice causes a weaker singer to avoid the rigors of ear training. The weaker singer follows the stronger singer, who may sing too loudly in order to "lead" the section. Weaker singers must be identified and trained. The well-intended, more experienced singers who intensify volume to strengthen the section sound should be advised to lead instead by example. Such skilled singers should sing as if they were giving demonstration lessons to the singers seated on either side of them.

For any choral conductor, it is very difficult to accommodate the strengths and weaknesses of each singer. If most of the singers in the choir are inexperienced, the conductor may choose to use the piano as a leveling tool, playing the notes on the keyboard to assist the reading of rhythms and melodic material. Rehearsal techniques that depend heavily on the piano as a means of teaching the notes may, however, foster inaccurate and/or nonlegato singing among the choir members. If it is possible for the conductor to sing the music, phrase by phrase, to the section, choral vocal technique will grow with the knowledge of the repertoire. The conductor need not be a masterful singer. Simple, clear, well-supported singing will convey the vocal information required.

Some conductors record the choral parts on cassette tapes for their singers to study outside of rehearsal. This too is a useful tool but should not be considered a means to an end. For reasons of vocal health and self-esteem, it is important to encourage listening and "audiation" for all singers. Guided trial and error demands patience and pedagogy, but speeds the process toward musicianship incrementally over time. All singers who learn their music by any form of passive listening are stifling their own musical growth. Just as solo singers "sing the music into their voices," choral singers must "sing" the individual contours of melody and rhythm into their voices.

If a choral singer complains of vocal fatigue or hoarseness after rehearsals, the physician, speech-language pathologist, or voice teacher must consider the singer's ability to sight-sing and the methods for music teaching practiced by the choral conductor. A good choral rehearsal does not result in tired, hoarse voices, but rather in well-educated, invigorated ones.

Text and Rhythm

The goal in healthy singing is the achievement of a flowing, legato line. Singing "on the breath" is the cornerstone of bel canto, or beautiful singing. In the papal choirs of the 16th and 17th centuries, the high art of bel canto singing was taught to young boys using exercises on vowel sounds only. Documents from the time indicate that the advanced singers were asked to demonstrate the steadiness of their legato singing techniques by singing a series of vowel sounds over a lighted candle. Each vowel sound was sung and a consistent crescendo to decrescendo or *messa di voce* (literally, a measuring of the voice) was performed. If the flame did not flicker, the voice was considered competent to learn the execution of consonant sounds. A voice capable of making measured dynamic changes without disruption of tonal quality is evidence of firm breath control and vowel purity. Pure vowel sounds were the first major guidepost on the road to legato singing, representing stability in the vocal tract. Consonants were a second step in vocal training involving the use of the articulators without a disruption of the vocal tract. The combination of these two skills determined the efficiency or stamina of the singing experience.

Most voice teachers agree that the teaching of vowels should precede the teaching of consonants, establishing a flow of tone before interrupting it with articulatory activities. Basic vocalises (exercises) are built from vowel patterns with consonants added subsequently, gradually. The teaching of solo repertoire often begins with singing the musical lines on "tone syllables" (la, na, du, etc) and thereafter on the vowel sounds of the text. This procedure establishes the right weight of tone throughout the registers and assists in developing adequate breath support. Developed over centuries, these pedagogic methods have proven their worth in the achievement of healthy vocal technique.

Lack of vocal training and the press of time too often preclude choral conductors from using the vocal wisdom of the ages in the teaching of choral repertoire. In all too many choral rehearsals, rather than teaching rhythmic skills, conductors assume that the text alone will guide inexperienced singers through the score. Most amateur choral singers do base their membership on a strong ability to imitate sound and memorize melody by ear, although they are generally novices in the area of rhythm. To some extent, the rhythm of choral music is founded on the rhythmic patterns of the text. In the belief that precious rehearsal time will be saved, misinformed choral conductors often introduce unfamiliar choral repertoire by asking the choir to sing it on the text. Less skilled singers may follow the words with little frustration, but they are likely to tire their voices and confuse their minds. Oddly enough, some choral conductors will use this method even with repertoire written in foreign languages containing uncommon sounds and symbols. This common choral method invites vocal harm through a "seek and find" pedagogic approach.

Rhythm is a fundamental construct for musical composition. It is the only unifying element between musical text setting and its accompaniment. The rhythm paces the text and intervals in the minds of the singers. Singers must learn to internalize the rhythm. A choral group must share a sense of inner rhythm for the music to be sung in tune, in tempo, and with unified expression. There are many methods for teaching rhythm, such as count-singing, conducting, tapping the fingers along the breastbone. It is essential that singers learn the rhythm of the music first before adding the text. Chanting the text in rhythm is an intermediate stage that will reinforce the learning and save the singing voices.

To summarize, singers cannot sing healthfully unless the mind understands the vowel shapes with proper pitch in the right rhythmic patterns. Slow, careful learning produces healthy, confident singing. Several hours of frenzied singing in a choral rehearsal can compromise overall vocal technique and health. If students of singing experience mental and vocal fatigue after choral rehearsal, the voice teacher should inquire about the method used for teaching repertoire.

Discipline

The personal charisma of a choral conductor attracts and nurtures the choristers in an ensemble. The conductor determines the nature of the organization, its aims, and its methods. A choir is not a democratic society, but a group of people governed by its leader. In some choirs, discipline during rehearsal is very strict. In others, singers are allowed to whisper or talk at will. Proper posture may be ignored. The level of discipline within the ensemble is of significance to the health and well-being of the individual choral singers. A gentle balance must be struck between method and delivery. If the discipline within the ensemble is firm enough to produce effective results but flexible enough to allow moments of relaxation, an atmosphere for good vocal instruction evolves. When discipline is lax, choral singers may abuse their voices. If the choral conductor has a tyrannical nature, a spirit of fear pervades the rehearsal, creating unwanted tensions detrimental to vocal health.

The conductor must be disciplined as well, emulating the singer each member of the choir should be. The conductor must stand in a good posture, avoiding the shifting of weight from foot to foot. Because the tapping of a foot disrupts the abdominal muscles that support the breathing mechanism, the conductor should not tap a foot while conducting. Singers see the conductor as the perfect example of a singing artist. Thus, the conductor must be consistent in word and deed.

Singing is a very complex mental and physical endeavor. Choral conductors who demand the attention by speaking or singing over choir members are simply wasting vocal energy. Singers cannot hear instructions and sing simultaneously. Furthermore, the frenzy of a shouting voice eliminates the possibility for concentration on either artful singing or verbal suggestions. The singing voice works by discrete mental signals that coordinate with the vocal tract through breathing and imaging. The instructions should be given before the singing ensues. The results are evaluated and adjusted accordingly after the singing stops.

It is important for the conductor to develop a helpful vocabulary, spoken in encouraging tones. A choir should not be stopped unless the conductor is prepared to assist with corrections through a pedagogic method. Knowing that the voices have been prepared for singing, the conductor's comments should be brief, targeted and well-spoken. After words of instruction or advice mingled with positive feedback, the choir should address its mistakes with a productive attitude. It is important for a conductor to monitor facial expressions and body language to ensure that messages to the group are clear and devoid of negative sparks. The atmosphere for the choral singer must be open to error without penalty. The conductor must be willing to simplify passages, repeat and confirm what is accurate while maintaining the concentration of the entire group. Not every mistake will be corrected immediately. With words of assurance, the conductor should table the passage and reconsider the obstacle for another rehearsal. Choral rehearsals should conclude with a sense of achievement. Singing should be remembered as a joyful activity. The use of a full-length mirror or a video camera can help a choral conductor understand the force of words, gestures, and tone of voice.

Studio teachers should be aware of the level of discipline in choral rehearsals attended by their students. If discipline is lacking, it may be the cause of vocal fatigue in the choral singer. If the learning environment is a healthy one, the studio teacher may wish to build upon its fine example as a means of structuring the student's practice regimen.

Breath Gesture

For decades, American choral conductors were taught orchestral conducting techniques. Adjustments to the choral setting were made on an "as needed" basis. Orchestral conductors rightly assume that each member of the orchestra has had private instruction on the instrument. Orchestras are organized by sections with leaders who provide hints about the execution of difficult passages to others in the section. The orchestral conductor indicates the tempo and the character of the music with a single flick of the baton. Instrumentalists have trained themselves to respond to the signal and produce tone on demand.

The singing instrument requires considerably more time and a great deal more coordination to prepare than most orchestral ones. Singers must hear the pitch, imagine the vowel shape, and prepare the breathing mechanism. The coordination of this set of activities in choral music is organized by the choral conductor's breath gesture.

Unfortunately, not every choral conductor has been taught this basic skill, as it is not always part of instrumental conducting technique (although it provides substantial benefit for instrumentalists, as well). Many conductors use orchestral conducting techniques, giving a downbeat and hoping for a choral sound. Unprepared, the singers gasp for breath to produce tone. This method of creating choral music can be very harmful to the singer. Forceful, poorly supported onset of vocal sound can be abusive to the voice.

If voice students present with a tendency toward glottal stops or hasty, noisy breathing habits, the studio teacher may wish to investigate the choral conducting techniques used in the student's choral ensemble.

Range and Tessitura

The selection of choral repertoire is a complicated process. Public choral concerts are expensive. The repertoire must appeal to the potential audience. In religious settings, the text must be appropriate to the worship event. Frequently, neither the disposition nor the skill of the singers is adequately considered. Often, the range and tessitura (where the range for the majority of the melodic material lies) of the music are ignored as well. Some choral conductors attempt to balance the choral sound by asking singers to depart from their normal singing ranges and join the ranks of other sections. Baritones may be expected to sing in falsetto for extended periods, thus strengthening an inadequate tenor section. Sopranos who read music easily might be used to stabilize a weak alto section. Altos sometimes try to sing tenor parts. An occasional, gentle venture out of one's range is not necessarily harmful to a skilled singer. A long departure (such as a season) from the normal classification, however, can be very detrimental to the overall health of a singer.

The repertoire and type of accompaniment must be appropriate to the size and ability of the choir, if healthy singing is to occur. A cappella singing tends to be the healthiest form of choral music making, based firmly in the bel canto tradition. Choral conductors and singers are, however, ambitious. Often the love for a particular work overrides reason, setting up vocal or intellectual demands that pose perils for the singers. For instance, smaller choirs may aspire to sing *Ein deutsches Requiem* by Johannes Brahms with an orchestra, but might be better served presenting the work with its duo-piano accompaniment. It is important to advise students and choral conductors about the negative effects on individual voices confronted with overwhelming instrumental accompaniments. Healthy choral singing is possible with any ensemble provided the conductor and choir are aware of the vocal demands and resources.

The range and tessitura of the repertoire have a significant impact on the comfort level of each singer in the choir. The range of a given vocal part may be reasonable; however, the tessitura may be at the extremes of the range. When choral singers are asked to produce voice in extreme tessitura for long periods of time, vocal fatigue or injury may result. Stamina in singing comes from well-coordinated vocal technique. It is not gained through prolonged full voice repetition at extreme tessitura. The vocal instrument is finite and must be given music to sing within a comfortable range and volume.

Choral singers have been known to complain of vocal fatigue after extended periods of singing choral repertoire. Studio teachers must create strategies for their students, advising about appropriate range and voice part within the choral idiom.

Seating

In the best circumstances, the experience of singing together can fortify the body, mind, and spirit of the choral singer. In less favorable settings, choral experiences have an adverse effect, inhibiting vocal growth and confidence. Group dynamics have a strong impact on choral singing. The abilities of singers vary widely. Competitive attitudes develop relative to personality traits, musicianship skills, and vocal gifts. If a choral conductor considers the personal, musical, acoustic, and vocal capacities of singers when organizing the sections of the choir, choral signing can promote positive personal and artistic growth. A singer's instrument responds best to a relaxed and receptive atmosphere.

Unfortunately, many choral conductors take little note of individual characteristics, positioning choir members within a section by height or by seniority. Other choral conductors allow singers to arrange themselves. Usually, leaving group dynamics to chance creates conflict between weaker and stronger personalities, placing the untrained singer at odds with the trained ones. Singers with lesser vocal gifts or training may refrain from singing, sensing competition with singers of more ability or experience. These inhibitions cause physical tensions that could compromise vocal health. Choral singers should be seated based upon the qualities of their sound and skill, with weaker singers nestled artfully among stronger ones. This practice builds a blended choral sound without intimidating the singers.

Choral singing is teamwork. Every member of the choir is an important element of the musical organization. The choral conductor should encourage this attitude with a welcoming, tolerant spirit. A studio teacher should be aware of a student's attitude toward the singers within a choral ensemble. One of singing's greatest challenges is confidence. A healthy choral organization engenders a positive self-image in every member.

Performance Schedule

Choral concerts are peak experiences. In preparation for performances, choral groups rehearse extra hours. Generally, choirs stand on risers, creating an uncomfortable elevation in somewhat cramped or even claustrophobic, circumstances. It is important to recognize the hazards for students of singing who participate in long rehearsals.

Choral folders may contain several pounds of music. Singers in the back row may extend their chins to see the conductor whose podium is several feet away. Conductors can (but often do not) mitigate these problems by spending a few extra minutes adjusting the position and posture of singers on the risers. Wise conductors speak openly to the choir about the need to conserve vocal and physical energy during the week leading up to performance. If the choral performance is to be a healthy experience, all forces must be in optimal condition.

Rehearsal Traditions

Until recently, singers were unaware of the negative impact certain food and beverages have on the singing voice. Most choirs have associated singing with socialization, designing rehearsal routines around a coffee break or period of fellowship. If the refreshments consumed contain chocolate, refined sugars, caffeine, or citrus, the voices of many of the singers will be at risk for the symptoms of gastroesophageal reflux disease (GERD) in the subsequent rehearsal time. When students of singing complain of hoarseness in the latter portion of choral rehearsals, reflux could be one source of distress and thus a reason to be evaluated by a laryngologist.

Benefits of Choral Singing

A choral rehearsal can be an ideal forum for strengthening musicianship skills, vocal technique, and self-esteem. The choral singer has the opportunity to relax within the choral tone, participating in arching phrases of greater length than any single voice can manage. The student of singing can develop a historical context for the solo repertoire being studied in private lessons. Because smaller voices perform as equals with larger ones, choral singing teaches acceptance and offers an increased sense of accomplishment.

The goals of choral singing are different from those of solo singing. Cooperation in choral singing demands that singers contribute to the choral sound but never dominate it. As ensemble members, choral singers respond to the artistic demands set by the conductor. In solo singing, the individual vocal, acoustic, and interpretive traits of the singer are paramount. An astute teacher of singing trains students to make adjustments in technique, attitude, and expectation appropriate to either setting. The ability to sing well in solo and ensemble settings is a sign of healthy technical and artistic vocal facility. There is nothing intrinsically "unhealthy" about singing in choirs, as long as solo singers have been properly trained.

The Role of the Voice Teacher in the Choral Context

Ideally, every singing teacher would be affiliated with a choral organization, acting as a consultant on vocal matters whenever possible. In order to advise students, singing teachers should be acquainted personally with the choral conductors within their immediate area. Solo singing and choral singing are compatible but different vocal activities. Teachers of singing and choral conductors must work together to ensure the vocal health of all singers.

The Role of the Laryngologist and Speech-Language Pathologist in the Choral Context

Laryngologists and speech-language pathologists who care for singers have important roles in the choral context. First, many medical professionals are enthusiastic singers themselves. Some are even trained in singing. Whether or not a laryngologist or speech-language pathologist is a skilled singer, it is helpful for medical professionals to participate personally in choral singing. If the medical professional is not a trained singer, the choral experience provides invaluable insights that assist in the evaluation and treatment of patients. In addition, the physician and speech-language pathologist should act as consultants for the choral conductor and choir members on matters of vocal health. The active participation of health professionals in a musical community fosters the kind of interdisciplinary collaboration among physicians, speech-language pathologists, singing teachers, choral conductors, and performers that is most likely to lead to effective voice building and healthy vocal performance. Good, secure choral conductors ordinarily not only welcome such collaboration, but moreover seek it out.

Study Questions

1. How are the demands of solo singing different from those of choral singing?

2. What is the purpose of a warm-up? A cool-down?

3. What are the major factors in vocal fatigue inherent in choral singing?

4. How should the piano be used during choral rehearsal?

5. How should choral repertoire be selected?

Reference

1. Ehmann W, Hassemann F. *Voice Building for Choirs.* Chapel Hill, NC: Hinshaw Music, Inc; 1980:ix.

For Further Reading

Demorest S. *Building choral excellence: Teaching sight-singing in the choral rehearsal.* New York, NY: Oxford University Press; 2001.

Ehmann W. *Choral directing.* G. Wiebe Trans. Minneapolis, MN: Augsburg Publishing; 1968

Finn W. *The art of the choral conductor.* Boston, Mass: CC Birchard & Co; 1939.

Sinclair C. *The effect of daily sightsinging exercises on the sightsinging ability of middle school choir students.* St. Paul, Minn: University of St. Thomas; 1996.

Swan H. *Choral conducting: A symposium.* Englewood Cliffs, NJ: Prentice-Hall, Inc; 1973.

CHAPTER

10

Voice Disorders Among Choral Music Educators

Brenda Smith

In 1993, the author completed a dissertation on the topic "The Performing Teacher," in recognition of the fact that musicians who wish to teach stand at considerable risk of injury due to personal and administrative stress. The scheduling of teaching, rehearsing, and preparing performances presents an enormous challenge. As a singer, voice builder, and choral pedagogue, the author has taken a special interest in the risks posed for those who teach the choral art. Proposing strategies that would ease the lives of choral music educators (choral music teachers, choral conductors, church musicians, and cantors) has become a major focus in workshops and in-service presentations on choral pedagogy given across the country with Dr Robert Sataloff, MD, DMA and Margaret Baroody, MM, a singing voice specialist active in Dr. Sataloff's practice. This chapter seeks to address the issues we have encountered among our audiences and create an awareness of the dangers within the working environment of choral music educators of all kinds.

Voice disorders are known to be one of the most prevalent occupational hazards among the global working population.[1-3] Because of the published results of several major research studies over the past decade, it has become widely recognized that classroom teachers represent a high percentage of those presenting with work-related voice injury. Medical and scientific research is beginning to study this subgroup of music educators. Because of the nature of tasks he or she performs, the choral music educator is at significant risk for permanent voice injury, greater than groups of classroom teachers that have been studied.

The human voice, central to every daily task, is a fragile but responsive instrument of communication. The voice is finite. Each of us in our youth has experienced long periods of voice use with minimal negative consequences. As we age, it is essential to understand that the larynx is one of the few organs in the human body that cannot be altered without significant loss of quality and stamina. For the choral music teacher, the voice is essential for two major life assignments— singing or speaking on the stage and singing and speaking in the classroom. Most working environments of choral music educators are hazardous to the voice. To date, research has proven the dangers to the voice with overwhelming results. Medical professionals and singing teachers have begun to make the information about vocal health and hygiene available to music educators when possible. To date, measures have been taken to reform the circumstances that place performing teachers at risk only after disabilities have been diagnosed.

The contributions of all music educators as band directors, choral or orchestral conductors are tremendous. These teachers work far beyond the normal weekly schedule, rehearsing evenings and weekends as well as arranging and chaperoning concert tours with their students. The budgets of most public schools concentrate funds on academic subjects, leaving teachers to raise funds for special educational opportunities for their ensembles. Often, the concerts of their group generate revenue for the school district but may not offer direct benefit to the music programs.

Furthermore, music educators tend to have extremely close contact with their students. Most students come to music groups through some sort of individual audition process. Music-making being a team effort, places music teachers in a coaching role comparable to that of athletic coaches. The delights of intense personal contact are great, yet at the same time, there are burdens to be borne that the general classroom teacher will never encounter. When music teachers attempt to rehabilitate their voices after an injury, the internal stopwatch presses toward a quick recovery for personal, financial, and musical reasons. Students, parents, and administrators seem to be standing on the sidelines tapping a foot until the teacher returns to work. A musical ensemble is not a democracy. It is shaped around the charisma, taste, and methods of the conductor. Thus, music educators stand apart from other teachers in positions of leadership and responsibility.

At a recent national convention of the American Choral Directors Association, Margaret Baroody, a singing voice specialist who works regularly with injured singers and conductors, described music teachers as, "the Clydesdales of educators—in the trenches working with heart, soul, mind, and voice to the benefit of others." Preserving the means of expression for teachers is as important as teaching pedagogic theory, technology skills, or discipline. If a teacher is beautifully trained as a musician and educator but cannot deliver the information with regularity and consistency to a classroom, the educational process has failed miserably.

The old saying "Delivery is everything" is especially important to a choral music educator. The choral conductor must demonstrate vocal models, speak within the rehearsal setting, address the audience in performance, and sell the program persuasively to potential donors and administrators. A hoarse or husky voice is unable to meet these assignments. In most public schools, the music wing is separate from the academic areas to "keep the noise confined." The band room may share a common wall with the choral rehearsal area. In churches, the choir room may adjoin the sanctuary and be treated with acoustic tile to dampen the sound. In either setting, the choral music educator is forced to execute vocal tasks over background noise. Known as the "Lombard effect," background noise causes the choral music educators to perceive that they cannot be heard. It is not uncommon for such educators to speak in a shrill or exaggerated manner, hoping to spin a tone above the sound of the neighboring ensemble.

For a choral music educator, the teaching profession is more than a job, it is a life. It demands additional responsibilities such as parental involvement, weekend and evening rehearsals, tour planning, plus concert publicity and programs, private coaching of student soloists, and the general pressure of frequent public performances. Within the church or synagogue, young people will ask for assistance with musical assignments outside the religious ones. Solos may be expected for special occasions such as weddings and memorial services. In the face of little rest, choral music educators present with a variety of voice complaints, including fatigue after elevating the volume; hoarseness; mucus in throat; throat pain; lack of stamina; inability to project above the noise; frequent voice breaks; absence of voice; and sick leave requests.

Such perceptions are real. The activities of the workday frequently cause a lessening of vocal power. By midweek, the voice begins to deteriorate sooner. At week's end, the voice is significantly less able to phonate. Choral music educators regularly commit a substantial amount of personal time, effort, and even money to maintain the integrity of programs that may be on the administrative chopping block. In the religious realm, counseling as well as teaching may be needed to assist the student. In emergency situations, the church musician may substitute for the pastor, rabbi, or religious educator. Voice abuse is directly associated with an extensive amount of time spent daily talking, often at elevated volume levels.

A choral music educator should consider purchasing an amplification device to ease the level of overall speech pressures. In negotiating work assignments, choral music educators should consider opportunities for vocal rest as a reason for release time. Days of rest should follow festival or performance activities. Regular voice lessons help maintain proper vocal habits. The choral music educator must be proactive in the care of the voice. As "performing teachers," choral music educators cannot afford to suffer the consequences of settings with poor acoustics or exceptional work loads.

A performing teacher is the best music educator, setting a role model for the students. A thoroughly educated artist has the most to share with the younger generation. The musical arts in public educational institutions unite students rather than divide them, bring life to the rigors of learning, and provide a skill useful for life—as a vocation or avocation. It has been studied and proven that the circumstances of music teachers in the classroom are in general abusive. Little if anything is being done to prevent vocal injury among teachers. However, the voice is fragile and finite. Once injured, it will not be the same. Prevention is more than an ounce of cure—it is the only cure.

Study Questions

1. What are the major factors in creating a healthy work environment within a classroom?

2. What are the emotional stresses of teaching? Of choral music teaching?

3. Name specific preventive measures for avoiding vocal injury, such as behavioral, dietary, and vocal regimens.

4. What are the symptoms of vocal fatigue?

References

1. Russell A, Oates J, Greenwod K. Prevalence of voice problems in teachers. *J Voice.* 1997;12(4):467–479,
2. Smith E, Lemke J, Taylor M, Kirchner HL, Hoffman H. Frequency of voice problems among teachers and other occupations. *J Voice.* 1997;12(4): 480–488.
3. Sala E, Laine A, Simberg S, Pentti J, Suonpää. The prevalence of voice disorders among day center teachers compared with nurses: a questionnaire and clinical study. *J Voice.* 2001;15(3):413-423.

PART III

The Vocal Approach to Choral Music

CHAPTER

11

Choral Singing and Children

Lifelong singing begins with the development of good vocal habits at an early age. Choral voice training creates the foundation for vocal growth by teaching relaxation, good posture, breathing technique, resonance, and registration. In addition, healthy choral singing experiences introduce children to musicianship tasks (rhythm, sight-singing and ear training) and teamwork, skills of value in academic and community life. When trained children's voices perform, audiences are inspired and excited. Few listeners recognize how diverse the individual talents of the children are. The challenge for the conductor of children is the melding of unchanged with changing voices, the training of ears that hear discretely and those that do not match pitch. Some of the children may have limited range; others have healthy access to upper and lower registers. Among the singers, there may be difficulties in speaking voice articulation such as stuttering or other impediments. Many youngsters are too inhibited to sing while others are eager to yell. Attention spans vary from child to child. This chapter should serve as a guide to conductors who work with children of all ages, offering a vision of vocal and musical possibilities and a caution regarding limitations.

Singing at every age requires mental, physical, and spiritual engagement. To paraphrase one of America's famous children's choir specialists, Helen Kemp: "Body, mind, spirit, voice–it takes all four to sing and rejoice!" The whole child must be brought to sing. To spark the powers of mental concentration and body awareness, relaxation is the first step. Insistence on proper posture and deep breathing frees the spirit, encouraging a vital, pleasing self-image. A beautifully resonant tone must be developed and trained. Identifying beauty in a vocal/ choral tone is an essential aspect of voice building in children. Youngsters are bombarded with noises of all kinds, not all of which are healthy or attractive models. The choral conductor must reinforce the positive vocal sounds children sing, encouraging and rewarding lilting, lyric tones. Exquisite intonation results when the conductor supplies the tools for tuning with patience and invention. If the positive elements of fine music making are taught with kindness and imagination, children will enjoy singing for a lifetime. Useful mental and physical discipline is the byproduct of a congenial yet concentrated learning atmosphere. The same essential elements for healthy voice building (ie, relaxation, posture, breath, resonance, taste, concentration, and discipline) form the scaffolding for acquiring knowledge in most areas of life.

Every children's choir rehearsal opens with a warm-up period, adjusting the use of the voice from speaking to singing and teaching the basics of singing. The order of the warm-up period activities is the same as with an adult choir: relaxation, posture, breathing, and resonance. The exercises and their duration are modified to meet the attention span and physical strength of the children in the choir. Exercises for children should be based in sounds already available through life experience such as laughing, giggling, sighing, and snoring. Storytelling that includes the imitation of barnyard animals or well-known imaginary characters will give the children a sense of confidence while exploring a variety of vocal sounds and colors. Selecting appropriate models is the secret to success in this approach. Using visual tools like puppets, ribbons, pictures, and banners enlivens the exercise period. This author has found the Pillsbury Doughboy to be a perfect example of proper body attitude and deep breath support for singers. The Doughboy is available in doll form complete with a battery operated giggle mechanism located in the abdominal region of the figure. Also, the models of this gleeful little helper come in T-shirt, platter, and ornament forms, to mention only a few. The spirit of play will make the learning fun and will extend the length of time the conductor can expect concentration from the choir.

There is no difference in choral vocal exercises prescribed for boys and girls. In children's voices, the basic ranges, sound ideals, and agility rates are the same. Some exceptions exist among children experiencing a growth spurt, but such differences have no influence on the exercises for the whole choir. In principle, unlike work with older singers, the training of many children varies little from the training of a single child. Basic good vocal, musical, and social habits are the goals.

Relaxation

Children need to find an appropriate degree of physical, mental, and spiritual relaxation. Many arrive at a children's choir rehearsal after a long day at school. Others may have spent time on a playground. In some situations, children's choral groups meet on Saturday or Sunday mornings when older children would be collecting an extra hour of rest. The physical condition of the children will determine the nature of the relaxation exercises needed. Gentle stretching of the extremities, such as toe touching, easy torso twists, and arm extensions, is always useful. With some children, a few moments of quiet meditation, eyes closed and deep breathing will center minds and hearts. In all exercises with children's choirs, it is very important to be imaginative, quick to shift from task to task, and positive about the assignments ahead.

A sense of anticipation and joy must emanate from a leader of young singers. Select from the list given in Chapter 12 under the heading "How is relaxation achieved?" the activities suitable for youngsters, being cautious to keep the activities brief. Remain alert to the results. Children are resilient; they will respond much more swiftly than older singers. The relaxation portion of the children's choir rehearsal need not be lengthy. If the conductor tells an engaging tale, asking the children to mimic the motions of a character or animal in the story, the children may be relaxed and eager for the rest of the rehearsal. Poetry, nursery rhymes, tongue twisters, and fables can be used to integrate singing with other art forms.

Posture

Posture is one of the basic skills each singer must master. Children benefit from the visual model presented by an accomplished choral conductor, whose erect posture becomes an unforgettable image to emulate. When conducting children, the conductor should monitor the behavior of the young singers in all rehearsal situations. Children need to learn a seated singing posture as well as a standing one. Children's choir conductors have a variety of ways to instill proper posture techniques in children, using puppets, hand signals, and verbal cues. No matter what method is used, attention to detail with each child is important.

Be aware that some children will not be tall enough to have both feet on the floor in a seated posture. The tendency will be to swing the legs or tuck the ankles. Neither of these behaviors is conducive to good singing habits. Design a series of signals that will teach relaxed seated posture, alert seated posture, and erect seated posture appropriate to each size of child. Young singers tend to overextend themselves, exaggerating the examples given. Avoid imagery such as giraffes, ostriches, and peacocks or other models that present with elongated postures. Maintenance of disciplined posture is important for the vocal growth of the child and the choir. Furthermore, good posture training enhances the ability of children to concentrate and remain alert during rehearsals and performances.

As with older singers, posture for a child involves centering the body weight on the metatarsals, with shoulders and rib cage expanded. To avoid tension, knees should be loose. Children should be admonished to loosen their knees frequently. It is common for children to lock their knees in moments of fear or boredom. When speaking to children about their singing, a friendly tone and encouraging words will help maintain a buoyant feeling in the feet and knees. The head should be balanced comfortably on the spinal column. Smaller children often stretch their necks to achieve a sense of maturity. Children experiencing a rapid growth spurt may have a tendency to slouch. Attention should be paid to good posture in all singers in every choir at every gathering of the ensemble.

Breathing

As with adult singers, breathing exercises should follow a period of relaxation and posture alignment. Recently, a nationally recognized clinician, speaking at a regional conference of accomplished choral conductors, forced everyone to promise verbally that no rehearsal should proceed to breathing activities unless good posture was prevalent throughout the choir. This is excellent advice for choirs of all ages. As discussed in earlier chapters, the musculature of the abdominal region should be loosened by panting, giggling, or sighing. Exhalation is always taught first, creating the need for a full inhalation of breath. To teach flexible, thorough exhalation, ask the children to puff away imaginary down feathers, blow out candles on a birthday cake, cool off a cup of hot cocoa, or any activity that requires the flexing of the abdominal muscles.

None of these exercises should be done for an extended period of time. One can incorporate a rhythmic pattern to hold the attention of the children and begin musicianship training right from the outset of the rehearsal. With children, the experience of a deep, centered breath may not be habitual. To encourage a low inhalation, invite the children to express surprise. Maintaining good posture for breath will be essential, avoiding high chest breathing. As above, breathing exercises should not be labored or lengthy. The goal is to instill an attitude toward deep breathing in an erect body. Breath management is done best with visual tools (stretching ribbons, pulling rubber bands, sending laser beams), chanting of text, or activities that use breath support such as blowing out birthday candles or cooling hot cocoa. Encourage children to blow out all remaining air at the end of these tasks to avoid hyperventilation or stiffness.

Resonance

Resonance involves connecting the breath mechanism to the vocal tone. The scientific aspects of resonance are discussed in Chapter 3 under the heading "Physiology of the Voice: How does it all work together to make a voice." In the aural environment of our time, children hear loud, complex noises, see violent explosions, and hear strident, screaming sounds that are poor examples for healthy voice use. Many children will not know that shrill, synthesized sounds are unhealthy or that extreme frequency or volume levels can be harmful. Exercises evoking resonant sounds can be found in the Chapter 12 in the section entitled "Resonance." As above, the concepts and exercises must be tailored to fit the range limits of children's voices. Children gladly imitate barnyard animals or motion picture characters. The selection of appropriate models will ensure the desired result. The choral conductor must demonstrate resonant tones that are freely produced and beautifully modulated. The conductor should model vocal examples in a range, dynamic, and character comparable to the range, dynamic, and character of young voices. Should the conductor be unable to generate such a tone healthfully, the assistance of another singer should be sought.

Musicianship Training

Unlike other musical instruments, the human voice must hear a pitch internally to approximate it. In music education, this activity is called "audiation," a process involving the recognition of pitch through imitation. The process is similar to language learning. The first step in learning a language is to hear the vocabulary, practice its pronunciation, and then understand its meaning. A young singer cannot sing a tone without hearing it in the "mind's ear." Thus, pitch matching is one of the first lessons in musicianship training. After considerable practice, the singers remember the pitches heard. Another essential task is the teaching of rhythmic skill. Rhythm quickens the attention of young singers, enhancing mental agility and discipline. Rehearsal techniques that instill good rhythmic skills in singers of any age are invaluable. A steady rhythmic pulse helps all singers pace the phrasing and breathing gestures of the music. Rhythm unifies the ideas of the conductor with those of the choral singers and an accompaniment where required. It is the guiding light through the labyrinth of any musical score. In our busy world, many children's choir conductors are turning to teaching tapes that allow singers to listen and absorb the melody, rhythm, and text of repertoire through an "osmosis" process. Such a teaching method discredits the minds and musical gifts of our children. The teaching of music fundamentals has been handed down from one generation to another for centuries. It is training that gives rich returns to any human being, whether music becomes a career choice or an avocation. Taking the time to teach young ears to hear and young hearts to recognize the pulse of music is one of the worthiest ambitions for a children's choir conductor. In our noisy environment, pitch matching is an ever more elusive action. Patience and diligence are the ingredients that help the young singer, dosed liberally with a smile of encouragement. Given time and proper instruction, every child can learn to match pitch. If rhythm is taught systematically, any child can become a rhythmically competent singer. Far too frequently, young people of significant vocal gifts advance to the college level without good aural or rhythmic training. The crisis of confidence that ensues can be avoided, if these basic musicianship issues are addressed from the outset of choral training.

Once aural and rhythmic fundamentals are learned, young singers will be eager to know how the music is portrayed on the page. Unlocking the mysteries of musical notation can be done through bright, colorful visual displays or with any number of jingles, games, or similar creative activity. Music-making is an art form that re-creates the musical thoughts of others, as documented in a musical score. For the youngster, the symbols for pitch and rhythm represent a puzzle to be solved.

Repertoire Learning

As in all productive teaching experiences, moving from simple to complex is useful. In music learning, getting a sense of the whole is also important. Guide the singers through the work to be learned, reading the text with inflection and meaning. Ask the children to express the ideas with physical responses. Elements of the text that are joyful can evoke a resonant "Alleluia!" or "Yippee!"; sad topics can bring a sigh or a hand upon the heart. Children can be encouraged to reflect the meaning of the words in their faces as well as their bodies without abandoning a good posture for singing.

In vocal music, the rhythm of the text determines the rhythm of the music. Therefore, the training of text should be done through rhythmic drills. Chanting the text, phrase by phrase, in the rhythmic patterns of the musical settings instills the spirit of the music and poetry. Next, one segment of the choir can be asked to present fragments of the text with the remainder of the group echoing the presentation. Depending on the age of the children, the melodic material may be sung phrase by phrase first on a neutral syllable and then with the text. If the children are capable of reading the melody, each phrase should be sung separately on a neutral syllable, correcting any wandering tones or tendencies, before the text is added. Please note that teaching text and music simultaneously at any age can instill erroneous associations between melody and vowel that are difficult to correct. Slow, methodical training in melody, rhythm, and text will pay rich rewards.

When the basic melodic and rhythmic structures have been taught, ask the children to sit tall on their chairs and sing softly the text they have learned in its musical context. To save time, the accompanist might play the harmonic structure quietly in the background. Note the weaker and stronger elements of this performance. Address the errors incrementally but persistently. "Repetition of the right act" as John Dewey said, is the essence of good learning. Do not ignore mistakes, but create a quick "divide and conquer" plan. Recognizing that the singers do not know what was right and what was inaccurate, praise the accurate execution of phrases first. Next, address the errors that are mere "blemishes" such as dotted rhythms that were sung evenly or singular words that were sung as plurals by a few. Finally, concentrate on the more egregious errors, beginning with the rhythm, next the notes on neutral syllables, and then the melody and text as one. Give words of encouragement for every improvement, but save effusions like "very good," "excellent," and "perfect" until those levels of competency are reached. "Good," "better," and "even closer" provide promises of greater success and set standards for excellence. Remember: Do not stop to correct the choir unless you are ready to identify the problem and explain its remediation. The children will learn from their mistakes if the conductor briefly explains the reason for stopping. The explanation should be concise with a swift return to an activity that will repair the misstep. Long lectures that explain or place blame are useless.

Holding the children's glance is important for maintaining their attention and fostering their self-esteem. Engaging the children in the acts that strengthen the music making will train them as singers and help them with problem-solving and critical thinking in other situations.

Study Questions

1. Name three (3) benefits available to children through singing in a choir.

2. What is the purpose of a choral warm-up for children? Is it different than for adults?

3. Create two (2) ways to demonstrate good posture to a child.

4. Why teach exhalation first? Describe one creative way to induce a thorough exhalation in a child.

5. Why is it important to define "beauty of tone" to children?

6. What is "audiation"?

7. Describe in order a method for teaching repertoire, beginning with rhythm.

8. What benefits are gained by children from a disciplined, congenial choral rehearsal?

For Further Reading

Kemp H. *A portrait of Helen Kemp.* [Video]. Garland, Tex: Choristers Guild; 2001.
Kemp H. *Of primary importance: A Practical Guide to Young Choristers.* Garland, TX: Choristers Guild; 1991.
Page S, *Hearts and Hands and Voices.* Tarzana, Calif: Fred Bock, Inc; 1997.

CHAPTER

12

Voice Building for Choirs

For decades, choral conducting was taught as an adaptation of orchestral conducting. By definition, orchestral players are accomplished musicians with years of study and practice on a particular instrument or instruments. The assumption that choral singers would be masters of their voices proved false. Most choristers are not technically trained musicians. They are simply persons with an aptitude and interest in vocal music, sometimes more interest than aptitude. Because they are not trained singers, they have not generally acquired the skills necessary to produce the sounds requested by conductors consistently or safely (avoiding vocal injury) without special guidance during choral rehearsals. Thus, the widely practiced transfer of orchestral rehearsal and conducting skills to choral groups was not adequate or advisable. An approach to the choral art by means of vocal pedagogical practices developed.

In his article entitled "The Development of a Choral Instrument," Howard Swan[1(p5-6)] wrote at length on this topic:

> Choral conductors, even more so than teachers of singing, are divided in their opinions concerning vocal technique. Some refuse to employ any means to build voices. Either they consider such procedures to be unimportant, or they are afraid to use an exercise which is related to the singing process. Sometimes the choral director cloaks his own ignorance of the singing mechanism by dealing directly with the interpretive elements in a score and thus avoids any approach to the vocal problems of

the individuals in his chorus. There are also those conductors who insist upon using only the techniques learned from a favorite teacher. These are applied regardless of the nature of a problem or its desired solution. Finally, there are some who without an orderly plan of procedure utilize a great number of vocalises, devices, and methods secured from many sources with the desperate hope that the tone of their chorus somehow will show a marked improvement.

Why does a choral conductor attempt to solve vocal problems by avoiding them? Perhaps he thinks that the requirements of a particular musical score will call forth from his chorus an appropriate response and the ability to master any technical difficulty. If a composition is sung correctly— if notes are right in pitch and duration—does this procedure guarantee automatically a beautiful sound? Strangely enough, this curious kind of thinking will reject the use of similar procedures by an instrumental ensemble, for all agree that some skill is necessary to play any instrument. Does not a singer also need a considerable measure of technical understanding to use his voice properly? It seems sensible to believe that a special quality of teaching and learning are essential for the development of a choral tone which is adequate for the demands of any musical composition.

One of the first vocal pedagogical approaches to choral music is known as voice building for choirs,[2] a systematic training program including warm-up procedures, rehearsal techniques, and cool-down exercises. It is a method based on the vocal experiences of life (sighing, sneezing, calling, whimpering) applied to the creation of healthy singing sounds. By engaging choral singers in simple tasks involving the production of supported, resonant vocal sounds, healthy singing concepts can be taught without conflicting with vocal technical terms learned in a solo singing context. Pedagogically, the method provides choral singers with a set of vocal tools for conquering singing assignments found in choral repertoires (legato, staccato, martellato, messa di voce, dynamics). The process builds the vocal instrument while inspiring confidence and self-esteem in the choral singer.

What is a voice builder?

A voice builder is a specialist with training in vocal pedagogy and choral conducting, an advocate for the amateur choral singer. It is a role designed by Frauke Haasemann (1922–1991). As a widow of World War II at age 26, she enrolled at the Church Music Institute of Westphalia in Herford, Germany to prepare herself for a professional life in music. At the invitation of the Evangelical Lutheran Church, Dr Wilhelm

Ehmann (1904-1989) had founded the school to rebuild the musical life of a devastated agricultural community. The church walls, steeple bells, and pipe organs had been damaged; the spirits of the congregations were in shreds. When asked about the school's earliest days, Dr. Ehmann always responded: "Aus dem Nichts kam es!" ("It came out of nothingness.") In the rubble that was Westphalia, the singing voice was the cheapest musical instrument. Dr Ehmann, a musicologist, philosopher, poet, and Flügelhorn virtuoso, resolved that the only ensemble he could build had to be a vocal one. Wisely, he called upon Frauke Haasemann, the youngest but most gifted student singer to train the voices of the choir. They called her contribution "Chorische Stimmbildung" or choral voice building. Thus began a 30-year cooperative effort to teach choral singing to the uninitiated singer.[2]

A fledgling collection of eight amateur singers soon became a choir of 36 accomplished musicians, known as one of the finest vocal ensembles in Europe. Voice building, the teaching of the nuts and bolts of singing distributed with generous doses of love and wit by Frauke Haasemann, was the potent strategy that brought Dr Ehmann's music to life, shaping an artful ensemble from a collection of shattered souls. In 1956, the Goethe Institute and the German Music Council selected Dr Ehmann and his Westfälische Kantorei as ambassadors of German culture throughout the world. From 1956 to 1977, the Kantorei sang in every country of the world except Russia and Australia. The group toured North America in 1960 and again in 1971, traveling by bus from New York City to San Francisco and back. Dr Ehmann recorded his first impressions of America in a monograph entitled: *Alte Musik in der Neuen Welt* or Early Music in a New World.[3]

Voice building, the collaboration between musicologist and singer or choral conductor and voice builder, was an invention of rarest quality. At once innovative and volatile, the concept defined a vocal rather than an instrumental approach to choral music. From its inception, choral conducting has rested its head upon the pillow of personal charisma. A choir devotes itself to the beliefs, knowledge, and musicianship of a single leader. A choral organization is not a democracy; it is a dictatorship, benevolent or bitter. Lyric spirits gravitate to the warmth of the conductor's campfire, whether cozy or fiery. Like clay to the potter, the choir's membership is the storehouse of ingredients to be molded to the sounds of the conductor's musical ear. Choral conductors, on the other hand, are musicians helplessly devoid of an instrument, living in musical silence until they are rescued by the audible expression of cooperative singers. The conductor's arms are empty unless filled with the swirl of song emanating from the choir. Like any dictator, benevolent or otherwise, many choral conductors are threatened by "competing" charismatic personalities and are reluctant to share power and authority. Thus, it was courageous of Dr Ehmann to allow Frauke Haasemann to build the voices of the choir. Although the need for an intermediary between the podium and the choir had been discussed in the letters of many church musicians throughout music history, the circumstances of post-World War II Westphalia forced the issue to a solution.[4,5] To put his historical, artistic ideas into practice, Dr Ehmann stepped aside, permitting healthy vocal principles to lay the foundation for the choral sound.

No one loved the camaraderie of choral music more than Frauke Haasemann. She stood among the singers as one of their own. In most situations, she served as translator and interpreter of the intellectual and social history poetically presented by Dr Ehmann. She simplified, codified, and applied his teaching, giving practical help and turning his inner voices into vibrant corporate song. Her vocabulary and pedagogical imagery were as graphic and basic as his thoughts were eloquent and profound. When he spoke of the sound ideals of the Papal Choir in the 16th century, Frauke responded by saying, "To make the sound of a young choir boy, round your lips to form the shape of a pig's snout." Instantly, voices of all ages and abilities melded together into one unified choral tone. The cryptic codes of Dr Ehmann's data had been broken, and the mysteries of perfectly modulated polyphony were revealed. Frauke humbly and happily returned to her seat, rejoining the ranks without rancor. The chemistry maintaining this gentle balance was a powerful potion. Both were abundantly gifted in specific aspects of the task, yet less able in the expertise of the other.

In the 1970s and 1980s, Dr Ehmann and Frauke Haasemann sought to plant seeds of pedagogical thought in the fertile ground of the American amateur singing tradition. Through a series of North American workshops, concerts, recordings, and publications, they hoped to amalgamate the ideas of choral conducting and voice building to answer the queries of choral conductors and church musicians. They taught singers and conductors of all levels of proficiency in remote corners of our land, shifting emphasis from the product to the process of choral singing. Their vocal tools were distributed with abundant good humor, assigning household names to vocal technical skills. The American choral world became filled with the sounds of cuckoo clocks, barking dogs, sighs, and yodels. Utterances heard in daily life were transformed systematically into singing skills, extending a welcoming hand to the amateur singer, regardless of talent or education.

The hope for a unified curriculum of choral conducting and vocal pedagogy has been realized in the concept of choral pedagogy. These remarkably clever approaches address effectively the problem of voice training in a choral setting. It is impossible to require years of traditional voice lessons from each choral singer and impractical to expect that choristers will practice singing regularly between rehearsals. Choral pedagogy involves techniques to reach a compromise between the untrained and fully trained singer, establishing the skills necessary to create predictable, consistent singing safely using methods that accomplish the desired results quickly, using only a few minutes of precious time at each rehearsal. In many ways, this challenge is even one more daunting than the task of training an individual singer in the studio over months or years. It places great responsibility on the conductor or voice building team and requires skill, thought, creativity, and flexibility in rehearsal design and technique.

Warm-up Procedures

The basics

The transition from speech to singing must be achieved through a series of well-chosen vocal exercises, establishing an atmosphere for learning, identifying physical fatigue, encouraging mental awareness, and centering concentration. Warm-up procedures are necessary at the beginning of a choral rehearsal to gather the minds and voices of the singers around a common goal. Each singer carries to the rehearsal myriad experiences of the day, the thoughts associated with responsibilities, struggles, and leisure activities. To erase the mundane or the stressful, pleasure or pain, the choral conductor must draw attention to the task at hand.

Are warm-up procedures necessary?

The warm-up process provides a transition between speaking and singing. The average choral singer has little recognition of habitual speech faults, breath flow, or articulatory tensions. Voices travel in tired bodies to most rehearsals. The vocal instrument must be given guidance to move from the confinements of poor speech patterns to the fluidity of lyric song. Singing requires a steady flow of breath, an elongation of vowel sounds, relative relaxation of the tongue, and controlled activity of the soft palate. These requirements demand mental and physical relaxation, proper posture, ready breath musculature, and open resonating chambers.

A warm-up session will address systematically, each of these four basic elements:

1. Relaxation
2. Posture
3. Breathing
4. Resonance

Warm-up procedures are also necessary medically. Singing is an athletic endeavor involving muscle groups throughout the body, including especially the chest muscles and related soft tissues in the neck. Singing a choral rehearsal can be much like running a marathon. Most people know enough about muscle physiology to warm up and stretch muscles before a foot race, and to stretch and cool down muscles after a race. Yet they do not recognize that the same principles apply to the muscles involved in singing.[6] Properly warming up and cooling down vocal muscles aids healthy development of the voice, vocal agility, application of good singing technique during rehearsal, and helps avoid vocal injury. While the warm-up process is addressing the four elements above, it is also preparing the body's muscles for safe use during the rehearsal.

How much time should be devoted to warm-up activities?

Once the four basic elements have been taught to a choir, no more than 5 to 7 minutes of rehearsal time are necessary to remind the singers of relaxation, posture, breath, and resonance and to accomplish adequate muscle preparation for safe rehearsal. Each warm-up session is designed to meet the vocal demands of the music to be sung. Warm-up activities should not become routine or predictable, but should set the tone for the rehearsal and the repertoire. The time spent preparing the choir vocally and spiritually will prove its worth by establishing concentration, increasing choral skills, and preserving vocal health.

Are certain exercises more appropriate than others?

It is important to select exercises appropriate to the age group and mentality of the choir. The use of fantasy can achieve simultaneous mental and physical relaxation. In some age groups, however, the use of imagination may inhibit singers. The choral conductor must select carefully the exercise, the manner of presentation, and the length of the activity.

What is the proper sequence for warm-up procedures?

The proper sequence for warm-up procedures is relaxation, posture, breath, and resonance. Warm-up procedures should build the vocal instrument by eliminating tension, establishing good posture, activating the breathing mechanism, and encouraging healthy tone production.

Why is relaxation essential as a preparation for singing?

Singing demands the mental concentration and physical coordination of any athletic activity. Using relaxation techniques, the mind and spirit of choral singers must be brought to a state of restful alertness. Next, the major muscle groups should be addressed, releasing tension systematically throughout the body. The relaxation portion of the warm-up period may be brief but should not be omitted. It is wasteful to use a choir's vocal resources unless a readiness for singing is established.

Choral singers rarely present themselves refreshed at a rehearsal. In public and private schools, the rehearsal of choral groups falls between many other academic activities. Vocal ensembles often meet before the school day begins to avoid conflicts with athletic events. In other cases, the rehearsals are scheduled at day's end, when all other requirements have been met. In the world of the choral amateur, rehearsals follow an entire day of work and travel, family and social commitments. The choral conductor must assist the singers in making a quick escape from the immediate past. A kind word, a cheerful tale, a welcoming smile from the podium will guide the singer from the stress and strain of the outside world. A short series of exercises can adjust the mood, order the mind, capture the remaining energies, and relax tense muscles that can alter singing technique and predispose the singer to vocal fatigue and injury.

How is relaxation achieved?

Relaxation is best induced through exercises addressing the major muscle groups. Below is a partial list of suggested activities. Additional suggestions for exercises that relax, energize, or develop the vocal system may be found in other sources.[7] Singers with injuries (especially back and neck) should be advised to omit any exercise that might be uncomfortable.

- Stretch the arms and legs, twist the torso, and rotate the head gently to ease tensions.
- Where appropriate, choir members can give one another a quick massage of the shoulders and upper arms.

- Tread in place, swinging the arms while imagining a sunny day in spring.

- Touch the toes, allowing the upper extremities to hang gently and stretch. With eyes closed, slowly lift the torso to its erect position. Open the eyes when the body is standing tall. Repeat when necessary.

- Imagine the body to be a marionette, pulled by imaginary strings. First the right shoulder and then the left are lifted from above and relaxed. Next lift the arms and legs.

- With fists clinched, pull the shoulders to ear level. Squeeze tightly and release.

- Clasping the hands together, stretch the arms forward as far as possible. Hold briefly and release. Then clasp the hands behind the back and pull backward as far as possible. Hold for a moment and release.

- With arms folded, cradle an imaginary child or pet. Rock the arms, bending the knees. Hum a gentle lullaby or coo softly.

- Rest comfortably on a chair, with eyes closed and arms folded across the midriff. Inhale deeply and snore.

- Pack a suitcase full of imaginary clothes of various sizes and weights.

- Hang wet laundry on a line, lifting each item from an imaginary basket.

- Act out the stages of a morning routine: stretching, yawning, showering, dressing.

- Walk an imaginary dog, meeting and greeting a variety of situations along the way.

- Practice golf or tennis swings. Bat and catch a ball.

- Imitate a swimmer's stroke or a skier's slide.

- Rest the right ear on the right shoulder and hold, eyes closed. Roll the head to the left side and repeat.

- Shadow box with an imaginary partner, knees flexed and feet active.

- Finger paint a broad area of an imaginary wall.

- Dance a few steps of a waltz or a tango with an imaginary partner.

- Practice twisting with an imaginary hula hoop about the waist.

- Stretch on tiptoe to reach an imaginary apple on a tree. Pick up one from the ground.

- Wave to friends on a departing train or in an automobile.

- Rake imaginary leaves, gathering them together into piles and sacks.

- Shovel imaginary snow, some heavy and some light.

- Take a stroll through the botanical garden, gazing at exotic flowers with sighs of wonder.

Do not ignore the smaller muscle groups. Here are some exercises for the facial muscles, the tongue, and the jaw.

- Make a very angry face with fists clinched, then release and smile.

- Imitate a clown face with elevated eyebrows and expansive smile.

- Stick out the tongue and touch the nose and the chin.

- Wiggle the tongue from side to side, and up and down.

- Make small circles with the jaw, first clockwise and then counterclockwise.

- Hum and chew simultaneously.

- Sing simple patterns on "blah, blah, blah," expressing boredom and release.

- Imitate a marionette with strings attached to a loose jaw segment.

- Bite an imaginary piece of fruit. Chew the fruit and spit out its seeds.

- Create the image of the smiling "Pillsbury Doughboy" with his characteristic giggle.

What concludes the relaxation segment of a warm-up procedure?

If the choir is capable of an easy, resonant sigh, unnecessary tensions have generally been released. Sighing is one of the body's most natural acts of relaxation. The releases of tension and breath plus the use of abdominal muscles for support make the sigh a very useful preparation for singing. When a choir sighs, the choral conductor learns a great deal about the physical, mental, and spiritual state of its members. If the singers struggle to release a single sigh, tension and fatigue are factors in need of further attention.

Posture

Posture determines the position of every aspect of the vocal instrument. Weight must be centered and equally distributed throughout the body. Most amateur singers have an habitual stance, but rarely do they have a balanced one. The body must be placed in a position of buoyant expectancy. The weight of the body should be balanced on the metatarsal heads (the balls of the feet), with knees loose and spinal column anchored, the scapulae (shoulder blades) and clavicle (collar bone) should be conceptualized as suspended at the nape of the neck, with the head balanced on the spine. The skeleton should be thought of as the scaffolding from which the body hangs. All muscle groups are freed for motion with no points of undue tension. For performance circumstances, singers may have to adjust their posture to accommodate various heights of heel and particular vantage points from the riser. If they are trained during rehearsals to sing with optimal posture, they will automatically try to maintain it as well as possible in awkward performance settings.

Imitation is a strong force. The choral conductor should exhibit good posture at all times, insisting upon it from singers at every moment of their singing. Good posture helps eliminate tensions, leaving the body buoyant, agile, and receptive. It also optimizes abdominal, back, and chest muscle function ("support"). Insistence upon erect posture for singing and speech will keep fatigue after vocal tasks to a minimum.

How does a choral singer achieve good posture?

To achieve good posture for choral singing, rise up on the metatarsal heads until balance is achieved. Rest easily on the heels with gravity centered. This places the singer's weight slightly forward on the feet. This is similar to the athlete "ready posture," practiced by a shortstop or tennis player. Next, tuck the buttocks gently, establishing a sense of firmness, but without overtensing the buttocks muscles. Extend the arms to either side, perpendicular to the floor, elevating the rib cage. Roll the thumbs back, exposing the palms of the hand. Lower and relax the arms, but maintain the expansive position of the upper body. Rotate the head lightly, seeking balance.

Is there a good sitting position for singing?

It is important to teach a sitting posture as well as a standing one. Singers should be asked to sit as far forward on the chair as possible, allowing the torso to be erect and balanced. The scapulae and clavicles should be maintained in the same expansive and relaxed position as for a standing posture. The head must be balanced easily on the spine. The singers should rest both feet comfortably on the floor in front of the chair with knees relaxed. While seated, each singer should be poised to rise into an erect standing posture. The conductor must insist upon this posture when singing occurs. Sections of the choir may sit in an "off-duty" position when not being called upon to sing.

Every choral conductor should take a few moments to sit in the rehearsal chairs and stand on the performing risers. The comforts and discomforts of both vary widely; conductors should also be familiar with the principles and pitfalls of chair design (see Chapter 7). It is important for a choir to receive clear instruction regarding acceptable accommodation for rehearsal and performing facilities. The conductor must find appropriate solutions to any awkward circumstances.

What exercises assist in training good posture?

- Pretend books or fruits are balanced on the head.

- Hold imaginary dessert plates on both palms held at shoulder height. Keep eye contact with both sides to maintain erect posture and to release neck tension.

- Imagine the head as a watchtower from which a beam of light travels. Move the body in a steady, circular motion to pass the beam of light across a shadowy space.

- Imitate the guards who watch at a palace gate, then relax to a singing posture.

- Imitate a drum major or member of a color guard, then return to a singing posture.

- Envision the head gear of Shakespearean actors with streaming cloth suspended from high, cone-shaped hats, with the head elevated, the neck relaxed, and the posture tall and stately.

- Imagine the body as a tolling bell, oscillating from side to side.

- With arms linked at shoulder height, create a line of imaginary "Rockettes."

- Evoke the position of a winning athlete at an Olympic event, standing proud during the flag ceremony.

- Using the arms, imitate the motions of a mighty tree in the midst of a powerful storm.

Gravity should be equally distributed throughout the body. Frequent reminders about steady, balanced posture are a benefit to all singers. The burdens of the day, its fatigue and care, may cause a contorted position. Good posture distributes the body weight properly upon the bone structure, easing pressure on muscle groups. Proper posture not only improves singing, but gives a concomitant sense of well-being.

Breathing

"To breathe is to sing and to sing is to breathe" is one of the oldest adages in vocal pedagogy. To that, one should add that the character of one's breath determines the character of one's singing. The openness of the throat and the readiness of the body during the process of exhalation and inhalation establish the circumstances for singing. Posture must be buoyant and erect, abdominal muscles supple and prepared. Thus, singers must be encouraged to relax when air enters the body and to move the air steadily, flexibly from the body. Any subconscious fears about breath must be anticipated and eliminated. If stiffness exists in any part of the body, its presence will be made known in the breath cycle.

Breathing is crucial to good vocal health. Most amateur singers have not been taught to breathe thoroughly. Many are apprehensive about managing breath while singing choral repertoire. The choral conductor must address the issues of breathing regularly, freely, and systematically. This book suggests approaches, but to address this complex subject expertly, it is helpful for the conductor to have studied singing. Failing that, if he or she is an expert wind instrumentalist, many of the same concepts about breathing and throat relaxation are applicable.

Is it possible to eliminate fears about vital capacity and breathing for singing?

The air in the lungs is divided into residual volume and tidal volume; combined they make up the total lung volume. Residual air is always in the lungs, even after forceful exhalation. The air that moves in and out of the body with each breath is called tidal air, the means by which the body maintains adequate oxygen in the blood. There is never a lack of air in the body. Fearing a deficit in air supply, choral singers often gather tension in the area of the clavicles and in the muscles of the abdomen. The conductor, exhibiting a relaxed but firm body posture, must insist on the same from the choir. Before each breathing exercise, the choir should be asked to exhale, thereby setting up the need for a low, thorough breath. It is helpful, at the point of inhalation, to invite each choir member to imagine a pleasant thought, one that would evoke a deep, calm breath. Referring to inhalation by its pedagogical designation "inspiration" may be encouragement enough.

The choral conductor should replace any reference to the "holding" of air with progressive suggestions, such as "releasing air over the course of the phrase," "spinning the tone throughout the line," "singing on the breath." At mere mention of breath management, untrained singers tend to tighten the abdominal muscles, lock the knees, and restrict the flow of air.

What is choral breathing?

Choral breathing is a corporate feeding of the choral tone. Choral repertoire is designed on the principle of choral breathing. Because of the teamwork of choral breath, choral phrases demonstrate expansive ranges and lengths. The structure of choral composition assumes that no one singer will necessarily execute any phrase in one breath. The combined effort of many voices gives choral music its scope, breadth, and depth.

A unified choral breath begins each passage and phrase. Within the context of a phrase, however, some singers breathe ("singing silences") while others sing audibly. Having left the choral tone temporarily, the singer continues to follow the progress of the music, its vowel, its dynamics, its text, and then re-enters the choral tone imperceptibly. Commonly called "staggered breathing," choral breathing allows each singer to offer the finest supported tone for as long as is comfortable. Relief and refreshment await at numerous locations along the melodic line.

Choral singers must be taught to breathe as frequently, freely, and quietly as possible. Amateur singers often view the need for choral breathing as a sign of weakness, a technical failure. Actually, choral breathing is the foundation of the choral art. It should be trained and encouraged.

When selecting locations for corporate breath in singing, be aware that voices use less air to sing higher passages, while lower passages require more air. Air use is more efficient for melodic material moving stepwise or following the contours of a triad than that for writing with larger or more awkward intervals. Air use is also more efficient when singing familiar material than when first learning a new work.

What is the first step in teaching breath management?

Relaxation of the abdominal muscles is the first step in teaching breath management. Many amateur singers carry a great deal of tension in the muscles of the abdomen. Exhalation and particularly inhalation will be hampered by such tension. Select a familiar song for the choir to perform on "f"[f], "sh"[ʃ], or "tsch"[tʃ]. Other useful activities that motivate flexibility and relaxation are panting, sighing, and yawning.

Why is exhalation taught before inhalation?

Exhalation is always taught first. Exhalation creates a need and an eagerness for deep inhalation. Amateur singers are capable of going through the motions of a full breathing cycle without actually inhaling air. Tension may be released but adequate air is not received. By exhaling at the outset, a full breath cycle must follow. The main difference between breath for singing and breath for life is the extended exhalation period needed to perform long singing passages. Singing occurs as the breath is exhaled, recycling the expelled air as a beautiful, resonant tone. Exhalation, therefore, is of primary importance in good singing technique.

What exercises improve exhalation?

Any task requiring an expulsion of air will be useful to the development of breath management for singing. Below are a few examples.

- Imitate the cooling of a hot beverage, a bowl of soup.
- Warm cold hands by blowing air across palms.
- Attempt to whistle.
- Blow out candles on a birthday cake.
- Blow up a balloon or a beach ball.
- Silence a noisy crowd with a sustained "sh" [ʃ].
- Create patterns of rhythms using the consonants "f" [f], "sh" [ʃ], "ts" [ts], or "tsch" [tʃ].

- Imagine a deep sleep. Exhale fully with eyes closed.

- Sigh at various levels of intensity.

- Imitate an inflated raft or tire as air escapes.

Good posture must be maintained during the execution of exhalation exercises. The chest should not fall nor should the knees lock. At each juncture in the process, the demeanor of every singer should indicate readiness.

How is inhalation taught?

Thorough exhalation creates the need for inhalation. Inhalation should be spontaneous and vigorous, involving expansion of the abdominal region without any disruption of posture. Air should be received gladly. The cheekbones express anticipation, while the tongue and jaw are passive. Eyebrows must not lift nor should foreheads furrow. Inhalation is an act of refreshment, nourishing the body and the spirit, and preparing the voice.

Is it best to inhale through the nose or through the mouth?

Breathing through the nose is the most healthy, allowing for the purification of the air inhaled. Breathing exclusively through the nose during singing is often impractical. It is time-consuming and may cause throat tension. Inhalation through the mouth presents other hazards because the air from the atmosphere is cold and impure. Furthermore, it is common for the amateur singer to engage the tongue in the act of oral inhalation. If air can be drawn through the nasal passages in a spirit of expectancy and with relaxation, the air passing the vocal folds will be warmed, filtered, and humidified, keeping the vocal folds relaxed. This technique must be taught and used whenever musical circumstances permit.

How is healthy inhalation taught?

- Drinking in the scent of an exquisite perfume or flower provides a fine image for proper inhalation.

- In a seated position, leaning forward, elbows placed on the knees, the singers will sense this expansion as they inhale. The muscles of the back expand during inhalation also. In a standing position, the same expansion can be felt.

- Describing the breath mechanism as a "ring" around the body, or a "cloud" of air upon which the vocal instrument floats, can be useful imagery for the amateur singer.

- Suggestion of daily activities that induce sighs or exclamations can be helpful: the unexpected arrival of a welcome guest, the completion of a project, the success of an athletic team, evoking expressions of surprise or delight.

- Some amateur singers wish to designate the memory of a singular event to help inhalation continue in a relaxed fashion from rehearsal to rehearsal.

The conductor must be vigilant about the nature of inhalation and exhalation within the choir. If the singers are fatigued or anxious, tension will interfere with proper inhalation. Audible breath is rarely noted by the singers, but is always heard by the audience and should never escape the attention of the conductor.

What is the goal in breath management for singing and speaking?

The ultimate goal of breath management is a thorough cycle of inhalation and phonation with little unused air remaining.

What is a choral breath gesture?

Unlike solo singing, choral singing requires a corporate breath. The choral conductor must indicate the time and nature of the breath, appropriate to the musical and expressive demands of the repertoire. The conductor presents a mirror image of buoyant singing posture, with arms elevated from the midriff. The eyes, mouth, and elbows coordinate in a single motion of anticipation and acceptance.

Choral conductors must be careful to exhibit good personal breathing habits. A relaxed approach to inhalation requires calmness and coordination. The hectic pace of a rehearsal and the relentless stream of questions and comments from eager choral singers may impede the conductor's ability to speak or sing with relaxed breath technique. It is essential that choral conductors practice obvious freedom in their own breathing process. Amateur choirs will follow the example given. "What they see is what you get" is the apt title of a teaching video by Rodney Eichenberger.[8] Conductors should rehearse choral gestures before a full-length mirror or video camera to ensure good modeling images.

Breath gestures occur at each major entrance of the choir and at any significant points of entry by individual voice parts. It is not possible to gesture for every phrase in every vocal line. The conductor must, however, maintain a physical demeanor reminiscent of good choral breathing techniques throughout any performance.

What vocal exercises promote good breath management?

- Laughing patterns to relax abdominal muscles and engage breath energy.
- Staccato singing to develop flexibility for the onset of the breath in singing.
- Calling and echoing to engage the breath mechanism for contrasting dynamics.
- Melodic patterns sung on "ng" or "n" ([ŋ] and [n]) to draw supported air to the resonators.
- Melodic patterns sung on lip trills "br" or "r" ([bɾ] or [ɾ]) to teach flexible support in all ranges.
- Sighing to coordinate mental image with breath readiness.
- Descending sliding patterns, known as glissandi to unite relaxation with phonation and breath support.
- Phrases sung on French nasals to connect breath mechanism and resonators.
- Panting to relax and activate abdominal muscles.
- Yawning to combine relaxation, breath, and phonation.

Resonance

Resonance means literally "to sound against." Resonance for singing occurs when the sound waves produced in the vocal mechanism travel through the higher structures of the vocal tract. The resonators (the pharynx, the oral cavity, and the nasal cavities) work together to shape the acoustic properties from the frequencies set forth by the vocal folds (voice source signal). The sensations of resonance are crucial to the training of a singing voice. The outer, acoustic circumstances vary constantly. Furthermore, the information gleaned aurally by the singer is only a portion of the tone quality a listener hears. The singer must learn to trust the sensations of resonance and the admonitions of the conductor. Under the guidance of the conductor, rehearsal—the experience of hearing and feeling again—creates a memory of coordinated thought and action and of sounds and sensations for the choral singer. In common parlance, the term "resonance" is used interchangeably with "placement," "nasal resonance," "singing in the mask," "focus," "ping," "ring," and other terms; each is intended to refer to the sensation of phonation in the region of the face and head.

How is resonance taught to a choral singer?

Sighing, yawning, and humming assist the sensations of resonance. Lip trills on "br" [bɾ] or "r" [ɾ] patterns sung on the consonants "l" [l], "n" [n], and "ng" [ŋ] as well as the sounds of French nasals, are useful. In addition, resonant sensations are felt in the imitation of the sounds of insects and animals, such as bees or mosquitoes buzzing, cows mooing, or dogs barking. These sounds can be shaped into choral exercises.

What range and patterns should be used for choral exercises?

It is preferable to begin exercises in the upper middle range of the voice, selecting simple descending patterns. Choose a pitch level slightly above the normal speaking tone to avoid the use of undue weight in the singing. The singing voice will respond most quickly to glissando passages such as the following:

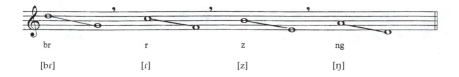

br	r	z	ng
[bɾ]	[ɾ]	[z]	[ŋ]

Once resonance has been established, proceed to syllables with simple combinations for consonants and vowels.

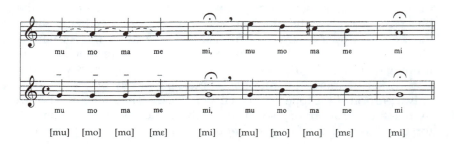

mu	mo	ma	me	mi,	mu	mo	ma	me	mi
mu	mo	ma	me	mi,	mu	mo	ma	me	mi
[mu]	[mo]	[mɑ]	[mɛ]	[mi]	[mu]	[mo]	[mɑ]	[mɛ]	[mi]

Why should ascending patterns not be used in the first moments of a warm-up?

Ascending patterns encourage the amateur singer to carry weight from the lower registers into the higher ones. It is always useful to warm up with descending patterns, beginning in the upper middle range. With the admonition to lighten the voice with each step, ascending material can be added thereafter. Also, amateur singers tend to lose concentration and support on descending melodic material much more frequently than during ascending passages. The regular study and practice of descending patterns develops consistency in registration and trains the ear. Ascending patterns must be taught and they require preparation.

What is phonation?

Phonation is the production of sound. The vocal folds act as lips on a brass mouthpiece, creating vibrations through interruptions to air powered through them from the lungs. In simplest terms, vibrating vocal folds turn air waves into sound waves, as discussed in greater detail in Chapter 3. Phonation occurs at the laryngeal level, while resonance takes place in the vocal tract (the pharynx, the oral and the nasal cavities).

When does phonation take place?

Phonation takes place in response to neurolinguistic signals. In singing, a mental image of a pitch sets off a series of signals, coordinated by the phonatory system, assisted by the breath mechanism. The singing sound begins when intelligent thought meets a responsive power source (breath and oscillator).

For conductors without singing experience, it is important to consider the following: to sing a pitch, amateur singers must have heard the pitch. Although singers introduce themselves as "sight readers" of music, they may not be sight-singers. Naming a note is quite different from maintaining an aural image of its representative pitch. No amount of vocal technique can suffice if the pitch to be sung is not known to the singer. Often, choral conductors with extensive keyboard or instrumental experience fail to realize the lack of experience amateur singers have with the "aural image" that is singing. Most amateur singers have sung along with recordings or with their neighbors, never practicing careful, quiet mental imaging of a pitch. The need for steady and concentrated attention to exquisite conscious pitch imaging is essential to good tone and tuning.

Why is humming difficult for amateur singers?

Good humming requires a loose, relaxed jaw and tongue. The teeth are kept gently apart with lips lightly closed. Many singers find it difficult to maintain an easy position in the oral cavity during humming, noting the increase in resonant sensations when the tongue and jaw are squeezed. It is essential that the choral conductor model humming well and monitor the humming of amateur singers very carefully. The vowel [ɑ] is useful for teaching humming technique. If the singer can learn to produce an open, relaxed [ɑ], he or she can be instructed to bring the lips together gently, changing nothing except the lip position. A good hum is a good [ɑ] with the lips barely touching one another.

What other exercises develop good, resonant singing tone?

- Place the hands firmly along the bony sides of the nose. Speak and sing sounds conceptualizing them as buzzing through the fingers.
- With hands clasped about the mouth, rehearse patterns of calling: "You, who?" or "Hello."
- Sing patterns using French nasal sounds: "bien," "bon," "lointain."
- Imitate a tolling bell, "Ding dong," allowing the body to rock from side to side.
- Sing short scale passages on the word, "Sing!"
- Sing a familiar tune on lip trills ("br" [bɾ], or "r" [t]).
- Ask the choir to remove an imaginary bathing cap from the head as a passage is sung.
- Placing the hands over the ears, sing a pitch while pulling imaginary headphones or ear muffs horizontally away from the body.
- Sing descending scale patterns using syllables beginning with "f" [f], "v" [v], "th" [ð], or "z" [z].
- Sing descending scale patterns on "l" [l] or "n" [n].

Conclusion

Voice building for choirs is a vocal approach to choral music, providing brief, practical vocal training and preparation for the amateur singer. Relaxation, posture, breathing, and resonance are the basic elements for building a choral voice.

Study Questions

1. Design a warm-up procedure including the four basic elements (relaxation, posture, breathing, and resonance) in sequence.

2. Define "choral breath" and "choral breath gesture."

3. What is a resonant tone?

4. In what range and directional pattern should choral exercises begin? Why?

5. Why is humming difficult? What teaching techniques are helpful?

References

1. Swan H. *Choral Conducting: A Symposium.* Englewood Cliffs, NJ: Prentice-Hall Inc; 1973: 5–6.
2. Ehmann W, Haasemann F. *Voice Building for Choirs.* Chapel Hill, NC: Hinshaw Music, Inc; 1980.
3. Ehmann W. *Alte Musik in der Neuen Welt.* Darmstadt, Germany: Merseberger Verlag; 1961.
4. Petzoldt R. *Heinrich Schütz und seine Zeit in Bildern.* Kassel, Germany: Bärenreiter Verlag; 1972: 30–33.
5. David HT, Mendel A. *The Bach Reader.* New York, NY: W.W. Norton & Co Inc; 1966:119–126, 137–149, 152–157.
6. Snyder C, DM, Saxon K, Dennehy CA. Exercise physiology: perspective for vocal training, In: Sataloff RT: *Professional Voice: The Science and Art of Clinical Care.* 2nd ed. San Diego, Calif: Singular Publishing Group Inc; 1997:775–782.
7. Raphael BM, Sataloff RT, Increasing vocal effectiveness. In: *Sataloff RT: Professional Voice: The Science and Art of Clinical Care.* 2nd ed. San Diego, Calif: Singular Publishing Group Inc; 1997:721–730.
8. Eichenberger R. *What They See Is What You Get: Linking the Visual, the Aural, and the Kinetic to Promote Artistic Choral Singing* (Video). Chapel Hill, NC: Hinshaw Music Inc; 1994.

For Further Reading

Voice Building for Choirs

Ehmann W. *Choral Directing.* Wiebe G, trans. Minneapolis, Minn: Augsburg Publishing House; 1968.

Ehmann W, Haasemann F. *Voice Building for Choirs.* Smith B, trans. Chapel Hill, NC: Hinshaw Music; 1980.

Gümmer, P. *Erziehung der menschlichen Stimme.* Kassel, Germany: Bärenreiter Verlag; 1970.
Lohmann. P. *Stimmfehler-Stimmberatung.* Mainz, Germany: B. Schott's Söhne; 1933.
Martienssen-Lohmann, F. *Das bewusste Singen.* Leipzig, Germany: CF Kahnt; 1923.
Martienssen-Lohmann. F. *Der wissende Sänger.* Zürich, Switzerland: Atlantis Verlag; 1963.

Relaxation

Brown WE. *Vocal Wisdom: Maxims of Giovanni Battista Lamperti.* Boston, Mass: Crescendo Press; Reprint 1973.

Posture

Barlow W. *The Alexander Technique.* New York, NY: Alfred A. Knopf; 1973.
Peterson P. *Natural Singing and Expressive Conducting.* Winston-Salem, NC: John F. Blair; 1966.

Breathing

Christy V. *Expressive Singing.* 3rd ed. 2 vols. Dubuque, Ia: Wm C Brown; 1974.
Proctor D. *Breathing, Speech and Song.* Vienna, Austria: Springer-Verlag; 1980.
Stampa A. *Atem, Sprache und Gesang.* Kassel, Germany: Bärenreiter Verlag; 1956.
Vennard W. *Singing: The Mechanism and the Technic.* 5th ed. New York, NY: Carl Fischer; 1967.

Resonance

Coffin B. *Overtones of Bel Canto.* Metuchen, NJ: Scarecrow Press; 1980.
Sable B. *The Vocal Sound.* Englewood Cliffs, NJ: Prentice-Hall; 1982.

CHAPTER

13

Choral Singing: The Singing Voice and the Choral Tone

Words are inadequate to describe or classify the phenomenon of the singing voice. Voices are designated as lyric or dramatic; singing sounds as pearl-shaped, rich and round, earthy, or celestial. A well-sung melodic passage might be described as a "thread of silver" sung from a "golden throat." Vocal timbres may be called light or dark, warm or cool, bright or covered, flutey or reedy, velvety or metallic. Sometimes, literal hues will be used to describe vocal colors, such as "dark red" or "pale pink." To interpret these poetic designations, the technical terms range, registration, and classification of a voice must be understood.

A singing tone is a complex sound, combining images with impulses, air with muscular energy. Phonation, the sound-making process, relies on a system of resonators and articulators to create an exquisite expression of the thought and feeling. Single singing sounds are bound together in strands of poetic phrase or abstract melodic passages to become music. The number of notes available to a singer, the ease of access to these notes, and the selection of an appropriate repertoire are crucial to the achievement of musical, vocal, and choral goals. In order to make wise repertoire and rehearsal choices, a choral conductor must be aware of the ensemble's expressive and vocal strengths and weaknesses as determined through range, registration, and voice type.

What is a "singer's range?"

The range of a singing voice is the number of notes, from the lowest to the highest pitch, a voice sings. With vocal training, the musically acceptable range of a voice will expand. The aging process may limit certain segments of the voice.

A singer's range will have a bearing on the solo or choral repertoire appropriate for the singer. It is, however, only one of the determining factors in voice classification. The register of the voice, the speaking range, the vocal timbre, the temperament, the intelligence, and the musicality of the singer, as well as the agility of the voice, are all of equal importance.

The approximate range of a voice classification is written in vocal and choral scores in the following fashion:

What does register mean?

The term "registration" comes from the terminology of pipe organ building. It refers to sounds that are alike, based on their essential timbres. For instance, reeds are one register, while strings are another. Commonly, the *registers* of the voice are called the chest voice, the middle or mixed voice, and the head voice. The chest voice is made up of pitches that sound below the general speaking range of a voice. The middle or mixed voice are those singing sounds that coincide with pitches heard in the speaking range. The head voice consists of singing sounds that ring above the speaking range. Additional registers known as the falsetto and the whistle voices are higher extensions of male and female voices, respectively. Scientists often use other terms to describe registers such as *vocal fry*, *modal*, and *loft*; the nature of different registers is still being researched.

What is falsetto?

Though generally associated with men's voices, falsetto is an extension of the upper range, available to voices of both genders. The sound of the falsetto voice is one of light, higher registration having a distinctive "brightness" of quality. Because of its unusual vocal color, the falsetto voice is best used sparingly. Not every singer has a reliable falsetto register. Others may find it difficult to move toward and away from the falsetto voice without perceptible, audible change (voice breaks).

The falsetto register in the female voice is not always accessible. An extension of the head voice register in the female is called the whistle voice.

What are appropriate uses of the falsetto voice?

The falsetto voice can be very helpful during the repetitive activities of a rehearsal, saving vocal energy in the musical passages within the upper range. When amateur singers are uncertain of pitch, vowel, or rhythm, the falsetto voice offers the possibility of supported, relaxed exploration without waste of vocal energy.

In particular musical circumstances, the use of the falsetto voice can expand the palette of dynamic colors, achieving extreme levels of soft singing. The demands of the repertoire and the abilities of the singers must be considered carefully before selecting falsetto singing at any specific juncture in musical performance.

What is improper use of the falsetto voice?

It is not advisable to request the use of falsetto singing for extended periods of time or in isolation from the other registers, or to require falsetto from singers who find it difficult. Furthermore, it can be unhealthy to use the falsetto voice if it is not produced in a relaxed, supported fashion.

What is the whistle voice?

The whistle voice is an upper extension of the female voice at and beyond F_6. Most prevalent in *coloratura* operatic repertoire, it is rarely used in choral singing.

How do the registers of the voice function?

For the human voice to negotiate the pitches throughout the singer's range, attention must be given to registration. Each register of the voice has its own color, weight, and character. In order to sing a vocal repertoire expressively, the specific qualities of each register must be melded together into a compatible series of vocal tones, allowing the voice to move imperceptibly from one register to another. Access to the highest and lowest pitches of a range is possible only through a mastery of the registers, within themselves and in relation to the others. Using various levels of breath energy and mental imaging, the singer modulates the voice through passageways from one register to another.

What are the ranges of the chest voice, the middle or mixed voice, and the head voice?

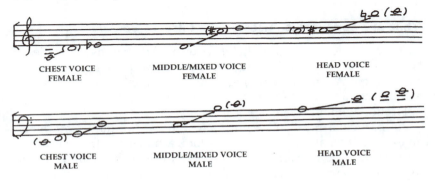

What choral exercises increase range?

Exercises that allow experimentation with pitches of high and low range include the following:

1. Imitate the sounds of a whimpering puppy, a barking St. Bernard dog, and a whole kennel full of dogs of various sizes and shapes.

2. Gently create the sound of a siren approaching and departing, allowing the pitch to rise and fall.

3. Sing the following notes in various transpositions, bending the knees as the singing approaches the crest of the phrase.

What is tessitura?

Tessitura describes the aspect of range used in a given piece of vocal music or in a given vocal line within a musical work. If a work or line is said to have a high tessitura, the notes assigned lie generally in the upper middle range or upper range of the voice. A work or line is said to have a low tessitura when the music involves primarily the lower notes of the range. Repeated or sustained notes in either extreme of the voice complicate the execution of the music. Thus, a work or passage may have a moderate range but a difficult tessitura, if, for example, the musical line stays on fairly high notes most of the time. Conversely, the music may demand a wide range but lie in a modest tessitura. Solo singers sometimes address problems of difficult tessitura when the key of a work is changed. Occasionally, in choral music, changing the key will help one section of the choir but may present difficulties for another.

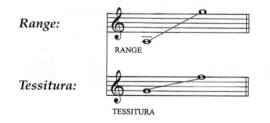

In defining the strengths of a single voice, the word tessitura is used to describe the regions of the range in which vocal coordination and colors are most available and most beautiful.

What is a register "break?" What is a "passaggio?"

Commonly called "break" or *"passaggio,"* the area of passage from one register to another usually creates a few unstable notes that are not solidly in either register. The vocal mechanism—with its coordinated cartilages, muscle tissue, and ligaments—positions the vocal folds for the production of tones at various pitch levels. The way the system produces sound is determined both by the way the vocal folds are organized and by the process of sound production at different pitches. Breath support and complicated, subtle laryngeal changes can maintain stability during the shifting process. It is common for the amateur singer to have audible difficulty at any register shifting point, thus the pejorative term "break." Through explanation, exercise, and practice, the proper proportions of energy and image will facilitate gentle passage through all the notes of a singer's range.

Choral singing ranges

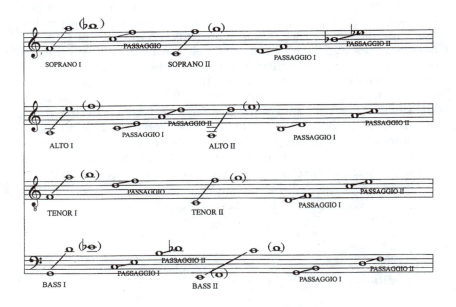

How is a "break" in a voice different from a "crack?"

As described above, a "break" is an unstable region of the range, lying between any two registers of the voice. A vocal tone is a complex sound, combining breath, mental imagery, and muscle coordination. Each element must be balanced in precise relation to the others. A voice "cracks" when muscular tension and breath managements become imbalanced resulting in sudden, uncontrolled changes in a given note, frequently including change into a different register. It is particularly difficult for the amateur singer to determine and maintain the right ratios of breath, thought, and relaxation at the points of register shift. Therefore, voices may be more likely to "crack" at the points known as "breaks." The same phenomenon can occur at any point in the range, and "cracks" are particularly common on very high notes. To remedy tendencies to crack, elements of breath, timbre, and muscle coordination should be isolated and corrected. In solo singers, this process may take years. Choral conductors must teach singers to compensate and overcome tendencies to crack much more quickly.

What exercises are used to teach proper registration?

General exercises:

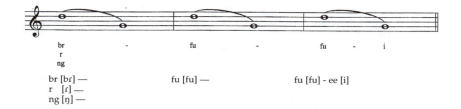

Exercises smoothing or "blending" the registers:

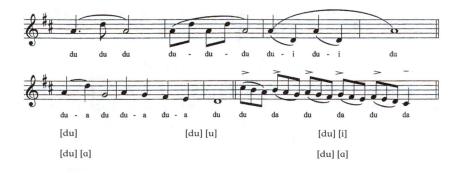

What is the meaning of the word "Fach?"

Fach is the German word for "drawer" or "shelf." In vocal terminology, the word *Fach* refers to the classification of a voice based on its timbre, agility, associated temperament, and performance. The basic classifications are: soprano, mezzo-soprano, alto, tenor, baritone, and bass. Within each *Fach* are further qualifications:

Soprano
Lyric soprano, Dramatic soprano, Coloratura soprano, Spinto

Mezzo-Soprano
Lyric mezzo, Dramatic mezzo, Coloratura mezzo

Alto
Alto, Contralto

Tenor
Lyric tenor, Dramatic tenor, Heldentenor, Spinto

Baritone
Lyric baritone, Bass-Baritone, Baritone

Bass
Bass-Baritone, Lyric bass, Basso profundo

Classification by *Fach* identifies the use of a given voice as appropriate to roles or selected works within the operatic or oratorio literature. Choral sections are not classified by *Fach* but by range (soprano, alto, tenor, bass). Individual singers within a choral ensemble, however, may readily refer to themselves by any of the designations given above.

Note: Divisi (divisions) within a choral section (Soprano I, Soprano II, and so on) do not signify a shift in *Fach*. Divisi are determined by range, timbre, balance, agility, and musicianship.

How are voices classified for choral singing?

Voices are classified for choral singing by function with specific subsections of the choir: Soprano I, Soprano II, Alto I, Alto II, Tenor I, Tenor II, Bass I, Bass II. A voice classified for solo purposes as a soprano voice may function within a choir as an alto for sake of range, balance, or color for a brief period.

When classifying voices for choral singing, choral conductors must consider the following factors: range, timbre, musicianship, and personal stability.

The basic *range* of a voice should be the first consideration. Refer above to the typical ranges for each classification and the points of passage between the registers. The vocal classification assigned should allow the singer to perform primarily in the most accessible registers of the voice. Even though a soprano and alto may have nearly the same range (highest and lowest notes), the alto will not be able to maintain comfortably the higher *tessitura* of the soprano line.

The *timbre* or color of the voice is an initial identifying signal for classification. Conductors may use the signal in combination with the range to create a particular quality within a given section of the choir. For example, if the repertoire to be sung is essentially that of the 19th century, a voice of warmest quality might be classified as a Soprano II. The same voice might be asked to sing Alto I in a repertoire of the Baroque, with fugal entrances requiring special coloration. Thus, timbre suggests balance as well as classification.

The *musicianship* of an amateur singer is a consideration in classification. If the singer sings fluently at sight, it is acceptable to assign a classification that will place the singer in extremes of range, rhythm, and pitch—especially if the singer is also skilled in vocal technique. A strong sensation for pitch, a cultivated aural image of timbre and tone, and a clear understanding of proper registration are aspects of an established vocal technique that will assist a voice in managing musical passages lying at the extremes of range. A trained soprano will know specifically how notes in the chest register should be sung, making an alto part possible. An alto with sufficient vocal technique can negotiate some soprano choral sections without applying excessive weight or color. If the singer is less proficient in basic musical skills, the voice should be protected from extreme demands. Amateur singer ambitions sometimes exceed technical or musical ability. Considerations of range, timbre, musicianship, and personal stability will guide the conductor to a wise choice.

Life has many seasons, each one affecting personal stability. There are amateur singers whose personal circumstances make it impossible for them to sing boldly or extensively. There are other singers whose physical fitness and mental attitude invite experimentation and exposure. For some, the musical demands of a harmony part are greater than their intellectual stamina can maintain. For others, a growing interest in musical matters may attract them to a harmony part.

When possible, a performance repertoire should be selected for the vocal forces available to the choir. Choirs also have productive periods and lean times. Successful programming will reflect the current state of the ensemble.

What is a choral soprano? A choral alto?
A choral tenor? A choral bass?

A choral composer's mind and ear are guided by a sound ideal for each voice part; this is comparable to an operatic composer's dramatic sense for each vocal role. The sound ideals have evolved through various historical style periods but have not moved far from the original point of departure.

In the history of Western singing, the tenor voice was the first choral sound, deriving its name from the Italian verb *tenere*, meaning "to hold." Young men delivering the chants of the Church sang in unison. During the course toward maturity, some of the men developed lower voices. While the higher ones held the *cantus firmus* (the thematic material), the lower ones created supportive material below the melodic line. Those voices were called *basso*, meaning "low." As musical training grew in sophistication and prominence, younger boys were included in the choral activities of the early Church. These voices sang descant parts higher than the tenor and were referred to as alto, meaning "high." The highest voices, known as soprano meaning "above," were the last enrichments of the choral structure.

Centuries of choral music were built on a pyramid formation, with the bass as foundation, the tenor as chief color component, and the alto and soprano as ornamentation to the tenor line. The influence of operatic singing (particularly the popularity of the *castrato*) in the 18th century enhanced interest in the idiomatic capabilities of each vocal part, giving equal importance to soprano, alto, tenor, and bass in choral compositions. The growth and development of singing societies in the 19th century both divided and united the ranks of singers, creating strong, secular ensembles for men's voices (*Männerchor*) and large a cappella choirs emancipating women to sing the soprano and alto parts (Berliner Singakademie).

Thus, choral classifications relate to choral roles within the repertoire, each singer offering elements of range, timbre, musicality, and spirit.

Choral sopranos in an amateur choir may be lyric voices, dramatic voices, or coloratura voices. Together, they carry primarily melodic or descant material. Choral sopranos are aware of their acoustic advantage over the rest of the ensemble. This exposure is inhibiting, causing most amateur sopranos to fear extremes of range and dynamics.

Amateur choral singers who prefer to sing alto are frequently soprano voices with a lack of ability or confidence in the upper range. Some are singers with a true devotion to singing harmony. Because the range of the alto voice shares that of the typical speaking voice, the alto section of a choir can assist the entire ensemble in delivering clear diction. Composed to accommodate harmonic needs, the material written for choral altos is often repetitive and uninteresting. This redundancy may cause weakness in rhythmic accuracy and tuning. The choral alto is the courier of lyric text to the audience, an invaluable choral role that is critical to the color of the choir's output. For example, the addition of one "dark" contralto to an amateur ensemble can add years to the maturity of the choral sound.

The limited quantity of true tenors is a fact of life. The bulk of choral repertoire was written to reveal the tenor line, thus in a high tessitura. Few in number and vocally taxed, choral tenors require special attention and treatment. They must not be expected to experiment with note-reading in high ranges. They should be allowed to rest at regular intervals during a rehearsal session. Their vocal forces are fragile but mighty. If tenor voices are to be preserved, they must be protected.

In most amateur choirs, the tenor section contains light, lyric baritones with easy access to the falsetto register. Occasionally, women's voices are used to balance the tenor part. Either remedy causes tuning complications. Acoustically, the brilliant timbre of the tenor voice dominates, cutting through the texture of the choral sound. Therefore, in terms of sheer numbers, it is possible to achieve a good balance with a smaller number of true tenors. It can be vocally unhealthy to substitute women or baritones for any extended length of time, and this practice should be permitted only under special circumstances with carefully selected voices. In recognition of this fact, many settings of simple standard repertoires have been arranged for soprano, alto, and bass.

Choral basses are low voices, appreciated for the richness and stability of their lowest notes. For this reason, choral basses seek to enhance the depth and weight of their sound. Lower voices tend to be less agile than higher ones, the bass being the least flexible of all. It is usual to find choral basses lagging behind the beat or pressing down upon the pitch. Descending intervals are more difficult for anyone to hear or sing than ascending ones. Finality in cadential figures is typically established by a descending leap in the bass line, punctuating the slow of melodic motion. Bass voices benefit from careful ear training and tuning exercises, and from coloratura agility exercises.

What factors determine divisi?

Divisi within a choral section are a matter of taste. A conductor may wish to divide choral sections by historical sound ideal, by vocal expertise within a given section, by timbre of singers, or by equitable units. Each historical style period requires a choral sound with more or less vocal color within particular sections of the choir. Choral conductors must adjust the divisi of the choir according to the requirements of the music. Some conductors ask weaker readers to sing musical assignments that will strengthen their skill. Others may place stronger readers in harmonically challenging locations, allowing weaker readers to carry melodic material. Repertoires vary in breadth of timbre. Equal or diverse divisi are implied through form and theme Polychoral works and fugal writings call for equal divisi. Works based on some *cantus firmus* suggest a more diversified divisi, increasing the voices that carry the theme, while decreasing those singing subordinate material.

Be aware that divisi can be used as means of achieving dynamic contrast. The addition or subtraction of voices, or the reassignment of some voices to other subsections of the choir, will adjust the dynamic level without challenging the skill of singers.

Singing and the Choral Tone

To achieve choral tone, a choir combines its corporate properties of voice, intellect, and musicianship, filtered and molded by the conductor. Like any singing sound, the choral tone is complex. Unlike solo singing, choral singing gives little emphasis to the singer's formant, neutralizing idiosyncracies of individual singers to create a blend of voices. Choral tone is a cultivated sound, specific to each choir, and each conductor. In a letter to the Collegiate Chorale, February 12, 1953, Robert Shaw wrote:[1(p108)]

> We've worked hard on musical disciplines. They aren't good enough. They never are—but all that we have accomplished is worth nothing at all unless it releases the spirit to sing and shout, to laugh and cry, or pray the primitive prayer. I earnestly believe, too, that the spirit—and only the spirit—can guide us to the sound. If hearts hymn, then the sound is illumined. If the inner necessity is large and compelling then the sound will be more than we need. People are only a little less movable than mountains, and the same thing moves them both.

How is choral tone achieved?

Vocal music of the Western world evolved from the earliest intonations chanted by religious people. On this foundation rests sacred and secular choral music of Western civilization. To develop choral tone, the choir must begin with unison singing. In the opinion of Wilhelm Ehmann, "The most basic and vital aspects of the choral art are to be learned from unison singing. . . . Unison singing is the preparatory school for polyphonic singing and requires the ultimate in terms of freedom and relaxation."[2(p152)] The common denominator of choral tone is the unified vowel sound. As a point of departure, begin by singing melodic material in unison on a single vowel. Move from simple to complex, using monosyllables and later words. Once unison singing affords a flowing, unified, choral tone, introduce the choir to the singing of canons. Unison singing and canon singing are perfect preparations for homophonic and polyphonic choral repertoires. There are many subtleties involved in shaping choral tone. The conductor influences singing technique, vowel formation, manner of attack and release, aspects of legato and articulation, and other factors that allow the sound to be molded to the conductor's intent.

What is blend?

A choral tone is a sound uniting or "blending" all participatory voices. It is a color, quality, and quantity of sound indicative of a particular set of choral forces—the singers and their conductor. The conductor selects for and against certain tendencies in the individual voices of the assembled singers. Through frequent repetition, the sum total of the conductor's selections is inscribed upon the aural memory of the choir. When speaking of the blend of the sound as the identifying tone, the choral fingerprint of the ensemble, Lloyd Pfautsch stated:

> The sounds of his chorus will be a commentary on his ability to transfer his knowledge, to enlarge and refine his pedagogical techniques, to arouse and maintain dedication to vocal and musical disciplines on the part of the singers, to shape the syllabic and melodic nuances, to expand the knowledge and technical proficiency of the chorus, and to lead the group to artistic performance.[3(p78)]

What are the elements of a blended sound?

1. *Color:* No individual voices are identifiable. Also, a distinct sound quality typifies each section and the whole choir.

2. *Balance:* Individual choral sections are balanced within the tonal texture.

3. *Tuning:* Voice leading is accurate, resolving points of tension clearly, and pitch is accurate and consistent among sections.

4. *Diction:* Vowels and consonants are pronounced uniformly and can be understood by an audience.

What is vibrato?

The natural undulation of tonal frequency within the parameters of the pitch, having no greater variation than about a semitone, is known as *vibrato*. It is a vital element in tone and tuning, a major consideration in blend. Vibrato is made regular and steady through practice. *Note:* The age and size of a voice and the overall physical condition of a singer may cause unappealing rates or frequency variations of vibrato.

How does seating affect tuning and blend?

A choral section is a unit made up of the individual properties of its singers, the properties being range, timbre, musicianship, and personality. Although not scientifically proven, experience has shown that the placement of certain voices based on the compatibility of vocal color, frequency, and formant affects tuning and choral blend.

In Western music, tuning is dictated by an instrumental standard, an arbitrary designation of 440 Hz or 442 Hz. Instrument builders have invented mechanical devices to enable players to tune their instruments. The human instrument, the voice, has an infinite number of pitches available to it, unlike the piano, which has only 88 at any given time. A singer has no frets (like a guitar) that point the way to the right notes. Singing correct notes requires an accurate ear and controlled ear-voice coordination. Some singers tune readily with others, while some struggle mightily. When voices are placed close to one another, a battle of frequencies ensues. This can work to the advantage or disadvantage of a choir.

A singing sound is a complex sound with aspects of a fundamental frequency surrounded by its overtones. Although oversimplified, vocal timbre may be thought of as the fundamental aspect of the tone. A voice with a substantial fundamental sound has a "darker," "heavier," "dramatic" quality. Voices with a lesser presence of the fundamental sound are "lighter," "brighter," more "lyric." Placed in the close proximity of a choral section, these contrasting vocal qualities collide with minute differences in pitch and of vibrato rates. Voices presenting comparable proportions of fundamental to overtone tend to conflict keenly with each other. Spaced between voices of contrasting proportions, such voices blend into a better ensemble.

In practice, the conductor should hear each voice in the section individually. Each singer sings a short segment on a vowel of the conductor's choice. Choose a simple scale pattern or a phrase from a well-known song. Every singer performs the same task, guiding the conductor toward valid comparisons. Group the singers within the section into units of darker and lighter voices. Within each subset, arrange the individual voices such that those with a greater presence of fundamental are flanked on either side with those of lesser. Arrange the subsets to suit vocal color preferences. Matters of vibrato rate, height, and personality will flavor final decisions about seating arrangements. It is rare to perform this process without observing like voices unconsciously listing away from one another. As human beings are not symmetrical, one ear dominates over the other, making it preferable for some singers to stand to the right or left of another. Making correct arrangements will improve with practice. The value of it will be obvious and audible. Sometimes other factors also influence seating. Voices influence the singers in front of them. Conductors may want to avoid the tendency to put strong singers, such as soloists and "ringers" (hired professionals) in the front, seating them instead behind the other singers in the section. Their influence over quality, pitch, and rhythms will be greater throughout the choir.

How are singers placed in a choir?

Based on the conductor's preference, the choral sections of a choir may be arranged in a number of ways. Performing circumstances may dictate the location of certain singers, the tallest and smallest taking back and front row positions. Matters of balance may be addressed by placing some choral sections at acoustical advantage to others. Tuning and blend are enhanced through prudent placement of voices as described above.

Below are illustrations of several possible configurations:

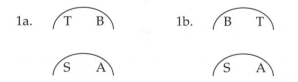

1a and 1b are configurations based on tuning needs. In 1a, the bass section strengthens the tuning capability of the alto section. In 1b, the bass and soprano sections confirm tonal contour with tenor and alto sections, creating harmonic color.

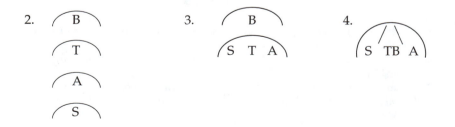

The configuration in example 2 is for large choruses, while that of example 3 achieves balance in a choir having few true tenors. Example 4 works best where singers toward the back of the risers cannot be heard as well as those in the front for acoustical reasons, such as curtains above or a low stage ceiling. Positioning the men toward the front may help achieve balance. If the choir normally uses configuration 1a above, configuration 4 works well by maintaining critical relationships as closely as possible.

Conclusion

Voices are classified by range, timbre, and temperament. Pitch frequency and vibrato rate are additional considerations in classifying and placing choral singers within an ensemble. The arrangement of singers within a section for rehearsal and performance influences choral tone, blend, and tuning and can correct the acoustical weaknesses of a performance space.

Study Questions

1. What is the relationship between the singer's formant and the choral tone?

2. What are the extended registers of the singing voice?

3. Name the characteristics of a choral soprano, alto, tenor, and bass. Are these classifications the same as those of *Fach* classifications?

4. How are divisi determined?

5. What factors influence the placement of singers in rehearsal? In performance?

References

1. Mussulman J. *Dear People* . . . Robert Shaw. Bloomington: Indiana University Press; 1979:108.
2. Ehmann W. *Choral Directing*. Wiebe G, trans. Minneapolis, Minn: Augsburg Publishing House; 1968:152.
3. Pfautsch L. The conductor and the rehearsal. In: Decker H, Herford J, eds. *Choral Conducting: A Symposium*. Englewood Cliffs, NJ: Prentice-Hall Inc; 1973:78.

For Further Reading

The Singing Voice

Articles

Vennard W, Hirano M, Ohala J. Chest, head, and falsetto. *The NATS Bulletin.* 1971;27(2): 30–38.

Waters C. Is there a break in your voice? *The Etude.* March 1967:149.

Books

Appelman DR. *The Science of Vocal Pedagogy.* Bloomington: Indiana University Press; Reprint 1974.

Bunch M. *Dynamics of the Singing Voice.* New York, NY: Springer-Verlag; 1982.

Denes P, Pinson E. *The Speech Chain: The Physics and Biology of Spoken Language.* Murray Hill, NJ: Bell Telephone Laboratories; 1963.

Duey P. *Bel Canto in Its Golden Age.* New York, NY: King's Crown Press; 1950.

Frisell A. *The Baritone Voice.* Boston, Mass: Crescendo Press; 1972.

Frisell A. *The Tenor Voice.* Boston, Mass: Bruce Humphries; 1964.

Helmholtz H. *On the Sensations of Tone.* Ellis A, trans. London, England: Longmans, Green; Reprint 1939.

Ladefoged P. *Elements of Acoustic Phonetics.* Chicago, Ill: The University Press; 1962.

Reid C. *Bel Canto: Principles and Practices.* New York, NY: Coleman-Ross; 1950.

Reid C. *The Free Voice.* New York, NY: Coleman-Ross; 1965.

Stubbs GE. *The Adult Male Alto or Counter-Tenor Voice.* London, England: Novello; 1908.

Sundberg J, ed. *Research Aspects on Singing.* Stockholm, Sweden: The Royal Swedish Academy of Music; 1970.

Zemlin W. *Speech and Hearing Science: Anatomy and Physiology.* 2nd ed. Englewood Cliffs, NJ: Prentice-Hall; 1981.

The Choral Tone

Miller R. *English, French, German and Italian Techniques of Singing.* Metuchen, NJ: Scarecrow Press; 1977.

Seashore C. *In Search of Beauty in Music: A Scientific Approach to Musical Aesthetics.* New York, NY: Ronald Press; 1947.

CHAPTER

14

Choral Singing Techniques

Poetry is the source of vocal music. The chosen text determines the mood, the melody, the rhythm, and the inflection of the music. The emotions of poetic thought evoke a broad spectrum of vocal colors. In addition, each historical style period has its own preferences for singing techniques. The basic three techniques of choral singing are legato, martellato, and staccato. Messa di voce is a technique used to articulate and express a text in certain style periods.

What is legato singing?

Legato refers to a connected, flowing line of vocal or instrumental music, a phrase of continuous vocal sound. The word legato is used synonymously with the words cantabile, sostenuto, and legato singing with cantilena. Legato is the first goal of vocal technique and the most preferred style of choral singing.

The practice of legato singing derived from the chanting of poems, hymns, and liturgy. As civilization expanded, audiences and architecture grew in size and scope. The only means of amplification for the cantor was an elevation of vocal pitch and volume, along with an extension of the vowel sounds within the text. The result was an undulating text, carried on a stream of breath and bearing deeper meaning through the sustained vowels. The spirit of the cantor's soul was communicated through this necessitated mode of presentation.

Legato singing rests upon a steady flow of breath, well-supported and free. It requires buoyant and erect posture, open and well-adjusted resonators, and relaxed and ready articulators. When singing a legato line, the singer coordinates perfectly the mental pitch signals with the vowel sounds to be sung. Consonants are sung quickly and efficiently.

The steady flow of breath and sound signals must be cultivated through diligent practice. Legato singing is much more than sustained speech; it is a physical, spiritual, musical, and mental process demanding concentration and confidence. A legato line may be described as a slender, supple thread of singing, a wide unfurled ribbon of sound, a string of perfect pearls of song.

What exercises promote legato singing?

1. a. Prepare by singing a sustained pitch on a lip trill.

br –

[bɾ]

b. Sing a sustained pitch on a single vowel.

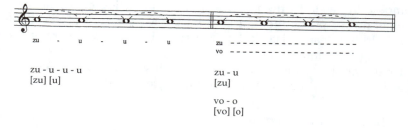

zu   -   u   -   u   -   u   zu –
                                  vo – – – – – – – – – – – – – – – – – – – .

zu - u - u - u   zu - u
[zu] [u]   [zu]

                                  vo - o
                                  [vo] [o]

2. a. Move from pitch to pitch with a gentle slide, using one vowel.

zu   -   zu   -   zu
vo   -   vo   -   vo

b. Move from pitch to pitch with a gentle slide, shifting from vowel to vowel.

zu   -   i   zu   -   i   zu   -   i   zu   -   i   zu   -

[zu] [i]

3. a. Singing with one vowel, move in stepwise motion and include one small leap.

	[zu]	zu –		zu –	zu
	[vo]	voh –		voh –	voh
	[la]	la –		la –	la

b. Sing the same passage and change the vowel at the point of the leap.

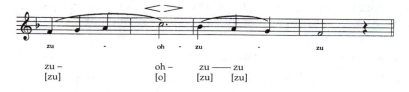

zu –   oh –   zu —— zu
[zu]   [o]   [zu]   [zu]

4. a. Invite the choir to cradle an imaginary child while singing a familiar lullaby on a single vowel.

[zu]   zu ———   zu ———   zu zu zu zu   zu

b. Sing the lullaby again, oscillating between two or three vowel sounds.

[zu] [u] [zo] [o]   [zu] [u] [zɑ] [ɑ]   [zu]   [zo] [zɑ] [zu]

5. Select more complicated patterns to be sung first on one vowel and then on several vowels. Use hand motions to promote forward flow of breath and thought. The hand motions might imitate the outlines of a rainbow, the long strokes of swimming, the tug of a rope.

6. Sing a line of music on the vowels only, allowing no breaks in the sound texture. Then add the consonants without compromising the vowel connections.

What is martellato? How is it sung?

Martellato means "hammering" in Italian. Developed in the Baroque period, martellato was used to affect word painting or to imitate the articulations of wind instruments, especially the reed instruments of the time. Passages to be sung in martellato style appear most frequently in works by Johann Sebastian Bach, George Frederick Handel, Georg Philipp Telemann, and Henry Purcell.

   Martellato singing rests upon a legato line. The connected, flowing vocal line is "hammered upon" by pulsations of breath. With gentle pressures from the abdominal and other support muscles, the vowel sounds are accentuated with clarity on a cushion of air.

What exercises train martellato singing?

1. Prepare by giggling, laughing, whimpering, or panting. Next, sing a short pattern of notes using staccato style. Finally, repeat the notes with legato singing, accenting each note slightly. The combining of staccato accentuation to legato singing is martellato technique:

Who?   Who?   Who?   Who?   Who!

[ᴍu]

2. Sustain a single pitch.

Who?- -.

Who? ——
[ᴍu]

3. Pulsate from the diaphragm on the single pitch.

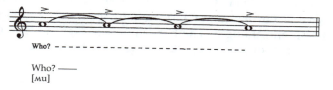

Who? -

Who? ——
[ᴍu]

4. Pulsate on the first pitch of each eighth note pair, reiterating the vowel sound for both notes of the pair.

You!You!You!You!You!You!You!You! You! You! You! You! You! You! You! You!   You!

You! You!
[ju]

5. Sing a passage of dotted notes, articulating all notes with abdominal pulsations.

du - u du - u du - u du - u   du

du – u
[du]

6. Pulsate on the first pitch of each 16th-note cluster, reiterating new vowel sounds for each note.

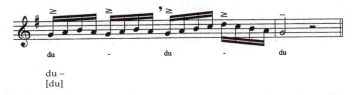

du   -   du   -   du

du –
[du]

Be very cautious that no aspirate "h" sounds are emitted. The singing should be supported by the breath and articulated by the abdomen, not by glottal stops.

What does staccato singing achieve?

Staccato singing is used for exercising the voice, developing coordination, and training accentuated articulations. Vocalises sung in staccato can assist in range extension, flexibility, relaxation, and breath activation. It may be used to strengthen weak aspects of a vocal mechanism. Frequent use of staccato exercises will eliminate breathy singing. Staccato exercises prepare singers to execute accented notes or patterns (sforzati, etc). It must be trained carefully, however, because attempts at staccato singing can be taxing or even dangerous if they are done with vocal strain and glottal (vocal fold) stops to interrupt the sound.

Staccato style appears only rarely in the context of choral performance.

What is messa di voce and how is it used?

Messa di voce, literally "measuring the voice," is a singing technique used in the training of young boys in the papal choirs of the 16th and 17th centuries. After years of basic vocal training, the stability and maturity of the voice were tested by singing a sustained pitch while achieving a steady increase and decrease in volume. A voice with "equal measurement" was capable of meeting the rigorous assignments of the papal choir. A voice that broke or wavered was not yet advanced enough in technique or age. The choral repertoire of the time was written for performance by the choirs of the church. Thus, the technique of messa di voce became the trademark of a mature singing technique.

Messa di voce gives life to a tone, expressing or embellishing the meaning of a word. It may be used as a tool for articulation in thematic material, especially fugal subjects.

The teaching and practice of messa di voce technique stabilize the pitch sense and the dynamic range of choral voices and enhance the choir's emotional palette.

What exercises train choirs to execute gradual dynamic changes (crescendo and diminuendo)?

1. Sing a single pitch on the vowel [u] or [ɑ].

   [u]
   [ɑ]

2. Sing a passage on the following chain of vowel sounds: [u], [o], [ɔ], [o], [u].

   [u] [o] [ɔ] [o] [u]

3. Sing the entire passage on [o], concentrating on a steady crescendo/ decrescendo of sound.

   oh —
   [o]

Dynamic changes occur as mental concentration and breath support unite around the emotion of the music. Choral singers will not achieve the desired degree of dynamic change on command. Individual singers have individual interpretations of the words "loud" and "soft," "forte" and "piano." When asked to increase volume, amateur singers press on their voices. Soft singing may lack energy, tempo, and resonance. It is helpful to conceive the desired dynamic gesture as a shape to be created by the voice. Concentration on the intensity of the vowels to be sung will maintain the integrity of the singing during dynamic variations.

What exercises assist choral singers in executing sudden dynamic changes?

Unlike the vocal and intellectual pacing of messa di voce (a gentle increase and decrease in dynamic), sudden dynamic changes require an emotional shifting of gears combined with an appropriate response from the voice and breath. For a forte sound, choral singers should be encouraged to call out with their voices, drawing an inward alertness. Imagining the body as a tolling bell will achieve body awareness and deep breath support. For a piano dynamic, the experience of an echo inspires mental and physical attention without a diminution of tonal color or character. A stage whisper reminds choral singers of the energy required to communicate important words with lowered volume. Below are some exercise sequences to develop various dynamic changes:

1. Exercises based on calls and echoes assist in establishing a context for dynamic changes.

2. Imitate a tolling bell. Imitate a single bell.

3. Announce a dramatic text. Repeat the text in a stage whisper. Sing the text loudly and softly on a single pitch.

Conclusion

Vocal music of the Western world evolved from the chanting of texts. Legato singing is the evolutionary result. It is the first goal in expressive singing. Martellato emerges as a singing technique in the Baroque period, emulating reed instruments. Staccato singing is rarely present in performance but is useful for training the voice. Messa di voce, a steady increase and decrease in volume on a given pitch, gives life and expression to text and tone. Dynamic changes in choral music increase vocal color and dramatic range.

Study Questions

1. Define the three singing styles: legato, martellato, and staccato. Describe the preparatory and teaching exercises used for each style.

2. What is messa di voce? How is it used?

3. What techniques assist gradual, even dynamic changes?

4. How do the basics of relaxation, posture, breathing, and resonance relate to legato singing? Martellato singing? Staccato singing? The execution of messa di voce?

5. What techniques encourage sudden dynamic changes to forte singing? Piano singing?

For Further Reading

Duey P. *Bel Canto in Its Golden Age.* New York, NY: Da Capo Press; 1980.
Jennings K. *Sing Legato.* San Diego, Calif: Neil A. Kjos Music Co; 1982.
Ware C. *Basics of Vocal Pedagogy: The Foundations and Process of Singing.* Boston, Mass: McGraw-Hill; 1998.

CHAPTER

15

Choral Diction

The main goal in teaching choral diction should be the establishment of techniques applicable to all singing languages, techniques that achieve articulate, flowing text. Choral diction demands a collaborative approach to vowel sounds, melding dialects and habits into one corporate vowel. Consonants must be rhythmic and timed. Through exercise, repetition, comparative listening, and careful imitation, choirs become proficient in the creation of any textual sounds.

How do choral conductors learn to pronounce foreign words?

The International Phonetic Alphabet (IPA)[1] is the elementary tool for the training of the conductor. A shorthand of comparative symbols, the IPA gives quick access to pronunciations and inflections. The IPA assumes an aural experience with the target language. The symbols assist in the recollection and refer to sounds in the target language comparable to those in the native language. It is important to remember that the symbols represent comparable, not identical, sounds. Inflective patterns and idiosyncratic consonant combinations create minute variations in vowel sounds unique to each language and culture.

The IPA symbols themselves must be memorized and practiced. When used in text analysis and score studies, the IPA symbols become one's own. The symbols for vowel sounds are the ones most frequently referenced. The IPA does not provide general rules or exceptions for pronunciation. Singers' diction textbooks are amply available, providing fundamental principles and musical examples. A listing of basic diction textbooks and references is given at the conclusion of this chapter. Most textbooks include a recording of basic sounds in the target language, as well as phonetic readings of standard poetry. Tapes of readings by excellent native speakers in combination with the symbols of the IPA would be an ideal preparation for teaching choral diction. Some professional tapes and videos of singers' diction are available, although none in English use native speakers in foreign languages. Anthologies of phonetic readings contain occasional texts arranged in choral settings.

Many foreign-language dictionaries use the IPA as the basic pronunciation guide. Note that the symbols appear in the target not the native language of a foreign-language dictionary; thus, if the dictionary is German to English, IPA will be given for English only.

How do choral singers learn to sing texts in foreign languages?

Choral singers learn to sing texts in foreign languages by imitation and repetition. It is generally not time-effective to expect choral singers to learn the International Phonetic Alphabet as their tool for pronunciation. Some zealous choir members may wish to include the symbols in their own factual baggage, but most will find it an impediment. Instead, the choir must rely on good examples spoken and sung by the conductor or a language assistant. The use of recorded texts is also helpful. For "live" assistance with the nuances of pronunciation and syntax, diction coaches or consultants can be retained. Books of nursery rhymes, children's songs, and tongue-twisters in foreign languages can be acquired at most foreign-language departments of local schools, colleges, and universities. These simple, rhyming texts make fine vocal exercises for choral diction.

How effective is recitation of the choral text in a foreign language?

Sung language is quite different from spoken language. It is essential that foreign phrases be formed as speech but performed immediately as song. The text should be taught in short units, relating words that rhyme or repeat. Speak the text segment slowly. Chant the text on a single pitch and then sing the text in its musical context. Be aware that the largest deviations in diction will be found in the choir's native language, where habits abide unnoticed. When foreign words relate closely to native words, the meanings should be pointed out early. Such cognate relationships are extremely common between Latin and English, and between German and English, for example. Awareness of the meanings adds a sense of familiarity, naturalness, and intelligence to the line and helps teach language and sound diction simultaneously.

How important is repetition in the training of choral diction?

Accurate repetition of the choral text is abundantly important. The articulators must become accustomed to forming the shapes of vowels and consonants in each new language. The more frequent the practice, the more ready and profound the skill.

What choral techniques make vowels pure and clear?

Vowel purity comes from exquisite imitation of a single sung sound. Clarity evolves from rhythmic accuracy. The conductor must be discreet and precise in executing the textual examples and in conducting the musical passages. For foreign sounds to become pure and clear, carefully monitored repetition is required. Singers whose native language is English should be made extremely aware of how impure (diphthong-laden) their habitual speech is and how that differs from a language like Italian.

What choral technique ensures consonant precision and expression?

Precision in the execution of consonants relates to rhythm. The choir must maintain an inner pulse, articulating the consonants within the context of the pulse. Engaging abdominal support under the consonants will ensure expression without vocal fatigue. The conductor dictates the length and expressive quality of consonants. The conductor also dictates the timing of the consonants within a musical line. For example, in a dramatic entrance, if the consonant is placed on the beat, the impact of the vowel may reach the audience late. Placing the consonant a split second early may enhance the dramatic impact of the entrance. The choir notes the dictated information in the score, coordinating the mind and body for impeccable choral diction. Regarding lyric choral diction, Wilhelm Ehmann[2] wrote:

> To achieve an *uninterrupted musical and verbal line* in speech and in singing, syllables and words must glide into each other. In this activity of meshing and coupling words, the last consonant of the final syllable

of a word is joined to the first consonant of the word that follows. This results in a sort of speech escalator or a moving conveyor belt. The unfurling of this speech belt would appear as illustrated in the following lines: "The morningstar beamsbrightly." "Inspring a youngman's fancy lightly turnsto thoughtsof love." One should concentrate on soft, smooth, and unbroken transitions, except where punctuation marks or other pauses are necessary for bringing out the sense of the word. Cold and lifeless individual words are melted, so to speak, by the warm, sustained breath into a flowing stream of living speech.

Choral Diction: Study Guide

Below are vowel sounds of general use and their IPA symbols. Note that spellings vary, although sounds are the same.

Vowel Sounds

[i]   seem, seen, scene, mean, beam, dream, team, scream

[ɪ]   chin, fin, grin, sin, thin, brim, rim, Tim, Quincy

[e]   chaotic, caper, Kate, cape, drape, fate, mate, sate

[ɛ]   bed, bet, red, thread, Fred, tread, dread, bread

[a]   tassel, hassle, task, flask, mask, crass, grass

[ɑ]   father, bother, blah, tra la la

[ɔ]   horse, force, course

[o]   moat, boat, mote, note, cloak, gloat, Coke, poke, rote

[ʊ]   book, hook, foot, soot, nook, brook, pull, full, luck

[u]   fool, prove, crew, shoe, sue, spool, tool, jewel

[ə]   abet, ahead, alone

[ʌ]   bun, fun, ton, blood, flood, nut, gut, mutt, sun

[y]   German: müde   French: une, lune, sur

[ʏ]   German: Glück

[ø]   German: schön   French: peu

[œ]   German: möchte   French: neuf

Note: [ʔ] = "stroked glottal"/pause

[ɒ]   = prefixes, suffixes, and final monosyllables that use the schwa [ə] and end in r
Example: bitter, better, matter, forward, foreword

[˜]   indicates a nasal sound

Vowel Combinations or Diphthongs

[aʊ]   plow, cow, gown, clown

[ɔɪ]   boy, ploy, toy, exploit, decoy, Detroit

[aɪ]   pile, style, tile, file, beguile, trial, mile

[eɪ]   pale, stale, tale, tail, fail, mail, sale, male, bail

[oʊ]   pole, stole, toll, sold, dough, know, sew

Note: [:] = elongation of preceding vowel

Consonants

[j]   yell, yield, yoke, youth, yen, yearn, yule,

[ŋ]   sing, singer, long, lung, swing, zing, hungry

[ŋk]   sink, sank, spank, tank, swank, sunk

[ŋg]   finger

[ʃ]   shade, should, shred, sugar, special, nation, fashion

[ʒ]   treasure, garage, azure, rouge

[tʃ]   match, chant, rich, choice

[dʒ]   fudge, justice, gem, joyous

[θ]   think, thin, thrifty, thrust, throw, cloth

[ð]   then, the, bother, brother, clothe

[ç]   German: ich, mich, Dich, ewig, möglich

[x]   German: ach, nach, doch, noch

[θ]   German: Spiel, Spiegel, Stuhl

[ɾ]   rolled/trilled

[ʁ]   velar/retroflex

Note: [:] appearing between double consonants indicates a stopped consonant combination
Example: Italian: tutti, frutti

Conclusion

Because of the manner of performance, choral diction differs from solo-singers' diction. Choral conductors use the International Phonetic Alphabet as a standard for pronunciation. Phonetic readings, audiotapes, videotapes, and dictionary references are available to assure the conductor of inflection and elision. Choral diction is expressed to the choir through imitation and repetition.

Study Questions

1. What are the sources for the learning and teaching of singer's diction?

2. How can the precision of consonants affect expression in choral singing?

3. What role do cognates play in teaching choral singers text in foreign languages?

4. Solo singers speak of good diction as "lyric diction." Define techniques for "lyric" choral diction.

5. Using the series of words given under each vowel, diphthong, and consonant combination, create strings of tongue-twisters or jingles that could be used for warm-up exercises.

References

1. *Principles of International Phonetics.* London, England: International Phonetics Society; 1949 (Reprint 1971):1–57.
2. Ehmann W. *Choral Directing.* Wiebe G, trans. Minneapolis, Minn: Augsburg Publishing House; 1968:62.

Singer's Diction Reference Materials

English

Marshall M. *The Singer's Manual of English Diction.* New York, NY: Schirmer Books; Reprint 1953.
Uris D. *To Sing in English.* New York, NY: Boosey & Hawkes; 1971.

French

Grubb T. *Singing in French.* New York, NY: Schirmer Books; 1977.

German

Odom W. *German for Singers.* New York, NY: Schirmer Books; 1981.
Siebs T. *Deutsche Bühneaussprache.* Berlin, Germany: Walter de Gruyter; 1969.

Italian

Colorni E. *Singer's Italian.* New York, NY: G Schirmer; 1970.

Latin

Hines R. *Singer's Manual of Latin Diction and Phonetics.* New York, NY: Schirmer Books; 1975.
Jeffers R. *Translations and Annotations of Choral Repertoire. Vol. I: Sacred Latin Texts.* Corvallis, Ore: Earthsongs; 1988.

Other Diction References:

Adler K. *Phonetics and Diction in Singing: Italian, French, Spanish and German.* Minneapolis: University of Minnesota Press; 1965.
Cox RG. *The Singer's Manual of German and French Diction.* New York, NY: G Schirmer; 1970.
Miller R. *English, French, German and Italian Techniques of Singing.* Metuchen, NJ: Scarecrow Press; 1977.
Moriarty J. *Diction: Italian, Latin, French and German.* New York, NY: EC Schirmer; 1975.
Wall J, Caldwell R, Gavilanes T, Allen S. *Diction for Singers: A Concise Reference for English, Italian, Latin, German, French and Spanish Pronunciation.* Dallas, Tex: Pst, Inc; 1990.

CHAPTER

16

Rehearsal Techniques

Rehearsal sessions are voice building opportunities, beginning with periods of warm-up, music-making, and cool-down. The choral conductor builds the choral instrument, singer by singer, exercise by exercise.

What is the significance of the warm-up and cool-down periods?

Warm-up activities assist the vocal mechanism in adjusting from speech to song. Cool-down periods relax the singing voice, adjusting pitch and muscle coordination toward the speaking range. They may be seen as gestures of welcome and farewell from conductor to choir.

The warm-up process centers each singer for the tasks at hand, preparing the body and shaping a spirit of readiness. The moments devoted to warm-up can be used as points of reference, a time for the conductor to take stock of the choir's level of physical and mental fatigue and to speak of the group's progress toward mutual performance goals. These introductory minutes can be used pedagogically to praise and remind the singers of good efforts or progress toward positive ends in previous rehearsals. The warm-up period offers the chance to train voices vigorously or perhaps to comfort and console the minds and hearts of the singers.

It is wise to vary the sequence of events in warm-ups, avoiding boredom and generating anticipation. Choral singers should arrive at the rehearsal eager to see and hear what the conductor has in store. A trip of fantasy or a heavy sigh to release tension, an awakening of good posture, a lively activation of the breath mechanism, and an invigorating sequence of vocal tones set the stage for imaginative, creative choral work. The atmosphere of the rehearsal should be hopeful and buoyant from the first instant, with the conductor embodying joyful anticipation.

The cool-down period can be brief but must not be forgotten. A steady, extended sigh from the highest to the lowest ranges of the voice, a gentle shrug of shoulders, or a simple recitation of poetry on a supported tone will prepare the singers for conversational speech and will help relax muscles just as cool-down exercises do after sporting events.

During the warm-up, the choir members give their voices to the care of the conductor. The conductor honors the gift by treating the choir's instruments with kindness, intelligence, and skill. At the point of cool down, the conductor graciously returns the voices to their donors.

A rehearsal is a performance for a choral conductor. For most choral singers, the warm-up period is the primary source of vocal technical information. It is a voice lesson in a corporate setting. Harsh words or bland instructions will stifle vocal progress, while friendly, engaging expressions coax and inform. When bad temper intrudes, relaxed and healthy singing disintegrates. Patient, orderly proceedings seasoned with good humor and wit benefit choir and conductor alike.

How does a choral conductor pace rehearsal time?

The pace of a choral rehearsal depends on tangible and intangible elements. As a rule, rehearsals with young singers move rapidly from one work to another, accommodating youthful attention spans. Choirs of sophisticated adults expect opportunities for inquiry. Other ensembles would prefer to sing steadily with little interruption. The successful conductor discerns the group dynamic, steadying and steering the course of the rehearsal accordingly.

Order the repertoire for a rehearsal with a sense of drama and with an eye to vocal difficulties. Rehearsals should end with tension resolved. Begin rehearsal preparation by considering the loveliest sentiment expressed in the texts to be studied. Using those words as a guide, arrange the other works to point toward the concluding selection either by comparison or contrast. If a choir is preparing a large work with a single theme, include a hymn, canon, or folk song with which to begin and end the rehearsal. The order and pace should vary from rehearsal to rehearsal. Conductors must be flexible. If the conductor's plan does not fit the choir's mood on any given night, the conductor needs to change the plan to use the time productively.

Vary the work on any given piece by beginning sometimes near the end and working forward, a technique especially useful in Baroque music where fugal themes congregate at the final cadence. In another work, select a short, difficult passage to deconstruct to its simplest terms. Teach the vocal principles involved, using a familiar exercise related to the vocal problems of the passage. When some aspect of the goal is reached, move to another piece. Never repeat difficult sections indefinitely unless progress is audible. Stamina in singing is limited; frustration is unlimited. Trial and error take a toll on voice and soul. Moving briskly from work to work, imparting clear information, and allowing serious effort is preferable to lengthy explanations and relentless repetitions.

Certain vocal tasks prepare the voice for others:

- When rehearsing a passion of Johann Sebastian Bach, work with the legato singing of a chorale to equip the choir with tools for the martellato ("hammered" legato) of the chorus movements.

- The singing of tuneful folksong arrangements or similar familiar works relaxes the choir after intense efforts with tuning or articulation in more difficult repertoires.

- Anthems of Purcell or Handel instill rhythmic drive and clarity to lighten the dense fugal and homophonic writing of 19th-century German composers (Brahms, Schumann).

- Double choruses of Heinrich Schütz, requiring a transparent sound ideal and wide dynamic range are models for the double choruses of Felix Mendelssohn. The vocal colors are quite different, but the structure and manner of performance are the same.

When arranging works in rehearsal order, consider the tessitura of the music, the repetitive passages in the repertoire, and the dynamic range. Amateur singers cannot sing high, sustained, repetitive music for extended periods of time without yielding diminishing returns.

What are the hallmarks of a "good rehearsal?"

The hallmarks of a "good rehearsal" are as follows:

1. Singers acquire "tools"of healthy, artistic choral singing.

2. Conductor and singer remain vocally refreshed.

3. Musicianship skills increase, including
   a. sightsinging,
   b. rhythm, and
   c. tuning.

4. Aspects of the text are revealed, giving context and insight to interpretation.

5. Musical form and style unite with creativity.

What are the "tools" of healthy, artistic choral singing?

The basics of relaxation, posture, breathing, and resonance are the first tools of healthy, artistic choral singing. The techniques of legato, martellato, and staccato are tools to be learned. Messa di voce is a guide to and facilitator of consistent dynamic changes. Choral singers must be taught to support articulated text and music with a steady flow of breath.

In every rehearsal, the choral conductor should distribute these tools through the activities of the warm-up and apply them systematically in the teaching and singing of the repertoire.

Positive reinforcement is the best tool. No repetition of a musical passage should occur without the conductor giving a reason for the repetition and an explanation of the tools to be used; however, spoken explanations should be kept very brief most of the time. Diligent, constructive attention to vocal technical detail produces cumulative results, bearing greater fruit season to season.

How do conductors and choral singers remain vocally refreshed?

Discipline is the short answer. Good posture, relaxed breathing, and proper tone placement will assist the conductor and the singers in remaining vocally refreshed. The conductor must stand or sit in an erect posture, taking time to breathe before giving instructions to the choir. It is essential to select a healthy, supported pitch and volume level. With helpful reminders from the conductor, the choral singer will sit and stand properly while singing. If a section is not needed during a rehearsal period, those singers should be allowed to relax comfortably. The conductor should maintain a mental image of a healthy, accomplished singer, someone seated erectly, breathing freely, and singing sonorously. As the choir's behavior deviates from the image, the conductor must act quickly to restore it.

What habits save the choral conductor's vocal energy?

Choral conductors should not sing along with the choir nor keep time with a foot. The conductor who sings cannot hear critically. By tapping a foot, the conductor maintains tempos at the expense of good posture. This also throws the conductor off balance, predisposing him or her to back and other muscle injuries. It also makes the conductor's appearance less authoritative than that achieved with a solid, balanced stance.

What habits save the choral singer's vocal energy?

When not involved in the act of singing, it is best to avoid whispering or talking. If other sections of the choir perform a passage alone, the silent sections are advised to think their lines rather than hum them or sing them softly.

Can sight-singing be taught in a choral rehearsal?

Like learning a foreign language, sight-singing improves with use. Incorporating some sight-singing into every rehearsal will yield benefits. Allow the entire choir to share in the reading at the octave of a difficult passage assigned to a single section. Teach the choir canons from time to time, training both eye and ear.

However, because of the brevity of rehearsals, it is essential to teach sight-singing at least at a basic level. Any well-conducted choir should sight-sing noticeably better in the second season of a year than in the first. Following are some suggestions to introduce an amateur choir to sight-singing:

1. Teach the singers what time signatures and measures are.

2. Teach the choir basic conducting patterns, emphasizing the importance of watching the conductor. Point out that whenever they see a down beat, they know they are at the beginning of a measure.

3. Teach the choir basic note values and how to read a rhythm. Practice reading rhythms on a spoken tone syllable, using music to be learned by the group. Point out that once the singers can read rhythms, they will always be in the right place, even if they are not able to sing the right note.

4. Teach horizontal reading. Point out how frequently the first note of a phrase repeats within the following patterns. By memorizing the sounds of pitches, singers can determine points of reference.

Scanning the line, point out the location of notes above and below the reference notes.

5. During the warm-up exercises, introduce intervals present in the works the choir will learn. Relate these intervals to familiar melodies, such as "Here Comes the Bride" for the interval of a perfect fourth.

Amateur singers rely on their tonal memory but welcome assistance with sight-singing. Choirs in academic settings may put to use one of the many solfege systems. Repertoires for children's choirs frequently teach tunes using *solfège* syllables or numbers.

How are notes and texts taught to a choir?

Note learning in a choral rehearsal must be taught systematically. First note the musical form of a work, where points of tension are established and resolved and where repetitions occur. Once the form is clear, the choir can embark more adventurously and more confidently on a discovery of the melodic material. Subdivide lengthy, complicated phrases. Present each theme in its simplest form and its more ornamented shape. During this period of investigation, it is best to sing the music on tone syllables rather than text. Syllables can be chosen to delineate the formal divisions of the work and to instill a vocal color fitting for the text and treatment. Note learning should move from simple to complex, beginning under the tempo. Allow the tempo of the work to increase due to familiarity with the music and its architecture. Observe all breath marks from their first introduction.

When text is added, read the text with beautiful inflection in a speaking tone. Next, chant the text in rhythm. In the case of a foreign text, each singer writes into the score both a word-by-word translation and a poetic interpretation of the text. Without detailed textual information, the choir is reciting and singing nonsense syllables.

Select intricate textual passages and create short exercises using the vowels of the words sung in their proper order. As the choir becomes more fluent in the singing of these vowel chains, add the consonants and the rhythm.

Note and text learning should move gently without haste. Time spent at the outset will be saved in the longer term. Bad habits in music or text are sources of confusion and consternation, obstacles to fine performance.

Why is rhythm important in choral singing?

Rhythm is the only unifying element between the choir and its conductor, its accompaniment unit, and its own sections. The choir has text, tone, and rhythm. Conducting gestures punctuate the rhythm. Accompaniment forces have rhythm and tone but no text. The relentlessness of rhythm swirls the musicians into one wave of sound. Furthermore, steady rhythm propels the flow of breath, the accuracy of pitch, the clarity of diction, and the power of expression. It is the pulse of the music aligned poetically with the heartbeat of the singer that drives the expressive engine of the choir.

Rhythm is the weakest musical skill in most amateur singers, resting on their imitative skill and tonal memory. That is another reason why teaching sight-singing begins with teaching the singers how to read rhythms and depend on them to keep their place. The pulse of the music must be made lively and active for choral singers. They must express rhythm as clearly as text or melody. Choral singers must breathe and sing rhythmically.

A rehearsal powered by rhythm remains in the muscle memory of the singer. A vocal repertoire derives its rhythm from the meter of the text. Chanting the text in rhythm gives clear insights into the rhythm of the melodic material.

How can a choir learn to tune with greater accuracy?

A note sung out of tune is a wrong note, a missed opportunity. Within the parameters of a given pitch, myriad tuning possibilities exist. Also, within a chordal context, one tuning of a pitch may be preferable to another. A choir relies on the expertise of the choral conductor to judge tuning accuracy. Singers do not hear themselves as clearly as the conductor can. Singers hear the "echo" of their own voice, a response that returns deceptive information. The choral conductor collects and sorts the sounds of the choir, suggesting tools to be used for pitch accuracy. Having put the tool to use, the singer memorizes the sensations of the proper act. Trial and error arrive at a workable solution. Training choir members to tune exquisitely is worth the time spent when measured over the course of a choir's existence. The time saved in achieving accurate timing and desired quality quickly will be its own well-deserved reward.

What simple remedies correct tuning problems?

When a choral tone is "sharp," some conductors ask the singers to round their lips. Thinking sad thoughts instead of happy, minor moods instead of major, may have the same effect. Conversely, if the pitch is "flat," the singers may lift the upper lip slightly, revealing the two front teeth. Putting a sense of joy into the tone or shifting moods from dark to light may help. Sometimes, just asking the choir to smile slightly is sufficient to lift the pitch. Flat singing on descending passages is common and can be easily avoided. Amateur singers think that high notes are hard and low notes are easy. When descending, they relax their mental concentration and their breath support simultaneously. Low notes need to sung with intelligence and abdominal support, too. This should be pointed out and emphasized with martellato exercises in lower ranges of the voice.

In simple terms, sharp singing derives from excessive energy and tension and an elevated larynx. Flat singing shows a lack of energy and a depressed larynx.

Singers respond positively to constructive tuning instruction. They rarely hear their error and require a tool for adjustment.

What musical circumstances present special tuning obstacles?

- Descending lines (diatonic or disjunct)
- Descending intervals
- Chromatic passages (descending or ascending)
- Leaps to and from registers
- Repeated notes
- Words with [ɛ] or [a] or [ɑ]
- Phrases within a passaggio
- Voice crossings
- Changes of dynamics (crescendo/decrescendo, messa di voce, echo)
- Music evoking extreme emotion

Why are textual context and interpretation essential to healthy choral singing?

The human voice portrays the meaning of words through color changes. If choral singers understand the context and interpretative possibilities of a text, they will develop instinctively its colors and contours. In addition, vocal skills develop slowly, requiring time and repetition. When a choral rehearsal addresses the deeper meanings of the music and its textual source, a singer gathers inspiration for continued vocal practice while absorbing philosophical insights.

What function does the piano have in choral rehearsal?

The piano is a useful accompaniment instrument but should never become a crutch to the choir or its conductor. The pianist should be fully aware of the conductor's goals, noting carefully the desired translations, interpretive breath and expression marks, and tempo expectations. By punctuality and readiness, the accompanist assists the conductor in setting an efficient, friendly tone to the rehearsal. However, it is very important to remember that the piano is a percussion and not a wind instrument. The tendency of amateur singers to lean on the piano for pitch and expression may result in nonlegato, inaccurate singing. The piano must be applied as a colorful accompaniment to the choir, as a confirmation of chordal structures and as a rhythmic reminder. The conductor should not allow it to provide a false sense of security among choral singers; even material written to be performed with accompaniment should usually be practiced a cappella at some time during the rehearsal process.

Conclusion

A choral rehearsal opens with a warm-up and moves logically from work to work. It concludes with a central thought, a sense of vocal accomplishment, and a quick cool-down. It offers abundant opportunities for teaching the "tools" of singing.

Study Questions

1. What is the purpose of a warm-up at the beginning of a rehearsal? Of a cool-down after a rehearsal?

2. What "tools" for singing can be taught in a choral rehearsal?

3. What vocal technical considerations determine the pacing of a rehearsal?
   What pedagogical philosophies order rehearsal plans?

4. Name typical tonal and textual tuning problems.

5. Create a rehearsal plan incorporating matters of vocal technique, musicianship, and repertoire considerations.

For Further Reading

Decker H, Herford J. *Choral Conducting: A Symposium.* Englewood Cliffs, NJ: Prentice-Hall Inc; 1973.

Ehmann W. *Choral Directing.* Wiebe G, trans. Minneapolis, Minn: Augsburg Publishing House; 1968.

Paine G, ed. *Five Centuries of Choral Music: Essays in Honor of Howard Swan.* Stuyvesant, NY: Pendragon Press; 1988.

Swan H. *Conscience of a Profession.* Chapel Hill, NC: Hinshaw Music Inc; 1987.

Bibliography

Children's Choirs

The study of choral pedagogy is intended as a preventive measure to ensure vocal health for future generations. Choral activities with young voices require special consideration. A selected bibliography of reliable sources in the field of children's choirs follows:

Articles

Adler S. Our best and most lasting hope. *The Choral Journal.* 1993;33:21.

Goldring M. An Englishman's view of North American youth and children's choirs. *The Choral Journal.* 1992;33:31.

Rao D. Children's choirs: a revolution from within. *Music Educators Journal.* 1993;80:44.

Sinclair R. Sing, sing, sing. *The Washingtonian.* 1990;32:86.

Tagg B. An interview with Gregg Smith. *The Choral Journal.* 1993;33:19.

Tagg B. Building the American children's choir tradition. *The Choral Journal.* 1993;33:7.

Books

American Choral Directors Association. *National Directory of Children's Choirs in America.* Lawton, Okla: Brooks G; 1991.

Bartle J. *Lifeline for Children's Choir Directors.* Toronto, Canada: GV Thompson; 1993.

Bourne P. *Instructional Techniques for Children's Choirs: A Curricular Model.* Ann Arbor, Mich: University Microfilms International; 1990.

Crocker E. *Essential Musicianship; A Comprehensive Choral Method: Voice, Theory, Sight-Reading, Performance.* Milwaukee, Wisc: Hal Leonard; 1996.

Farrior C. *Body, Mind, Spirit, Voice: Helen Kemp and the Development of the Children's Choir Movement.* Ann Arbor, Mich: UMI Dissertation Services; 1995.

Ingram M. *Organizing and Directing Children's Choirs.* New York, NY: Abingdon Press; 1959.

Jacobs R. *The Successful Children's Choir.* Tarzana, Calif: HT FitzSimons Co; 1995.

Kemp H. *Of Primary Importance: Information, Preparation, Application.* Garland, Tex: Choristers Guild; 1989.

Killian J. *Essential Repertoire for the Young Choir.* Milwaukee, Wisc: Hal Leonard; 1995.
MacKenzie J. *Keep 'em Singing.* Grand Rapids, Mich: Zondervan Publishing House; 1993.
McRae S. *Directing the Children's Choir: A Comprehensive Resource.* New York, NY: Schirmer Books; 1991.
Page S. *Hearts and Hands and Voices: Growing in Faith Through Choral Music.* Tarzana, Calif: HT FitzSimons Co; 1995.
Rao D. *Choral Music Experience.* Farmingdale, NY: Boosey & Hawkes; 1987.
Sinclair C. *The Effect of Daily Sightsinging Exercises on the Sightsinging Ability of Middle School Choir Students.* St. Paul, Minn: University of St. Thomas; 1996.

Recordings

Celebrate the Best of the Boys' Choir of Harlem. New York, NY: Boys' Choir of Harlem; 1995.
Chicago Children's Choir. Chicago, Ill: Chicago Children's Choir; 1972.
Colorado Children's Chorale Performing Small Miracles. Denver, Colo: Colorado Children's Chorale; 1987.
Kemp H. *Children's Choir Methods.* Crofton, Md: Recorded Resources Corp; 1986.
Kemp H. *Children's Choirs. Sessions 1–3.* Louisville, Ky: Southern Baptist Theological Seminary; 1989 (Audiovisual, 4 video cassettes).
Moore M. *Teaching Children to Sing.* Nashville, Tenn: Convention Press; 1989.
Nelson R. *The Children's Choir.* New York, NY: American Guild of Organists; 1985.
Skiles J. *Developing a Children's Choir.* Nashville, Tenn: Gaylor Multimedia; 1995.
Toronto Children's Chorus. New Orleans, La: HIS Recording; 1987 (Audiovisual).

Choral Conducting

Articles

Crutchfield W. Mining veins of vocal gold to build choral splendors. *NY Times.* January 17, 1993; 2–23.
Smith P. Importance of chorus directors. *Opera News.* 1990; 54:5.
Young P. A choral cornucopia. *Maclean's.* 1989;102:59.

Books

Armstrong K. *Choral Musicianship and Voice Training.* Carol Stream, Ill: Somerset Press; 1986.
Busch B. *The Complete Choral Conductor: Gesture and Method.* New York, NY: Schirmer Books; 1984.

Decker H, Kirk C. *Choral Conducting: Focus on Communication.* Englewood, Cliffs, NJ: Prentice–Hall; 1988

Ehmann W. *Choral Directing.* Wiebe G, trans. Minneapolis, Minn: Augsburg Publishing Co; 1968.

Finn W. *The Art of the Choral Conductor.* Boston, Mass: CC Birchard & Co; 1939.

Garretson R. *Conducting Choral Music.* Boston, Mass: Allyn & Bacon; 1961.

Gordon L, *Choral Director's Complete Handbook.* West Nyack, NY: Parker Publishing Co; 1977.

Hammar R. *Pragmatic Choral Procedures.* Metuchen, NJ: Scarecrow Press; 1984.

Lopez R. *A Guide to Resources for the New Choral Conductor.* Ann Arbor, Mich: University Microfilms International; 1985.

Poe F. *Teaching and Performing Renaissance Choral Music: A Guide for Conductors and Performers.* Metuchen, NJ: Scarecrow Press; 1994.

Glossary

This glossary was developed from the authors' experience and also from a review of glossaries developed by Johan Sundberg (personal communication, June 1995), Ingo Titze (*Principles of Voice Production*, Englewood Cliffs, NJ: Prentice-Hall Inc; 1994:330–338), and other sources. It is difficult to credit appropriately contributions to glossaries or dictionaries of general terms, as each new glossary builds on prior works. The authors are indebted to colleagues whose previous efforts have contributed to the compilation of this glossary.

This glossary contains definitions, not only of terms in this text, but also of terminology encountered commonly in related literature. Readers are encouraged to consult other sources, and these additional definitions are included for the convenicence of those who do so.

abduct: To move apart, separate.

abduction quotient: The ratio of the glottal half-width at the vocal processes to the amplitude of vibration of the vocal fold.

absolute voice rest: Total silence of the phonatory system.

Adam's apple: Prominence of the thyroid cartilage in males.

adduct: To bring together, approximate.

affricate: Combination of plosive and fricative.

allergy: Bodily response to foreign substances or organisms.

alto: (See **contralto**)

amplitude tremor: Regular (periodic) long-term amplitude variation (an element of vibrato).

anabolic steroids: Primarily male hormones that increase muscle mass and may cause irreversible, masculinization of the voice. Anabolic steroids help cells convert simple substances into more complex substances, especially into living matter.

antagonist (muscle): An opposing muscle.

anterior: Toward the front.

anterior commissure: The junction of the vocal folds in the front of the larynx.

antibiotics: Drugs used to combat infection (bodily invasion by a living organism or virus).

anticoagulant: Blood thinner.

antihistamines: Drugs used to combat allergic response.

aphonia: The absence of vocal fold vibration; this term is commonly used to describe people who have "lost their voice" after vocal fold injury. In most cases, such patients have very poor vibration, rather than no vibration; they typically have a harsh, nearly whispered voice.

appoggio: translated as "support;" in the terminology of vocal technique, refers to the point of appoggio, whether it be of the abdominal or the thoracic region where the maximum muscular tension is experienced in singing (appoggio at the diaphragm, appoggio at the chest).

arthritis: Inflammation of joints in the body.

articulation: Shaping of vocal tract by positioning of its mobile walls such as the lips, the lower jaw, the tongue body and tip, the velum, the epiglottis, the pharyngeal sidewalls, and the larynx.

arytenoid cartilages: Paired, ladle-shaped cartilages to which the vocal folds are attached.

aspiration: (1) In speech, the sound made by turbulent airflow preceding or following vocal fold vibration, as I [hɑ]. (2) In medicine, refers to breathing into the lungs substances that do not belong there such as food, water, or stomach contents following reflux. Aspiration may lead to infections such as pneumonia, commonly referred to as *aspiration pneumonia.*

asthma: Obstructive pulmonary (lung) disease associated with bronchospasm and difficulty expiring air.

baritone: The most common male vocal range; higher than bass and lower than tenor. Singer's formant around 2600 Hz.

basement membrane: Anatomic structure immediately beneath the epithelium.

bass: (See **basso**)

bass baritone: In between a bass and a baritone. Not as heavy as basso profundo, but typically with greater flexibility. Must be able to sing at least as high a F_4.

basso: The lowest male voice; singer's formant around 2300 to 2400 Hz.

basso profundo: Deep bass; the lowest and heaviest of the bass voices. Can sing at least as low as D_2 with full voice. Singer's formant around 2200 to 2300 Hz.

bel canto: Literally means "beautiful singing;" refers to a method and philosophical approach to singing voice production.

benign tumors: Tumors that are not able to metastasize or spread to distant sites.

Bernoulli's principle: If the energy in a confined fluid stream is constant, an increase in particle velocity must be accompanied by a decrease in pressure against the wall.

bilateral: On both sides.

bilateral vocal fold paralysis: Loss of the ability to move both vocal folds caused by neurologic dysfunction.

bleating: Fast vibrato, like the bleating of a sheep.

body: With regard to the vocal fold, the vocalis muscle.

bravura: Brilliant, elaborate, showy execution of musical or dramatic material.

breathy phonation: Phonation characterized by a lack of vocal fold closure, which causes air leakage (excessive airflow) during the quasiclosed phase, producing turbulence that is heard as noise mixed in the voice.

bronchitis: Inflammation of the bronchial tubes in the lungs.

bronchospasm: Forceful closing of the distal airways in the lungs.

bruxism: Grinding of the teeth.

bulimia: Self-induced vomiting to control weight.

cancer: An abnormality in which cells no longer respond to the signals that control replication and growth. This results in uncontrolled growth and tumor formation, and may result in spread of tumor to distant locations (metastasis).

cartilage of Santorini: Small cartilage flexibly attached near the apex of the arytenoid, in the region of the opening of the esophagus.

cartilage of Wrisberg: Cartilage attached in the mobile portion of each aryepiglottic fold.

castrato: A male singer castrated at around age 7 or 8, so as to retain alto or soprano vocal range.

chest voice: Heavy registration with excessive resonance in the lower formants.

coloratura: In common usage, refers to the highest of the female voices, with range well above C_6; may use more whistle tone than other female voices. In fact, coloratura actually refers to a style of florid, agile, complex singing that may apply to any voice classification. For example, the bass runs in Handel's *Messiah* require coloratura technique

complex sound: A combination of sinusoidal waveforms superimposed on each other. May be complex periodic sound (such as musical instruments) or complex aperiodic sound (such as random street noise).

complex tone: Tone composed of a series of simultaneously sounding partials.

component frequency: Mathematically, a sinusoid; perceptually, a pure tone. Also called a partial.

compression: A deformation of a body that decreases its entire volume; an increase in density.

concert pitch: Also known as international concert pitch.

contact ulcer: A lesion with mucosal disruption most commonly on the vocal processes or medial surfaces of the arytenoid. Caused most commonly by gastroesophageal reflux laryngitis and/or muscular tension dysphonia.

contraction: A decrease in length.

contralto: The lowest of the female voices; able to sing F_3 below middle C, as well as the entire treble staff. The singer's formant is at around 2800 to 2900 Hz.

conus elasticus: Fibroelastic membrane extending inferiorly from the vocal folds to the anterior superior border of the cricoid cartilage. Also called the cricovocal ligament. Composed primarily of yellow elastic tissue. Anteriorly, it attaches to the minor aspect of the thyroid cartilage; posteriorly, it attaches to the vocal process of the arytenoid.

convergent: With regard to glottal shape, the glottis narrows from bottom to top.

corner vowels: [ɑ], [ɪ], and [u]; vowels at the corners of a vowel triangle; they necessitate extreme placements of the tongue.

countertenor: A male voice that is primarily falsetto, singing in the contralto range.

cover: (1) In medicine, with regard to the vocal fold, the epithelium, and superficial layer of lamina propria. (2) In music, an alteration in technique that changes the resonance characteristics of a sung sound, generally darkening the sound.

cranial nerves: Twelve paired nerves responsible for smell, taste, eye movement, vision, facial sensation, chewing muscles, facial motion, salivary gland and lacrimal (tear) gland secretions, hearing, balance, pharyngeal and laryngeal sensation, vocal fold motion, gastric acid secretion, shoulder motion, tongue motion, and related functions.

creaky voice: The perceptual result of subharmonic or chaotic patterns in the glottal waveform. According to IR Titze, if a subharmonic is below about 70 Hz, creaky voice may be perceived as pulse register (vocal fry).

crescendo: To get louder gradually.

cricoid cartilage: A solid ring of cartilage located below and behind the thyroid cartilage.

cricothyroid muscle: An intrinsic laryngeal muscle that is used primarily to control pitch (paired).

crossover frequency: The fundamental frequency for which there is an equal probability for perception of two adjacent registers.

cycle: A 360° rotation; same as a *period* in periodic motion.

cysts: Fluid-filled lesions.

damp: To diminish or attenuate an oscillation.

dB: (See **decibel**)

decibel: One tenth of a bel. The decibel is a unit of comparison between a reference and another point. It has no absolute value. Although decibels are used to measure sound, they are also used (with different references) to measure heat, light, and other physical phenomena. For sound pressure, the reference is 0.0002 microbar (millionths of one barometric pressure). In the past, this has also been referred to as 0.0002 dyne/cm^2 and by other terms.

decrescendo: (See **diminuendo**)

dehydration: Fluid deprivation; dehydration may alter the amount and viscosity of vocal fold lubrication and the properties of the vocal fold tissues themselves.

diaphragm: A large, dome-shaped muscle at the bottom of the rib cage that separates the lungs from the viscera. It is the primary muscle of inspiration and may be coactivated during singing.

diminuendo: Gradually reducing in loudness or force.

displacement flow: Air in the glottis that is squeezed out when the vocal folds come together.

diuretics: Drugs used to decrease circulating body fluid generally by excretion through the kidneys.

divergent: With regard to the vocal folds, the glottis widens from bottom to top.

divisi: Literally "divided," used in choral scores to indicate that a section is to be divided into two or more parts; generally intended for the rendering of fuller harmony.

dizziness: A feeling of imbalance.

dorsal: Toward the back.

dramatic soprano: A soprano with powerful, rich voice suitable for dramatic, heavily orchestrated operatic roles; sings at least to C$_6$.

dramatic tenor: A tenor with heavy voice, often with a suggestion of baritone quality; suitable for dramatic roles that are heavily orchestrated. Also referred to as *Heldentenor,* a term used typically for tenors who sing Wagnerian operatic roles.

dynamics: (1) In physics, a branch of mechanics that deals with the study of forces that accelerate object(s). (2) In music, it refers to changes in the loudness of musical performance.

dysmenorrhea: Painful menstrual cramps.

dyspepsia: Epigastric discomfort, especially following meals; impairment of the power or function of digestion.

dysphonia plica ventricularis: Phonation using false vocal fold vibration rather than true vocal fold vibration. Most commonly associated with severe muscular tension dysphonia. Occasionally may be an appropriate compensation for profound true vocal fold dysfunction.

dystonia: A neurological disorder characterized by involuntary movements, such as unpredictable, spasmodic opening or closing of the vocal folds.

edema: Excessive accumulation of fluid in tissues, or "swelling."

electroglottography (EGG): Recording of electrical conductance of vocal fold contact area versus time; EGG waveforms frequently have been used for the purpose of plotting voice source analysis.

electromyography (EMG): Recording of the electric potentials in a muscle, which are generated by the neural system and which control its degree of contraction; if rectified and smoothed, the EMG is closely related to the muscular force exerted by the muscle.

elongation: An increase in length.

embouchure: The shape of the lips, tongue, and related structures adopted while producing a musical tone, particularly while playing a wind instrument.

endocrine: Relating to hormones and the organs that produce them.

endometriosis: A disorder in which endometrial tissue is present in abnormal locations outside the uterus. Typically causes excessively painful menstrual periods (dysmenorrhea) and infertility.

epiglottis: Cartilage that covers the larynx during the act of swallowing.

epithelium: The covering, or most superficial layer, of body surfaces.

erythema: Redness.

esophagus: Tube leading from the bottom of the pharynx to the stomach; swallowed food is transported through this structure.

extrinsic muscles of the larynx: The strap muscles in the neck, responsible for adjusting laryngeal height and for stabilizing the larynx.

Fach (German): Literally, subject or box. It is used to indicate voice classification. For example, lyric soprano and dramatic soprano are each a different Fach.

false vocal folds: Folds of tissue located slightly higher than and parallel to the vocal folds in the larynx.

falsetto: High, light register, applied primarily to men's voices singing in the soprano or alto range. Can also be applied to women's voices.

flow: The volume of fluid passing through a given cross-section of a tube or duct per second; also called volume velocity (measured in liters per second).

flow glottography: Recording of the transglottal airflow versus time, ie, of the sound of the voice source. Generally obtained from inverse filtering, FLOGG is the acoustical representation of the voice source.

flow phonation: The optimal balance between vocal fold adductory forces and subglottic pressure, producing efficient sound production at the level of the vocal folds.

flutter: Modulation in the 10 to 12 Hz range.

F_0: Fundamental frequency.

focal: Limited to a specific area. For example, spasmodic dysphonia may be focal (limited to the larynx), or part of a group of dystonias that affect other parts of the body such as the facial muscles or muscles involved in chewing.

force: A push or pull; the physical quantity imparted to an object to change its momentum.

formant: Vocal tract resonance; the formant frequencies are tuned by the vocal tract shape and determine much of the vocal quality.

formant tuning: A boosting of vocal intensity when F_0 or one if its harmonics coincides exactly with a formant frequency.

functional residual capacity (FRC): Lung volume at which the elastic inspiratory forces equal the elastic expiratory forces; in spontaneous quiet breathing, exhalation stops at FRC.

frequency tremor: A periodic (regular) pitch modulation of the voice (an element of vibrato).

fricative: A speech sound, generally a consonant, produced by a constriction of the vocal tract, particularly by directing the airstream against a hard surface, producing noisy air turbulence. Examples include s [z] produced with the teeth, s [s] produced with the lower lip and upper incisors, and th [θ] produced with the tongue tip and upper incisors.

functional voice disorder: An abnormality in voice sound and function in the absence of an anatomic or physiologic organic abnormality.

fundamental: Lowest partial of a spectrum, the frequency of which normally corresponds to the pitch perceived.

fundamental frequency (F_0): The lowest frequency in a periodic waveform; also called the first harmonic frequency.

gastric: Pertaining to the stomach.

gastroesophageal reflux (GER): The passage of gastric juice in a retrograde fashion from the stomach into the esophagus. These fluids may reach the level of the larynx or oral cavity and may be aspirated into the lungs.

gastroesophageal reflux disease (GERD): A disorder including symptoms and/or signs caused by reflux of gastric juice into the esophagus and elsewhere. Heartburn is one of the most common symptoms of GERD. (See also **laryngopharyngeal reflux**)

glissando: A "slide" including all possible pitches between the initial and final pitch sounded. Similar to portamento and slur.

globus: Sensation of a lump in the throat.

glottal chink: Opening in the glottis during vocal fold adduction, most commonly posteriorly. It may be a normal variant in some cases.

glottal resistance: Ratio between transglottal airflow and subglottal pressure; mainly reflects the degree of glottal adduction.

glottal stop (or click): A transient sound caused by the sudden onset or offset of phonation.

glottis: The space between the vocal folds.

glottis respiratoria: The portion of the glottis posteriorly in the region of the cartilaginous portions of the vocal folds.

glottis vocalis: The portion of the glottis in the region of the membranous portions of the vocal folds.

granuloma: A raised lesion generally covered with mucosa, most commonly in the region of the vocal process or medial surface of the arytenoid; often caused by reflux and/or muscle tension dysphonia.

halitosis: Bad breath.

harmonic: A frequency that is an integer multiple of a given fundamental. Harmonics of a fundamental are equally spaced in frequency; partial in a spectrum in which the frequency of each partial equals *n* times the fundamental frequency, *n* being the number of the harmonic.

harsh glottal attack: Initiating phonation of a word or sound with a glottal plosive.

Heldentenor: (See **dramatic tenor**)

hemorrhage: Rupture of a blood vessel; this may occur in a vocal fold.

hormones: Substances produced within the body that affect or control various organs and bodily functions.

hyoid bone: A horseshoe-shaped bone known as the "tongue bone." It is attached to the muscles of the tongue and related structures, and to the larynx and related structures.

hyperfunction: Excessive muscular effort, for example, pressed voice or muscular tension dysphonia.

hypernasal: Excessive nasal resonance.

hypofunction: Low muscular effort, for example, soft breathy voice.

hyponasal: Deficient nasal resonance.

hypothyroidism: Lower-than-normal output of thyroid hormone. This condition is commonly referred to as an "underactive thyroid," and often results in malaise, weight gain, temperature intolerance, irregular menses, muffling of the voice, and other symptoms.

infraglottic: Below the level of the glottis. This region includes the trachea, thorax, and related structures.

infraglottic vocal tract: Below the level of the vocal folds. This region includes the airways and muscles of support. (Infraglottic is synonymous with subglottic.)

infrahyoid muscle group: A collection of extrinsic muscles including the sternohyoid, sternothyroid, omohyoid, and thyroid muscles.

intensity: A measure of power per unit area. With respect to sound, it generally correlates with perceived loudness.

interarytenoid muscle: An intrinsic laryngeal muscle that connects the two arytenoid cartilages.

intercostal muscles: Muscles between the ribs.

interval: The difference between two pitches, expressed in terms of musical scale.

intrinsic laryngeal muscles: Muscles in the larynx responsible for abduction, adduction, and longitudinal tension of the vocal folds.

intrinsic pitch of vowels: Refers to the fact that in normal speech, certain vowels tend to be produced with a significantly higher or lower pitch than other vowels.

jitter: Irregularity in the period of time of vocal fold vibrations; cycle-to-cycle variation in fundamental frequency; jitter is often perceived as hoarseness.

lamina propria: With reference to the larynx, the tissue layers below the epithelium. In adult humans, the lamina propria consists of superficial, intermediate, and deep layers.

laryngeal ventricle: Cavity formed by the gap between the true and false vocal folds.

laryngectomy: Removal of the larynx. It may be total, or it may be a "conservation laryngectomy," in which a portion of the larynx is preserved.

laryngitis: Inflammation of laryngeal tissues.

laryngocele: A pouch or herniation of the larynx, usually filled with air and sometimes presenting as a neck mass. The pouch usually enlarges with increased laryngeal pressure as may occur from coughing or playing a wind instrument.

laryngologist: A physician specializing in disorders of the larynx and voice. In some areas of Europe, the laryngologist is primarily responsible for surgery, while diagnosis is performed by phoniatricians.

laryngopharyngeal reflux (LPR): A form of gastroesophageal relux disease in which gastric juice affects the larynx and adjacent structures. Commonly associated with hoarseness, frequent throat clearing, granulomas, and other laryngeal problems, even in the absence of heartburn.

larynx: The body organ in the neck that includes the vocal folds; also called the "voice box."

laser: An acronym for "light amplification by stimulated emission of radiation." A surgical tool using light energy to vaporize or cauterize tissue.

lateral cricoarytenoid muscle: Intrinsic laryngeal muscle that adducts the vocal folds through forward rocking and rotation of the arytenoids (paired).

lesion: In medicine, a nonspecific term that may be used for nearly any structural abnormality.

lift: A transition point along a pitch scale where vocal production becomes easier.

loft: A suggested term for the highest (loftiest) register; usually referred to as falsetto voice.

Lombard effect: Modification of vocal loudness in response to auditory input, for example, the tendency to speak louder in the presence of background noise.

longitudinal: Along the length of a structure.

longitudinal tension: With reference to the larynx, stretching the vocal folds.

loudness: The amount of sound perceived by a listener; a perceptual quantity that can only be assessed with an auditory system. Loudness corresponds to intensity and to the amplitude of a sound wave.

lung volume: Volume contained in the subglottic air system; after a maximum inhalation following a maximum exhalation, the lung volume equals the vital capacity.

lyric soprano: A soprano with flexible, light vocal quality, but one who does not sing as high as a coloratura soprano.

lyric tenor: A tenor with a light, high flexible voice.

malignant tumor: Tumors that have the potential to metastasize, or spread to different sites. They also have the potential to invade, destroy, and replace adjacent tissues. However, benign tumors may have the capacity for substantial local destruction, as well.

marcato: Each note accented.

marking: Using the voice gently (typically during rehearsals) to avoid injury or fatigue.

martellato: A technique for singing melismatic passages in music in which certain notes are accentuated within the context of legato singing, generally found in works of the Baroque period.

medial (or mesial): Toward the center (midline or midplane).

menopause: Cessation of menstrual cycles and menstruation. Associated with physiologic infertility.

menstrual cycle: The normal, cyclical variation of hormones in adult females of child-bearing age, and bodily responses caused by those hormonal variations.

messa di voce: A traditional exercise in Italian singing tradition consisting of a prolonged crescendo and diminuendo on a sustained tone.

mezza voce: Literally means "half voice." In practice, means singing softly, but with proper support.

mezzo-soprano: A range of the female voice, higher than contralto but lower than soprano.

middle (or mixed): A mixture of qualities from various voice registers, cultivated to allow consistent quality throughout the frequency range.

middle C: C_4 on the piano keyboard, with an international concert pitch frequency of 261.6 Hz.

modal: Used frequently in speech, refers to the voice quality used generally by healthy speakers, as opposed to a low, gravelly vocal fry or high falsetto. Modal register describes the laryngeal function in the range of fundamental frequencies most commonly used by untrained speakers (from about 75 to about 450 Hz in men; 130 to 520 Hz in women).

modulation: Periodic variation of a signal property; for example, as vibrato corresponds to a regular variation of fundamental frequency, it can be regarded as a modulation of that signal property.

mucosa: The covering of the surfaces of the respiratory tract, including the oral cavity and nasal cavities, as well as the pharynx, larynx, and lower airways. Mucosa also exists elsewhere, such as on the lining of the vagina.

mucolytic: A substance that thins mucous secretions.

mucosal disruption: With reference to the vocal folds, a tear of the surface of the vocal fold; usually caused by trauma.

muscle tension dysphonia: Also called muscular tension dysphonia. A form of voice abuse characterized by excessive muscular effort, and usually by pressed phonation. A form of voice misuse.

mutational dysphonia: A voice disorder. Most typically, it is characterized by persistent falsetto voice after puberty in a male. More generally, it is used to refer to voice with characteristics of the opposite gender.

myasthenia gravis: A neuromuscular junction disease associated with fatigue.

myoelastic-aerodynamic theory of phonation: The currently accepted mechanism of vocal fold physiology. Compressed air exerts pressure on the undersurface of the closed vocal folds. The pressure overcomes adductory forces, causing the vocal folds to open. The elasticity of the displaced tissues (along with the Bernoulli effect) causes the vocal folds to snap shut, resulting in sound. "Myoelastic" refers to the muscle (myo) and its properties. "Aerodynamic" refers to activities related to airflow.

nasal tract: Air cavity system of the nose.

nervous system: Organs of the body including the brain, spinal cord, and nerves. Responsible for motion, sensation, thought, and control of various other bodily functions.

neurotologist: Otolaryngologist specializing in disorders of the ear and ear-brain interface (including the skull base), particularly hearing loss, dizziness, tinnitus, and facial nerve dysfunction.

nodules: Benign growths on the surface of the vocal folds. Usually paired and fairly symmetric. They are generally caused by chronic, forceful vocal fold contact (voice abuse).

objective assessment: Demonstrable, reproducible, usually quantifiable evaluation, generally relying on instrumentation or other assessment techniques that do not involve primarily opinion, as opposed to subjective assessment.

open quotient: The ratio of the time the glottis is open to the length of the entire vibratory cycle.

oral contraceptive: Birth control pill.

organic voice disorder: Disorder for which a specific anatomic or physiologic cause can be identified, as opposed to psychogenic or functional voice disorders.

origin: The beginning point of a muscle and related soft tissue.

oscillation: Back-and-forth repeated movement.

oscillator: With regard to the larynx, the vibrator that is responsible for the sound source, specifically the vocal folds.

otolaryngologist: Ear, nose, and throat physician.

overtones: Partials above the fundamental in a spectrum.

papillomas: Small benign epithelial tumors that may appear randomly or in clusters on the vocal folds, larynx, and trachea and elsewhere in the body. Believed to be caused by various types of human papillomavirus (HPV), some of which are associated with malignancy.

parietal pleura: The outermost of two membranes surrounding the lungs.

partial: Sinusoid that is part of a complex tone; in voiced sounds, the partials are harmonic, implying that the frequency of the nth partial equals n times the fundamental frequency.

passaggio (Italian): The shift or break between vocal registers.

period: In physics, the time interval between repeating events; shortest pattern repeated in a regular undulation; a graph showing the period is called a waveform.

pharyngolcele: A pouch or herniation of part of the pharynx (throat), commonly fills with air in wind players.

pharynx: The region above the larynx, below the velum, and posterior to the oral cavity.

phonation: Sound generation by means of vocal fold vibrations.

phonetics: The study of speech sounds.

phonosurgery: Originally, surgery designed to alter vocal quality or pitch. Now commonly used to also refer to all delicate microsurgical procedures of the vocal folds.

pitch: Perceived tone quality corresponding to its fundamental frequency.

pleural space: The fluid-filled space between the parietal and visceral pleura.

plosive: A consonant produced by creating complete blockage of airflow, followed by the buildup of air pressure, which is then suddenly released, producing a consonant sound.

polyps: Sessile or pedunculated growths; usually unilateral and benign, but the term is descriptive and does not imply a histological diagnosis.

posterior: Toward the back.

posterior cricoarytenoid muscle: An intrinsic laryngeal muscle that is the primary abductor of the vocal folds (paired).

power source: The expiratory system including the muscles of the abdomen, back, thorax, and the lungs. The power source is responsible for producing a vector of force that results in efficient creation and control of subglottal pressure.

pressed phonation: A type of phonation characterized by low airflow, high adductory force, and high subglottal pressure; not an efficient form of voice production. Pressed voice is often associated with voice abuse and is common in patients with lesions, such as nodules.

psychogenic: Caused by psychological factors, rather than physical dysfunction. Psychogenic disorders may result in physical dysfunction or structural injury.

pulmonary system: The breathing apparatus including the lungs and related airways.

pulse register: The extreme low end of the phonatory range. Also known as vocal fry or Strohbass, characterized by a pattern of short glottal waves alternating with larger and longer ones, and with a long closed phase.

quadrangular membrane: Elastic membrane extending from the sides of the epiglottic cartilage to the corniculate and arytenoid cartilages. Mucosa covered, it forms the aryepiglottic fold and the wall between the pyriform sinus and larynx.

recurrent laryngeal nerves: The paired branches of the vagus nerve which supply all the intrinsic muscles of the larynx except for the cricothyroid muscles. The recurrent laryngeal nerves also carry sensory fibers (feeling) to the mucosa below the level of the vocal folds.

reflux laryngitis: Inflammation of the larynx due to irritation from gastric juice.

registers: A weakly defined term for vocal qualities; often, register refers to a series of adjacent tones on the scale that sound similar and seem to be generated by the same type of vocal fold vibrations and vocal tract adjustments. Examples of register are vocal fry, modal, and falsetto, but numerous other terms are also used.

Reinke's space: The superficial layer of the lamina propria.

relative voice rest: Restricted, cautious voice use.

resonance: Peak occurring at certain frequencies (resonance frequencies) in the vibration amplitude in a system that possesses compliance, inertia, and reflection; resonance occurs when the input and the reflected energy vibrate in phase. The resonances in the vocal tract are called formants.

resonator: With regard to the voice, refers primarily to the supraglottic vocal tract, which is responsible for timbre and projection.

sensory: Having to do with the feeling or detection of other nonmotor input. For example, nerves responsible for touch, proprioception (position in space), hearing, and so on.

singer's formant: A high-spectrum peak occurring between about 2.3 and 3.5 kHz in voiced sounds in Western operatic and concert singing. This acoustic phenomenon is associated with "ring" in a voice and with the voice's ability to project over background noise, such as a choir or an orchestra. A similar phenomenon may be seen in speaking voices, especially in actors. It is known as the speaker's formant.

singing teacher: Professional who teaches singing technique (as opposed to *voice coach*).

singing voice specialist: A singing teacher with additional training and specialization in working with injured voices, in conjunction with a medical voice team.

sinusitis: Infection of the paranasal sinus cavities.

skeleton: The bony or cartilaginous framework to which muscle and other soft tissues are connected.

soft glottal attack: Gentle glottal approximation often obtained using an imaginary [h].

spasmodic dysphonia: A focal dystonia involving the larynx; may be of adductor, abductor, or mixed type. Adductor spasmodic dysphonia is characterized by strain-strangled interruptions in phonation. Abductor spasmodic dysphonia is characterized by breathy interruptions.

spectrum: Ensemble of simultaneously sounding sinusoidal partials constituting a complex tone, a display of relative magnitudes or phases of the component frequencies of a waveform.

spectrum analysis: Analysis of a signal showing its partials.

speech-language pathologist: A trained, medically affiliated professional who may be skilled in remediation of problems of the speaking voice, swallowing, articulation, language development, and other conditions.

spinto: Literally means "pushed." Usually applied to tenors or sopranos with a lighter voice than dramatic singers, but with aspects of particular dramatic excitement in their vocal quality, Enrico Caruso being a notable example.

staccato: Each note accented and separated.

steroid: Steroids are potent substances produced by the body. They may also be consumed as medications. (See also **anabolic steroids**).

stroboscopy: A technique that uses interrupted light to simulate slow motion. (See also **strobovideolaryngoscopy**)

strobovideolaryngoscopy: Evaluation of vocal folds utilizing simulated slow motion for detailed evaluation of vocal fold motion.

Strohbass (German): Literally "straw bass;" another term for *pulse register* or *vocal fry*.

subglottal pressure: Air pressure in the airway immediately below the level of the vocal folds. The unit most commonly used is centimeters of water. The distance in centimeters that a given pressure would raise a column of water in a tube.

subglottic: The region immediately below the level of the vocal folds.

subjective assessment: Evaluation that depends on perception and opinion, rather than independently reproducible quantifiable measures, as opposed to objective assessment.

support: Commonly used to refer to the power source of the voice; includes the mechanism responsible for creating a vector force that results in efficient subglottic pressure; includes the muscles of the abdomen and back, as well as the thorax and lungs; primarily the expiratory system.

superior laryngeal nerves: Paired branches of the vagus nerve that supply the cricothyroid muscle, and supply sensation from the level of the vocal folds superiorly.

supraglottic: Vocal tract above the level of the vocal folds. This region includes the resonance system of the vocal tract, including the pharynx, oral cavity, nose, and related structures.

suprahyoid muscle group: One of the two extrinsic muscle groups. Includes the stylohyoid muscle, the anterior and posterior bellies of the digastric muscle, the geniohyoid, the hyoglossus, and the mylohyoid muscles.

temporomandibular joint: The jaw joint; a synovial joint between the mandibular condyle and skull anterior to the ear canal.

tenor: The highest of the male voices, except countertenors; must be able to sing to C_5. Singer's formant is around 2800 Hz.

testosterone: The hormone responsible for development of male sexual characteristics, including laryngeal growth.

thoracic: Pertaining to the chest.

thorax: The part of the body between the neck and abdomen.

thyroarytenoid muscle: An intrinsic laryngeal muscle that comprises the bulk of the vocal fold (paired). The medial belly constitutes the body of the vocal fold.

thyroid cartilage: The largest laryngeal cartilage. It is open posteriorly and made up of two plates (thyroid laminae) joined anteriorly at the midline. In males, there is an anterior, superior prominence known as the "Adam's apple."

tidal volume: The amount of air breathed in and out during respiration (measured in liters).

timbre: The quality of a sound. Associated with complexity, or the number, nature, and interaction of overtones.

tonsils: Paired masses of lymphoid tissue located near the junction of the oral cavity and pharynx.

tonsillitis: Inflammation of the tonsils.

tracheobronchial tree: The air passages of the lungs and trachea (commonly referred to as the windpipe).

tremor: A modulation in activity.

tremolo: An aesthetically displeasing, excessively wide vibrato.

trill: A vocal or instrumental ornament involving an oscillation of pitch within a discrete range.

trillo: The repetition of a given pitch with frequent interruptions; a vocal ornament of the late Medieval and early Renaissance.

tympanic membrane: The eardrum.

vector: A quantity made up of two or more independent items of information, grouped together.

velar: Relating to the velum or palate.

velum: A general term that means "veil" or "covering." With regard to the vocal tract, it refers to the region of the soft palate and adjacent nasopharynx that closes together under normal circumstances during swallowing and phonation of certain sounds.

ventricle of Morgagni: Also known as laryngeal sinus and ventriculus laryngis. The ventricle is a fusiform pouch bounded by the margin of the vocal folds, the edge of the free crescentic margin of the false vocal fold (ventricular fold), and the mucous membrane between them that forms the pouch. Anteriorly, a narrowing opening leads from the ventricle to the appendix of the ventricle of Morgagni.

ventricular folds: The "false vocal folds," situated above the true vocal folds.

vibrato: In classical singing, vibrato is a periodic modulation of the frequency of phonation. Its regularity increases with training. The rate of vibrato (number of modulations per second) is usually in the range of 5 to 6 per second. Vibrato rates over 7 to 8 seconds are aesthetically displeasing to most people and sound "nervous." The extent of vibrato (amount of variation above and below the center frequency) is usually 1 or 2 semitones. Vibrato extending less than ±50.5 semitone is rarely noted in singers, although it is encountered in wind-instrument playing. Vibrato rates greater than 2 semitones are usually aesthetically unacceptable and are typical of elderly singers in poor artistic vocal condition, in whom the excessively wide vibrato extent is often combined with excessively slow rate.

viscera: The internal organs of the body, particularly the contents of the abdomen.

visceral pleura: The innermost of two membranes surrounding the lungs.

vital capacity: The maximum volume of air that can be exchanged by the lungs with the outside; it includes the expiratory reserve volume, tidal volume, and inspiratory reserve volume (measured in liters).

vocal cord: An old term for vocal fold.

vocal fold (or cord) stripping: A surgical technique, no longer considered acceptable practice under most circumstances, in which the vocal fold is grasped with a forceps, and the surface layers are ripped off.

vocal fold stiffness: The ratio of the effective restoring force (in the medial-lateral direction) to the displacement (in the same direction).

vocal folds: A paired system of tissue layers in the larynx that can oscillate to produce sound.

vocal fry: A register with perceived temporal gaps; also known as *pulse register* and *Strohbass*.

vocal ligament: Intermediate and deep layers of the lamina propria. Also forms the superior end of the conus elasticus.

vocal tract: Resonator system constituted by the larynx, the pharynx, and the mouth cavity.

vocalis muscle: The medial belly of the thyroarytenoid muscle.

voce coperta: "Covered registration."

voce di petto: Chest voice.

voce di testa: Head voice.

voce mista: Mixed voice.

voice abuse: Use of the voice in specific activities that are deleterious to vocal health, such as screaming.

voice coach: (1) In singing, a professional who works with singers, teaching repertoire, language pronunciation, and other artistic components of performance (as opposed to a singing teacher, who teaches singing technique); (2) The term voice coach is also used by acting-voice teachers who specialize in vocal, bodily, and interpretive techniques to enhance dramatic performance.

voice misuse: Habitual phonation using phonatory techniques that are not optimal and then result in vocal strain. For example, speaking with inadequate support, excessive neck muscle tension, and suboptimal resonance. Muscular tension dysphonia is a form of voice misuse.

voice source: Sound generated by the pulsating transglottal airflow; the sound is generated when the vocal fold vibrations chop the airstream into a pulsating airflow.

volume: "Amount of sound," best measured in terms of acoustic power or intensity.

waveform: A plot of any variable (eg, pressure, flow, or displacement) changing as time progresses along the horizontal axis; also known as a time-series.

wavelength: The initial distance between any point on one vibratory cycle and a corresponding point of the next vibratory cycle.

whisper: Sound created by turbulent glottal airflow in the absence of vocal fold vibration.

whistle voice: The highest of all registers (in pitch); it is observed only in females, extending the pitch range beyond F_6.

wobble: A slow, irregular vibrato; aesthetically unsatisfactory. Sometimes referred to as a *tremolo*, having a rate of less than 4 oscillations per second and an extent of greater than ±2 semitones.

Index

A

Acetaminophen, 52
Afrin, 52
Aging and voice, 33–34
  audiation (mental hearing), 65
  choir positioning, 66
  chord revoicing, 66
  deep breathing, 62
  dynamic, 65–66
  execution speed, 65
  lifetime skills, 64, 66
  and melisma, 65
  posture, 62
  range, 65–66
  resonance enhancement, 62–63
  staccato exercises, 63
  tone quality improvement, 64–65
  vocal warm-ups, 62
Akenfield (Blythe), 4
Alcohol, 37
Alexander technique, 84
Allergies, 43
Alto, 178, 180
Amateur singing, 4–6, 180–181
Amenorrhea, 73
American Choral Directors
     Association, 135
Analgesics, 52
Anatomy, 28
  diaphragm, 21–22
  larynx, 15–20
    cartilages, 16, 17, 20
    nerves, 16
    soft tissues, 20, 21
  pharynx, 16
  Reinke's space, 20
  vocal folds, 16
    mucosa, 20, 21
Anorexia, 72
Antibiotics, 44–45, 50
Anticoagulants, 35
Antihistamines, 35, 43, 44, 50–51
Anxiety, 38
Aspirin, 35, 52
Asthma, 37, 73, 76
Asthma inhalers, 35, 37
Axid, 37

B

Bach, Johann Sebastian, 11
Baritone, 178, 181
Barium esophagogram, 36–37
Baroody, Margaret, 135
Bass, 178, 180
Benadryl, 52
Berliner Singakademie, 11
Bernoulli force, 23
Beta-adrenergic blocking agents, 38
Botulinum toxin injection, 49
Breathiness, 40
Breathing
  breath gesture, 126–127, 164–165
  childhood choral singing, 144–145
  choral, 161–162
  deep, 62
  exercises, 62, 144–145
  inhalation exercises, 162–163
  inhalation teaching, 163–164
  management teaching, 162, 165
  overview, 160–161
  wind players, 74–75
Bulimia, 72

C

Cancer, 35, 49–50
Childhood choral singing
  breathing, 144–145
  exercises, 142–143
  musicianship training, 145–146
  overview, 141–142
  posture, 143–144
  relaxation, 143
  repertoire learning, 146–148
  resonance, 145
  warm-up, 142
Choral pedagogy, *See also* Voice
    building
  breath gesture, 126–127, 164–165
  breath management, 162, 165
  educator health risks, 133–136
  inhalation, 163–164
  laryngologist role, 130
  music selection, 122–123
  range, 127–128, 176
  resonance, 166
  rhythm, 124–125
  speech-language pathologist (SLP)
    role, 130
  tessitura, 127–128
  text, 123–125
  vocal health, 117–130, *See also main*
    heading Vocal health *for details*
  voice teacher role, 130
Choral sound
  and camaraderie, 11–12
  conductor-choir symbiosis, 10
  development, 10
Choral tone, *See also* Singing voice
  achievement of, 182–183
  blend, 183
  and positioning, 184–186
  and singer configuration, 184–186
  tuning/blend, 184–185
  vibrato, 183–184
Cimetidine, 37
Coffee, 37
Conducting
  and breath gesture, 164
  choral sound, 10

communication, personal, 10
discipline, 125–126
foreign pronunciation, 197–198
friendship/harmony fostering, 12
group symbiosis, 10
pedagogical tools, 9–10
singing *versus* instrumental, 126–127
and speech milieu, choir, 10
and voice building, 151–153
Conductors
  and aging singers, 63–64, 66
  on amateur singers, 4–5
  and contractual singers, 7
  as educational resource, 34–35,
    57–58
  health issues, 77–78
  voice problems of, 78
Contracts, 6–7
Contralto, 181
Cool-down, 7
Corticosteroids, 42, 44, 51
Cough medications, 43
Cysts, 39, 41–42, 53

D

Dance medicine, 72–73
Decongestants, 50
"The Development of a Choral
    Instrument" (Swan), 149
Dewey, John, 147
Dexamethasone, 51
Diabetes, 44
Diction
  consonants, 199–200, 201
  diphthongs, 201
  foreign pronunciation, 197–199
  International Phonetic Alphabet
    (IPA), 197–198, 200–201
  recitation, 198–199
  vowels, 199, 200–201
Diphenhydramine hydrochloride, 52
Diuretics, 51
Dysphonia, *See also* Spasmodic
    dysphonia
Dystonia, extrapyramidal, 48

I

Ibuprofen, 52
Infection
  herpes, 33
  upper respiratory tract, 43
Inhalants, 35, 37, 52
International Conference of
    Symphony and Opera
    Musicians (ICSOM), 71, 83
International Phonetic Alphabet
    (IPA), 197–198, 200–201
IPA, *See* International Phonetic
    Alphabet (IPA)
Isaac, 11

J

Journal of Singing, 69, 117
Journal of Voice, 69

K

Kemp, Helen, 142

L

Lansoprazole, 37
Laryngeal trauma, 47
Laryngitis
  and asthma inhalers, 35
  gastroesophageal reflux, 36, 43, 49
  infectious, 44–45
  noninfectious, 44
  with serious vocal fold injury,
      43–44
  sicca (dry voice), 44, 52
  treatment, 45–46
  voice rest, 45
  without serious vocal fold injury,
      44–45
Larynx, *See also* Vocal folds
  anatomy, 15–20
    cartilages, 16, 17, 20
    nerves, 16
    soft tissues, 20, 21
  physiology

cartilages, 26–27
  muscles, 19–20, 26
von Leden, Hans, 53
Lotti, 11
Lully, Jean-Baptiste, 77
Lump in throat sensation, 36, 43

M

The Man (Mandal), 83
Medications
  acetaminophen, 52
  Afrin, 52
  analgesics, 52
  antibiotics, 44–45, 50
  anticoagulants, 35
  antihistamines, 35, 43, 44, 50–51
  aspirin, 35, 52
  asthma inhalers, 35, 37
  Axid, 37
  Benadryl, 52
  beta-adrenergic blocking agents, 38
  cimetidine, 37
  corticosteroids, 42, 44, 51
  cough medications, 43
  decongestants, 50
  dexamethasone, 51
  diphenhydramine hydrochloride,
      52
  diuretics, 51
  Entex, 51
  famotidine, 37
  guaifenesin, 51
  hormones, 35
  Humibid, 51
  ibuprofen, 52
  Inderal, 38
  inhalants, 35, 37, 52
  lansoprazole, 37
  methylprednisolone, 51
  mucolytics, 50–51
  nizatidine, 37
  NSAIDs (nonsteroidal anti-
      inflammatory drugs), 52
  omeprazole, 37
  oral contraceptives, 38

Treatment *(continued)*
  psychotherapy, 46
  spasmodic dysphonia, 49
  steam inhalation, 45
  ultrasound, 46
24-hour pH monitoring, 37

U

Unions, 6

V

Vibrato, 93, 183–184
Vocal abuse, 33, 38–39, 44, 136
Vocal fatigue, 27
  after choral singing, 121
  overview, 32
  and vocal nodules, 40
Vocal fold paralysis, 47–48, 55
Vocal folds
  anatomy, 16
    mucosa, 20, 21
  atrophy of, 34
  edema of, 44
  erythema (redness) of, 44
  fundamental frequency, 25, 27
  harmonic partials, 25
  hemorrhages of, 35, 38, 44, 46–47
  hyperadduction, 48
  injury
    with laryngitis, 43–44
  lesions of, 33
  myoelastic-aerodynamic
    mechanism, 24–25
  overtones, 25
  physiology, 23–25
  voice source signal, 25
Vocal health
  audiation (mental hearing), 120
  breath gesture, 126–127, 164–165
  and choral repertoire teaching,
    122–130
  choral singing benefits, 129–130
  church musician issues, 121
  cool-down, 120
  and discipline, 125–126

evaluation questions, 118
and GERD (gastroesophageal
  reflux disease), 129
and musical repertoire, 122–123
and performance schedule, 129
and posture, 122
and rhythm, 124–125
and seating, 128–129
tessitura, 127–128
and text, 123–125
warm-up, 118–120
Vocal nodules, 37, 39, 40–41, 53
Vocal polyps, 39, 42–43, 53, 54
Vocal tremor, 35
Vocal wobble, 34
Voice building
  breathing, 160–165
  humming, 168
  and phonation, 167
  posture, 158–160
  relaxation, 155–158
  resonance, 165–168
  voice builder specialist, 150–153
  warm-up, 153–158, 167
Voice Building for Choirs (Ehmann and
    Hassemann), 119
Voice disorders
  and aging, 33–34
  and allergens, 35
  and allergies, 43
  and anxiety, 38
  arthritis, laryngeal joint, 33
  and bad habits, 34
  and barium esophagogram, 36–37
  choking, 33
  among choral music educators,
    133–136
  and dehydration, 35
  dystonia, extrapyramidal, 48
  and endocrine system, 38
  environmental irritants, 35, 39
  evaluation, 27
  and foods, 35
  gastroesophageal reflux disease
    (GERD), 129
  and gastroesophageal reflux
    laryngitis, 36, 43, 49

Wind players
  airflow rate, 75
  asthma, 73, 76
  breath support, 74–75
  exercise, 75
  fatigue, 73
  and larynx, 74
  mouth pressure, 75
  open throat playing, 74

  pain, 73
  respiratory disease, 75–76
  respiratory dysfunction, 73–76

Z

Zacconi, Ludovico (16th century), 93
Zantac, 37